MASTER THE™ CLEP®

Introductory Psychology Exam

PETERSON'S®

About Peterson's

Peterson's has been your trusted educational publisher for more than 50 years. It's a milestone we're quite proud of as we continue to offer the most accurate, dependable, high-quality educational content in the field, providing you with everything you need to succeed. No matter where you are on your academic or professional path, you can rely on Peterson's for its books, videos, online information, expert test-prep tools, the most up-to-date education exploration data, and the highest quality career success resources—everything you need to achieve your education goals. For our complete line of products, visit **www.petersons.com**.

For more information, contact Peterson's, 4380 S. Syracuse St., Suite 200, Denver, CO 80237; 800-338-3282, ext. 54229; or visit us online at **www.petersons.com**.

Contents

Before You Begin

OVERVIEW
- Why You Should Use This Book
- How This Book Is Organized
- Peterson's Publications
- Give Us Your Feedback

WHY YOU SHOULD USE THIS BOOK

Peterson's *Master the™ CLEP® Introductory Psychology Exam* is designed by test experts and educators to fully prepare you for test-day success. This helpful guide includes the following:

- **Essential test information:** We take the stress out of planning for a CLEP exam by providing all the information you'll need to know before the big day in one place—including how to register, where to go, and what to bring on the day of the exam.
- **Comprehensive coverage of the exam format:** After using this book, you'll know the structure and format of the *CLEP Introductory Psychology exam* from start to finish.
- **Expert tips, advice, and strategies:** Our test-prep professionals are veteran educators who know what it takes to prepare well for CLEP exams—you'll get expert tools and strategies that have proven to be effective on exam day, giving you the confidence to get the credit you deserve. Consider this your inside edge as you jump-start your education or career advancement journey.
- **Test topic review:** You'll get a review of the concepts presented in each exam domain and advice on creating an effective study plan for reaching your goal score. Not only will there be no surprises on test day, but you'll also have the confidence that comes with being thoroughly prepared.
- **Diagnostic and practice tests to support your study plan:** Take a diagnostic test to help you determine your strengths and weaknesses and target your study time effectively. Then, build your confidence

with Readiness Check reviews and Test Yourself practice questions at the end of each chapter. When you're close to test day, take the practice test to gauge your progress and determine what to study in your final review.

Peterson's *Master the™ CLEP® Introductory Psychology Exam* is an excellent review tool to prepare you, but it is not designed to teach you the subjects covered on the exam—all CLEP exams are intended for students who have at least some working knowledge of a topic rather than complete beginners. Before signing up to take any CLEP exam, be sure to review the appropriate "Resource Guide and Sample Questions" PDF on the College Board CLEP website (**https://clep.collegeboard.org**) to verify your familiarity with the subjects and terminology presented in the outline. That said, if you are new to the topic of psychology and nonetheless want to try to pass the exam, this book can serve as a great overview of the topics you'll need to dive into deeper as you prepare.

We know that doing well on the CLEP exam is important, and we're here to help you through every step of your journey. Consider this book your test-prep compass—it will guide you through preparing for your CLEP exam and get you started earning your well-deserved college credits.

HOW THIS BOOK IS ORGANIZED

Peterson's *Master the™ CLEP® Introductory Psychology Exam* provides information about the exam, tips and strategies for exam day, a diagnostic test, subject-matter review, and a practice test.

- **CLEP exam overview:** Chapter 1 tells you all you need to know about CLEP exams. You'll learn about the purpose of the exams, how to register, what to do on test day, and more. We've also included a specific breakdown of what you can expect to see on the CLEP Introductory Psychology exam.
- **Tips and strategies:** Chapter 2 covers a variety of study strategies and test-taking tips. We encourage you to look over this chapter periodically throughout your study to remind yourself of these tips and strategies.
- **Diagnostic test:** The diagnostic test (Chapter 3) consists of 24 multiple-choice questions (approximately a quarter of the number in the full CLEP exam), followed by an answer key and detailed answer explanations. This test is designed to measure your current knowledge.

- **Diagnostic test evaluation:** These scoring charts, examples, and instructions are designed to help you identify the areas you need to focus on based on your test results and serve as the starting point as you build a study plan to achieve your target score.
- **Psychology content review:** Each of the eight content review chapters (Chapters 4–12) centers on one or more of the 13 scoring categories represented in the CLEP Introductory Psychology exam, providing a general overview of important psychology subjects, topics, and terminology.
- **Key terms:** The **bold key terms** throughout identify psychology-specific names, concepts, and terminology. If a term is unfamiliar, look up how it is used in the context of the social sciences and add it to your study list. You may also use these terms to help guide any outside research you may need to do if you're new to the topic of psychology.
- **Readiness Checks:** Readiness Checks near the end of each content review chapter (Chapters 4–12) feature questions about key concepts that you need to understand for each scoring category on the exam. While these don't cover every single question that might come up, they are a useful way to evaluate your knowledge of the main topic.
- **Test Yourself practice questions:** The Test Yourself sections at the end of each content review chapter (Chapters 4–12) consist of five practice questions from the psychology topics covered in that chapter. Use the Test Yourself questions alongside the Readiness Checks to evaluate your knowledge.
- **Practice test:** The practice test (Chapter 13) consists of 48 multiple-choice questions (approximately half the number in the full CLEP exam), followed by an answer key and detailed answer explanations. This test is designed to measure your progress after studying, but you can take it whenever it suits your study needs.

We recommend starting with the test overview in Chapter 1 and the tips and strategies in Chapter 2. Then, move on to the diagnostic test in Chapter 3. The diagnostic test is designed to help you figure out what you already know and what you need to study. It contains 24 multiple-choice questions like the ones found on the CLEP exam, and they should provide you with a good idea of what to expect and how much you need to study before the official exam.

Once you take the diagnostic test (Chapter 3), check your answers to see how you did. Read the brief answer explanations to see why a specific answer is correct, and in many cases, why other options are incorrect. Use the scoring and evaluation charts to identify the categories of questions you missed so that you can spend your study time reviewing the information that will help you the most. As with any exam, knowing your strengths and areas for improvement greatly improves your chances of success. The sections following the diagnostic test will help you evaluate your results and create a study plan tailored to your specific needs.

Each of the eight content review chapters (Chapters 4–12) addresses one or more of the 13 categories covered in the CLEP Introductory Psychology exam: history, approaches, and methods; biological bases of behavior; sensation and perception; states of consciousness; motivation and emotion; cognition and learning; developmental psychology across the lifespan; personality; psychological disorders and health; treatment of psychological disorders; social psychology; and statistics, tests, and measurement. Each of these chapters summarizes the category or categories covered and various relevant subtopics. As you read these chapters, some of the information may be familiar, but take note of anything unfamiliar so that you can adequately prepare to understand the concepts as well as someone who has completed a semester-long course in psychology.

After studying the topics covered on the exam, you should be ready to take the practice test (Chapter 13). Revisit Chapter 2 after you review the content chapters to remind yourself of the tips and strategies you want to use. We recommend taking the practice test toward the end of your studying to see how much you've improved since the diagnostic test and to identify any areas you may need to prioritize during your final review. The practice test consists of 48 multiple-choice questions (approximately half the number in the full CLEP exam) that reflect the distribution of question types and categories in the official exam. Be sure to read the answer explanations following the test for additional information and details, even if you answered a question correctly. The questions you'll find throughout this book—in the diagnostic test, end-of-chapter Test Yourself sections, and the practice test—amount to more than the approximately 95 questions on a full-length CLEP Introductory Psychology exam. For additional test prep, including full-length practice tests, videos, and interactives to support your study, visit **www.petersons.com/testprep/product /clep-practice-tests-introductory-psychology.**

PETERSON'S PUBLICATIONS

Peterson's publishes a full line of books—career preparation, education exploration, test prep, study skills, and financial aid. You'll find Peterson's titles available for purchase at major retailers or at **www.petersons.com**. Sign up for one of our online subscription plans and you'll have access to our entire test-prep catalog of more than 150 exams *plus* instructional videos, flash cards, interactive quizzes, and more! Our subscription plans allow you to study at your own pace.

GIVE US YOUR FEEDBACK

Peterson's publications can be found at your local bookstores and libraries, high school guidance offices, college libraries and career centers, and at **www.petersonsbooks.com**. Peterson's books are now also available as e-books.

We welcome any comments or suggestions you may have—your feedback will help us make educational dreams possible for you and others like you.

Good luck!

Chapter 1

All about the CLEP Introductory Psychology Exam

OVERVIEW
- What Is CLEP?
- Why Take a CLEP Exam?
- How Does CLEP Work?
- CLEP Test Centers
- How to Register for a CLEP Exam
- How to Prepare for a CLEP Exam
- Test Day
- Introductory Psychology Exam Overview

WHAT IS CLEP?

The College-Level Examination Program (CLEP) provides an opportunity for people to earn college credit for what they have learned outside of a traditional classroom. Accepted or administered at more than 2,900 colleges and universities nationwide and approved by the American Council on Education (ACE), CLEP allows people to use their existing knowledge to fast-track their educational and professional goals.

WHY TAKE A CLEP EXAM?

CLEP is designed to address the fact that some individuals enrolling in college have already learned part of what is taught in college courses through job training, independent reading and study, noncredit adult courses, and advanced high school courses. CLEP provides these individuals a chance to show their mastery of college-level material by taking exams that assess their knowledge and skills.

CLEP is available to people in all stages:
- Adult learners
- College students
- Military service members
- Nontraditional students

Many adult learners pursuing college degrees face unique circumstances, including demanding work schedules, family responsibilities, tight budgets, and other constraints. Yet many adult learners also have years of valuable educational and work experience that could be applied toward a degree. CLEP exams allow adult learners to capitalize on their prior learning and move forward with more advanced coursework.

CLEP exams also benefit students who are currently enrolled in or are about to enroll in a college or university. With tuition costs on the rise, most students face financial challenges. The fee for a CLEP exam starts at $93 (plus any administrative fees of the testing facility)—significantly less than the average cost of a 3-hour college course. Students can maximize tuition savings by taking CLEP exams to earn college credit for introductory or mandatory coursework. With a passing score on a CLEP exam, students can move on to higher-level coursework in that subject, take desired electives, or focus on courses in a chosen major. Additionally, many nontraditional students find that CLEP exams allow them to determine their own learning pace.

Including tuition and fees, the average cost of 1 college credit hour for students in 2022–2023 was
- $161 at two-year public in-district schools,
- $456 at four-year public in-state colleges,
- $1,177 at four-year public out-of-state colleges, and
- $1,642 at four-year private nonprofit colleges.

Source: Jennifer Ma and Matea Pender, *Trends in College Pricing and Student Aid 2022* (New York: College Board, 2022), https://research.collegeboard.org/media/pdf/trends-in-college-pricing-student-aid-2022.pdf.

Members of the armed services can initiate their post-military careers by taking CLEP exams in the areas in which they have experience. As an additional incentive, CLEP exams are funded for active military personnel through the Defense Activity for Non-Traditional Education Support (DANTES) program.

A variety of savings and benefits are available to help military service members, eligible spouses, and civil service employees reach their education goals:

- **Funded exam fees:** Eligible first-time test takers will have their exam fees funded by DANTES.
- **Waived administration fees:** Eligible test takers will have their administration fees waived at DANTES-funded test centers and all on-base military test centers.
- **Free examination guides:** Eligible test takers who register for a CLEP exam will receive a free CLEP exam guide through DANTES.

Finally, the CLEP program helps many students who might otherwise feel like college is out of their reach because of the time, money, or effort required to earn the necessary credits for a degree. CLEP exams take two hours or less to complete. With good preparation, a test taker could earn credit for multiple college courses in a single weekend.

HOW DOES CLEP WORK?

CLEP offers 34 exams that cover material related to specific introductory-level college courses in history, social science, English composition, literature, natural science, mathematics, business, humanities, and world languages. Visit **https://clep.collegeboard.org/clep-exams** to explore the full catalog of exams.

Given the wide variety of subjects, it is important to know which colleges and universities offer credit for CLEP exams. It is likely that a college or university in your area offers credit, but you should confirm by contacting the school before you take an exam. Then review the list of CLEP exams to determine which ones are most relevant to the degree you are seeking and to your knowledge base.

Once you've confirmed that your school offers credit for CLEP exams, you can request that a copy of your score report be sent from College Board to the school you attend or plan to attend. The school will evaluate your score and determine whether to award you credit for or exempt you from the relevant course.

If the school awards you credit, the number of credits you have earned (ranging from 3 to 9, depending on the test subject) is recorded on your permanent record, indicating that you completed work equivalent to a course in that subject. If the school grants you an exemption to the course without credit, you'll be allowed to replace that course with one of your choice.

If you don't score enough points on the exam to earn credit from your school, take heart. You can retake the exam three months after the initial exam date. Even after paying the fee again, you'll still come out ahead in terms of time, money, and credit when you pass the exam.

CLEP TEST CENTERS

You can find CLEP testing locations at community colleges and universities across the country. Contact your local college or university to find out if the school administers CLEP exams or visit **https://clep .collegeboard.org/find-a-test-center-and-schedule-your-test** to find a convenient location. Keep in mind that some colleges and universities administer CLEP exams only to enrolled students or waive administration fees only for military service members whose exam fees are funded by DANTES. CLEP testing is also available to service members at military installations around the world.

CLEP Exams with Remote Proctoring

Test takers have the option to take CLEP exams at home with remote proctoring. Remote-proctored CLEP exams have the same timing, content, format, and on-screen experience as those administered at a test center. For registration and eligibility details, go to **https://clep.college board.org/about-remote-proctoring/take-clep-exam-remote-proctoring**.

HOW TO REGISTER FOR A CLEP EXAM

Follow these steps to register for a CLEP exam:

1. Sign in to My Account at **https://prod.idp.collegeboard.org** to choose your exam and the school(s) you want to receive your scores. (Test takers may send score reports to two institutions for free when they register. There is a $20 fee per score report for each additional institution.)
2. Pay for your exam(s).
3. Print your registration ticket.
4. Schedule your exam at your preferred test center. Write the test center address, contact information, and exam appointment details in the spaces provided on your ticket. Bring the ticket with you on test day.

Registering for a CLEP exam and scheduling it with a test center are separate steps.

Register, pay the fee, and print your ticket for the exam through the College Board website. Contact a test center directly to schedule the exam.

HOW TO PREPARE FOR A CLEP EXAM

Even if you are knowledgeable in a certain subject, you should still prepare for the exam to ensure that you achieve the highest score possible. The first step in studying for a CLEP exam is to find out what will be on the specific exam you have chosen. Test takers can find information regarding exam content in the individual CLEP exam's resource guide, accessed at **https://clep.collegeboard.org/clep-exams**. Each resource guide outlines the topics covered on the exam as well as the approximate percentage of questions on each topic. Each resource guide also provides numerous sample questions like those you'll see on test day so you can get a basic sense of what to expect. Test questions are multiple choice with one correct answer choice and four incorrect answer choices.

In addition to the breakdown of assessed topics and sample questions, the resource guide also lists CLEP-recommended reference materials. If you do not own the recommended books, check college bookstores. Avoid paying high prices for new textbooks by looking online for used textbooks. Don't panic if you can't locate a specific textbook listed on the fact sheet; the textbooks are merely recommendations. Search for comparable books used in university courses on the subject. Using current editions is ideal and using at least two different references when studying for a CLEP exam is a good idea. The subject matter provided in this book will offer a sufficient review for most test takers, but if you determine that you need additional information as you read this book, finding a few other references is recommended.

The resource guide also includes information about the number of credit hours that ACE has recommended be awarded by colleges for a passing CLEP exam score. However, not all colleges and universities adhere to the ACE recommendations for CLEP credit hours. Some institutions require higher exam scores than the minimum scores recommended by ACE.

This book is your one-stop pocket guide to all the things you'll need to know for the exam. Each chapter provides an overview of one or more of the scoring categories, and **bold terms** throughout the book will identify the most important things you'll need to know. Use these terms to keep track of words and names that are likely to be on the exam and to guide any additional study you may need to do as you learn what the exam will include.

TEST DAY

Once you've reviewed the material and taken practice tests, you'll be ready to take your CLEP exam. Follow these tips for a successful test day experience.

1. **Arrive on time.** Not only is it courteous to arrive on time at the CLEP test center, but it also gives you plenty of time to take care of check-in procedures and settle into your surroundings.
2. **Bring proper identification.** CLEP testing facilities require that test takers bring a valid government-issued identification card with a current photo and signature. The first and last name on your ID must match the name on your registration ticket.
   - Acceptable forms of identification include a current driver's license, passport, military identification card, or state-issued identification card. Individuals who fail to bring proper identification will not be allowed to take the exam. For a detailed list of acceptable identification, visit **https://clep.collegeboard .org/test-day/what-to-bring-on-test-day**.
   - Military test takers should bring their Geneva Conventions Identification Card. For more information on IDs for active-duty service members, spouses, and civil service employees, visit **https://clep.collegeboard.org/clep-military-benefits**.
3. **Bring the items you will need.** Be sure to have the following items with you:
   - A valid registration ticket printed from the My Account registration portal
   - Any required test center registration forms or printouts (Be sure to fill out all the necessary paperwork before test day!)
   - Any additional administration fees (Each test center charges an additional fee and sets its own policy for payment.)

4. **Leave prohibited items at home.** These items are *not* allowed at the test center:
   - Electronic devices including smartphones, cell phones, mobile digital devices (e.g., iPad devices or tablets), cameras, headphones, smartwatches, and fitness bands
   - Reading material, textbooks, reference materials (including dictionaries and other study aids), scratch paper, and any other outside notes
   - Personal calculators (Calculators are integrated into the CLEP exam software where necessary.)
5. **Take the test.** During the exam, take the time to read each question and answer choice carefully. Eliminate the choices you know are incorrect to narrow down the number of potential answers. If a question completely stumps you, take an educated guess and move on to make the most of the time you have for the exam.

INTRODUCTORY PSYCHOLOGY EXAM OVERVIEW

The CLEP Introductory Psychology exam assesses your knowledge of information covered in a standard one-semester introductory-level college psychology course. The exam does not require an understanding of advanced psychological concepts but instead draws on your knowledge and understanding of the subject's basic facts, concepts, and general principles. Questions on the exam follow the classifications, diagnostic criteria, and treatments contained in the *Diagnostic and Statistical Manual of Mental Disorders*, Fifth Edition (DSM-5).

According to the College Board (**https://clep.collegeboard.org/clep -exams/introductory-psychology**), you must be able to
- demonstrate knowledge of terminology, principles, and theories of psychology
- comprehend, evaluate, and analyze problem situations; and
- apply psychological concepts to new situations.

The 90-minute exam contains approximately 95 questions, some of which are pretest questions that will not be scored. The exam divides questions into 13 categories. These are the categories and subcategories and their relative weights on the exam as listed on the College Board website:

History, Approaches, and Methods (11%–12%)

- History of psychology
- Approaches: biological, biopsychosocial, behavioral, cognitive, humanistic, and psychodynamic
- Research methods: experimental, clinical, and correlational
- Ethics in research

Biological Bases of Behavior (8%–9%)

- Endocrine system
- Etiology
- Functional organization of the nervous system
- Genetics
- Neuroanatomy
- Physiological techniques

Sensation and Perception (7%–8%)

- Attention
- Other senses: somesthesis, olfaction, gustation, and vestibular system
- Perceptual development
- Perceptual processes
- Receptor processes: vision and audition
- Sensory mechanisms: thresholds and adaptation

States of Consciousness (5%–6%)

- Hypnosis and meditation
- Psychoactive drug effects
- Sleep and dreaming

Learning (8%–9%)

- Biological bases
- Classical conditioning
- Cognitive process in learning
- Observational learning
- Operant conditioning

Cognition (8%–9%)

- Intelligence and creativity
- Language
- Memory
- Thinking and problem solving

Motivation and Emotion (5%–6%)

- Biological bases
- Hunger, thirst, sex, and pain
- Social motivation
- Theories of emotion
- Theories of motivation

Developmental Psychology across the Lifespan (8%–9%)

- Dimensions of development: physical, cognitive, social, and moral
- Gender identity and sex roles
- Heredity-environment issues
- Research methods: longitudinal and cross-sectional
- Theories of development

Personality (7%–8%)

- Assessment techniques
- Growth and adjustment
- Personality theories and approaches
- Self-concept and self-esteem

Psychological Disorders and Health (8%–9%)

- Affective disorders
- Anxiety disorders
- Dissociative disorders
- Eating disorders
- Health, stress, and coping
- Personality disorders
- Psychoses
- Somatoform disorders
- Theories of psychopathology

Treatment of Psychological Disorders (6%–7%)

- Behavioral therapies
- Biological and drug therapies
- Cognitive therapies
- Community and preventive approaches
- Insight therapies: psychodynamic and humanistic approaches

Social Psychology (9%–10%)

- Aggression/antisocial behavior
- Attitudes and attitude change
- Attribution processes
- Conformity, compliance, and obedience
- Group dynamics
- Interpersonal attraction
- Stereotypes, prejudice, discrimination, and prosocial behavior

Statistics, Tests, and Measurement (3%–4%)

- Descriptive statistics
- Inferential statistics
- Measurement of intelligence
- Reliability and validity
- Samples, populations, and norms
- Types of tests

American Council on Education Credit Recommendations

Subject: Introductory Psychology

Credit Hours: 3

Minimum Score: 50

Source: American Council on Education. "College Board's College-Level Examination
  Program," https://www.acenet.edu/National-Guide.
Note: Each institution may set its own credit-granting policy, which may differ from the
  ACE recommendations.

Chapter 2

Study Strategies and Test-Taking Tips

OVERVIEW

- Study Strategies
- Mindset Strategies
- Test-Taking Tips

To do well on a CLEP exam, having knowledge of the subject is paramount, but there are also ways to improve your chances of achieving a high score. This chapter will cover some study strategies, mindset strategies, and test-taking tips that can help with timed testing generally and with preparing for your CLEP Introductory Psychology exam using this book. Once you've reviewed the advice in this chapter, use the diagnostic test in Chapter 3 to evaluate your current skills and make a study plan.

STUDY STRATEGIES

There are myriad ways to approach studying for a CLEP exam. You've made a smart first step by purchasing this book or, perhaps, by signing up for more comprehensive study assistance at **www.petersons.com**. That said, learning the material is only part of the equation since you also need to be able to recall information in a high-pressure, timed testing environment. Being able to recall information when you need it is generally the result of effective studying and repetition. Use the following strategies to help you make the most of the significant effort you'll put into studying for your CLEP exam.

General Strategies

- **Don't wait until the last minute—start early!** Come up with a reasonable study plan and calendar early in your test-prep process and stick to it. Having a study plan allows you to make sure you understand the exam, evaluate what components you need to work on, and have plenty of time to review what you know and learn anything new.
- **Spread out your study sessions over time.** Most people are better served by several shorter study sessions spread out over time than by lengthy cram sessions. It takes time to move things you learn into long-term memory, and the more time you give yourself to learn and review different concepts, the better you'll be able to recall them on test day. Because your brain needs time to process what it learns, spreading out your studying across multiple sessions is the best way to retain what you've learned.
- **Study regularly.** People need to regularly return to information they have learned to ensure that they remember it, so learners who complete periodic reviews of what they've learned can better retain the information. Studying regularly leading up to your exam is the best way to do this—it is far more effective than cramming, which offers few opportunities to practice recalling information, or studying sporadically, which leaves gaps during which you may forget what you've learned.
- **Study intensely rather than passively.** There is a documented relationship between stress and performance. Low-stress and high-stress situations both tend to affect performance negatively. However, there is a sweet spot: the right amount of pressure and intensity can improve performance, especially when learning. To study efficiently, you are best served by short, intense intervals. Languidly skimming over notes for hours on end will do significantly less than an hour of intentional, active retrieval combined with paraphrasing, mind mapping new concepts, or answering timed practice questions.
- **Develop active learning practices.** Active learning involves planning, monitoring, and reflecting on your learning process. Here are some tips for active learning:
    - Plan out your work time.
    - Read carefully and strategically.
    - Take notes in some form.
    - Assess your progress regularly.
    - Spread out your study time.

- ○ Keep a regular schedule.
- ○ Create something while studying.
- ○ Use metacognition techniques (such as reflective questions) to think about what you've learned so far and how you learned it.

- **Eliminate distractions.** Humans can multitask, but not very well—your divided attention is often the weakest of your attentive modes. To truly focus on the task of learning, you need to be able to isolate what you're trying to learn from other stimuli so that what you learn can register properly. One of the most significant distractors for many (but not all) people is language, whether the lyrics of a song or the dialogue of a TV show playing in the background. If your brain struggles to filter out other voices, remove yourself from environments with lots of noise and leave your phone in another room so you won't be distracted. Remember that you don't need to do this for long periods of time since your studying is more productive in intense bursts (an hour at a time) rather than in long, drawn-out cram sessions.

- **Encode new information meaningfully.** Memory always involves a process called encoding, wherein information moves from your senses to storage for later use. There are several tricks and tips for getting information to stick around, but one of the most effective ways is elaborative encoding. When you make information meaningful to you by connecting it to your own life and interests, it is easier for your brain to store that information for later use. For example, if you think about a real-life situation relevant to your own experiences that relates to the concept you are learning, you are more likely to remember it because you've encoded it in a way that holds meaning for you.

- **Divide tasks and information into chunks.** This technique can help anyone but is especially helpful for those who have trouble focusing. Divide topics into smaller chunks of information rather than large blocks so you can deal with one chunk at a time. Resources (like this book) have organizational structures that may or may not suit your learning objectives. A chapter may cover a wide array of topics too extensive for your studying load on a given day or may not align with what you are trying to learn. In that situation, try focusing on one section, chart, or exercise at a time. Use different study strategies for different chunks of information so you don't feel overwhelmed. Reorganize resources in your notes and study materials based on relationships you see, not necessarily on what the resource prescribes. Consider what you can cover in the time you have for a given study session and focus only on that information.

- **Vary topics and weave them together as you learn.** Alternate between topics while you study rather than dedicating large portions of time to a single topic. This strategy applies to both what you review and self-quiz in your notes as well as to practice questions. While you're at it, look for connections between different topics. How does understanding one idea help you approach another? How do different concepts relate to each other? Reflecting on these connections as you study helps solidify concepts in your mind.

- **Create new materials as you study.** To retain and understand information, you need to both be able to recall it and be able to apply it. Exposure to information in different forms and in different ways helps your brain process what you're learning, but doing something with the information you're trying to learn really helps. Taking practice tests is one of the best ways to study, but mixing your methods before you get to the practice test can have positive results. You can try a variety of methods:

    ○ Create something using new information you acquire (e.g., write your own practice questions or tests).

    ○ Develop a visual aid that helps you make sense of new information.

    ○ Use different sensory modes—auditory, visual, or physical—to study.

    ○ Seek out additional resources to expand your research and understanding.

    ○ Create materials that help you engage in repetitive learning (e.g., make flash cards).

- **Assess your retention and understanding regularly.** Periodically check in with yourself and look for ways to test or elaborate on what you've learned so far. Find ways to assess your retention and understanding of new concepts using practice questions and tests or by trying to explain the concepts as if you were teaching them to someone else. Reflect on which categories and topics you have learned well and which may still need improvement.

- **Review and summarize what you learned at the end of each study session.** This form of metacognition helps you make the most of your study time. By reflecting on what you learned and your thought processes and by summarizing new information, you are encoding that new information so you can recall it later. If you can't summarize a concept you've just studied, devote more time to it in a future study session.

Strategies for Using This Book

In addition to using the general study strategies, there are some specific ways you can use this book to help you prepare for your CLEP Introductory Psychology exam.

- **Use the Readiness Check and Test Yourself sections to help you assess your retention and understanding of new concepts.** Use these sections at the end of each content review chapter to practice evaluating what you have learned and take note of what you need to review further.
- **Use the bold terms throughout this book to guide your study.** Each time you encounter a bold term in one of the content review chapters, use the opportunity to assess your knowledge. For each bold term you encounter, ask yourself the following questions:
  - Is this term completely new to me, or have I heard it before?
  - If I've heard the term before, in what contexts have I heard it used?
  - Can I define the term in my own words based on what I know or have read?
  - What contextual information surrounds the term that can help me make sense of why it's important to the study of psychology?
  - Do I need to do further research to understand why this term is important?
  - Could there be a specific definition of this word that is important to psychologists or a specific way the term is used within the social sciences?
- **Do additional outside research while you read this book.** This book attempts to cover the general information that any test taker needs to know for the CLEP Introductory Psychology exam, but no single book can be a complete substitute for a semester-long course. Use this book to help you figure out what you know and what you need to learn, then dive deeper if a topic seems unfamiliar. Visit your local library to find resources or talk to knowledgeable librarians who can help you find information on topics that are new to you or that you don't fully understand.
- **Consider field-specific terminology when reviewing key terms and doing outside research.** In any field, specific terms are used in contexts that would be immediately recognizable to scholars of that subject but not necessarily to outsiders. Don't assume you know what a term means because you've seen it before; instead, try and figure out how psychologists use it. Add search terms like *psychology* or *social sciences* to find field-specific uses of a term when searching definitions online.

- **Use this book to guide your discussions with people who have taken an introductory psychology course.** If you know someone who has taken a course or the CLEP Introductory Psychology exam, ask them about the topics that are unfamiliar to you and about topics they encountered most frequently. They will likely have insights that can help you and may even have materials you can borrow (such as class notes or old textbooks) as you study and do outside research.

MINDSET STRATEGIES

No matter which CLEP exam you take, maximizing the efficiency of your study time and approaching the test with the proper mindset can make a big difference in your performance.

Manage Your Time

While CLEP exams have rather forgiving time constraints compared with other standardized tests, time management is still a key issue, and having the right mindset about it is important. A timed test does not have to cause anxiety or make you feel rushed—plan ahead so you feel confident about how you will manage your time. For the CLEP Introductory Psychology exam, test takers have 90 minutes to complete approximately 95 questions—this means that you should aim to answer each question in about 45 seconds or less. Many questions will be easy to answer and will take less time, leaving you more deliberation time for harder questions. Aim to eliminate the answer choices you know are incorrect, and make your best guess if you find yourself spending more than a minute or so on a question. Look for ways to save yourself time and move through the test efficiently without sacrificing accuracy.

Practice Testing Conditions

Test takers don't always think about the conditions under which they'll be testing on exam day, but the more you can mimic those conditions in practice, the more comfortable you'll be on test day. The diagnostic and practice tests in this book provide structure and time limits that can help re-create those conditions, but you may also want to consider your environment when you take the tests—try to mimic a testing environment and limit distractions that won't be present on the day you take the CLEP exam. By deliberately practicing testing under similar conditions, you will be rehearsing the mindset you want to have during the CLEP exam.

Evaluate the Stakes

You should approach the CLEP exam with careful consideration of what is at stake for you. For example, if you must pass the exam to graduate or enter a program with prerequisites, the stakes are probably higher for you than for someone taking it on a whim to bypass an expensive elective course. Higher stakes do not mean you must have a higher level of anxiety—assessing what is at stake should help you determine the appropriate amount of time and effort to devote to preparation. Depending on your circumstances, you may be able to take the exam multiple times, but each attempt requires time and energy, so make the most of your opportunity. During the exam, you can remind yourself of how well you prepared for your goal.

Build Confidence

Your goal is to be as certain as possible about the correct answer when you answer a question. Numerous strategies—many of which are in this book—can help you feel confident about your knowledge, but you need to know what they are and practice them. The good news is that as you become more adept at using these strategies, you will also become more confident in your ability to perform well on your exam. Confidence correlates positively with test performance, and building confidence is a valuable part of your test preparation.

TEST-TAKING TIPS

To maximize your performance on test day, there are several things to keep in mind in addition to your knowledge of the subject matter. Prioritizing these test-taking tips will help you manage important tasks on test day and perform your best on the exam.

Before Test Day

- **Understand the directions.** Luckily, the directions for the CLEP Introductory Psychology exam are straightforward—simply select the best of the five answer options for each multiple-choice question.
- **Know the expectations for each topic category.** Each of the content review chapters in this book (Chapters 4–12) covers one or more of the 13 testing categories of the CLEP Introductory Psychology exam, so reading this book will ensure that you understand what's expected of you. Revisit these chapters in the days leading up to your exam

to remind yourself how questions for each topic differ, how many questions to expect from each category, and how to apply the strategies you developed during your study to approach different types of questions.

- **Make sure you are rested and ready.** No one wants to take an exam hungry or groggy. Plan far in advance to make the night before your exam a relaxing one: don't study that night (you'll be well prepared by then), have a filling and nutritious dinner, get to sleep early, wake in time for a similarly filling and nutritious breakfast, and then get to your testing site early so you can settle in and relax your mind before the exam begins.

On Test Day

- **Answer every question before time is called.** Follow your time management plan to ensure you answer every question. There is no penalty for guessing, so don't leave any questions unanswered. You can always note which answers you guessed and review them later. If you're running out of time, spend the last few minutes of your exam guessing on all the questions that remain. Take time to eliminate answers you're pretty sure are incorrect first to improve your chance of guessing correctly—if you can eliminate two choices you know are incorrect, your chance of guessing correctly jumps from 1 in 5 to 1 in 3.
- **Use all the time you're allotted.** There is no such thing as "finishing early" with a timed test—use every minute you're given!
- **Make time for review.** Save time for review by following your time management plan. Use the time you have left to review your answers and return to more difficult questions, particularly those on which you had to guess.
- **Prioritize the questions you can answer with confidence.** As you take the exam, prioritize the easiest questions and those you feel most confident about first, then move on to harder questions. This way, you maximize the number of questions you are likely to get right. After you have answered all the questions, flip this priority arrangement—start by reviewing the questions you feel least confident about and then review those about which you feel more certain.
- **Be certain of your answers.** Don't just select an answer that seems right and call it a day. Review all the answer options and eliminate incorrect options as best you can so you can be more certain of the answer you do select even if you end up having to guess. Even when

you feel confident about an answer, read the other options to make sure there isn't a better answer.

- **Guess as few answers as possible.** While it is better to guess than leave a question blank, your goal should still be to maximize the number of questions you can answer confidently. The more you practice time management and the more answer choices you can eliminate, the fewer answers you will have to guess.

These study strategies and test-taking tips will help you as you prepare for your CLEP exam. The more familiar you are with them and comfortable you are practicing them, the easier they will be to implement on test day. Return to this chapter as you read through the content chapters of this book and before you take the practice test in Chapter 13. By using these strategies and tips as you prepare, you'll be able to perform your best on your CLEP Introductory Psychology exam.

Chapter 3

Diagnostic Test

OVERVIEW

- Diagnostic Test
- Answer Key and Explanations
- Interpreting Your Diagnostic Test Results
- Evaluating Your Strengths and Areas for Improvement
- Setting Goals
- Creating a Study Plan
- Using This Book

An answer sheet for this test can be found on page 257.

DIAGNOSTIC TEST

This diagnostic test and the time allotted are approximately a quarter of the length of a full CLEP Introductory Psychology exam.

24 Questions—23 Minutes

Directions: Each of the questions or incomplete statements below is followed by five suggested answers or completions. Select the one best answer for each. The Answer Key and Explanations will follow.

---

1. Psychoanalysis relies on the idea that each person has a conscious, a subconscious, and an unconscious mind that impact their behavior and cognition, a theory developed by

   A. Carl Jung
   B. René Descartes
   C. Sigmund Freud
   D. Franz Joseph Gall
   E. Alfred Adler

2. Which of the following represents the highest level of Maslow's hierarchy of needs?

   A. Social belonging
   B. Self-esteem
   C. Safety needs
   D. Self-actualization
   E. Physiological needs

3. A patient experiences serious damage to the right hemisphere of his brain. Following the injury, he struggles to understand metaphorical language and figurative meaning within conversations. Which of the following brain functions explains this change in personality?

   A. Neuroplasticity
   B. Neurogenesis
   C. Synaptic pruning
   D. Synaptogenesis
   E. Lateralization

4. Which of the following involves top-down processing?

A. Perceiving the redness of an apple
B. Experiencing discomfort when diving into a cold pool
C. Misinterpreting an optical illusion
D. Perceiving the distance of an object with one eye closed
E. Selectively paying attention to one feature of the visual field

5. Psychedelic substances, such as MDMA and psilocybin mushrooms, have increasingly been the subject of research interest in psychology and psychiatry. Which of the following mechanisms likely contribute to the efficacy of these drugs for the treatment of mental health conditions, such as PTSD, in a clinical setting?

A. Increased activity in the default mode network
B. Decreased activity in the default mode network
C. Increased activity in the salience network
D. Decreased activity in the salience network
E. Increased activity in the central executive network

6. Which of the following theories posits that the depletion of the body's energy stores motivates individuals to engage in behaviors that will restore energy equilibrium and homeostasis?

A. Appraisal theory
B. Drive-reduction theory
C. Cannon-Bard theory
D. James-Lange theory
E. Gate control theory

7. A child watches their favorite television program and begins to imitate the phrases and actions of one of the program's main characters, indicating the child is engaged in

A. reinforcement learning
B. punishment learning
C. observational learning
D. generalization learning
E. discrimination learning

8. While walking his dog, Keith sees a car drive by that looks like his grandmother's car, which reminds him that her birthday is coming up later in the month. Which of the following processes is responsible for Keith's association?

   A. Memory priming
   B. Selective attention
   C. Divergent thinking
   D. Convergent thinking
   E. Availability heuristic

9. "The formation of new neural connections" describes the process of

   A. synaptic pruning
   B. synaptic growth
   C. neural plasticity
   D. neurogenesis
   E. habituation

10. Which of the following is true of behavioral observation compared with other methods of personality assessment?

    A. It involves more self-reporting.
    B. It relies on an individual's own awareness of their personality traits.
    C. It is less prone to the introduction of bias.
    D. It has more clinical applications.
    E. It involves analyzing larger sets of data.

11. Which of the following is not considered an anxiety disorder?

    A. Agoraphobia
    B. Selective mutism
    C. Panic disorder
    D. Social phobia
    E. Antisocial personality disorder

12. The basic goal of cognitive behavior therapy (CBT) is to help a person

    A. change thought and behavior patterns that may be affecting their well-being

    B. access subconscious or unconscious thoughts

    C. correct chemical imbalances that affect brain function

    D. memorize mantras that can be applied to stressful situations

    E. face their phobias through exposure

13. Changing one's behavior in response to direct requests or explicit social pressure is called

    A. obedience

    B. conformity

    C. compliance

    D. internal attribution

    E. external attribution

14. Meghan becomes upset when her new coworker shows up late to work on her first day. Meghan is always on time for work, and she assumes her coworker is not serious about this position and did not care enough to try to show up on time. Meghan's perception of her coworker's behavior is influenced by which of the following?

    A. Actor-observer bias

    B. Confirmation bias

    C. Negative stereotypes

    D. Fundamental attribution error

    E. Outgroup homogeneity effect

15. When designing an experiment, a researcher carefully selects a large number of study participants to ensure that the findings of the study are generalizable to the wider public. Which of the following terms describes this approach to participant selection?

    A. Representative population

    B. Normative population

    C. Variable sample

    D. Representative sample

    E. Normative sample

16. Which of the following statements is true of correlational studies?

   A. They rely heavily on the experimental method.
   B. They rely heavily on case studies.
   C. They are focused on determining causation.
   D. They use datasets to analyze issues that would be difficult or unethical to assess using experimental methods.
   E. They use experimental methods to analyze issues that would be difficult or unethical to assess using datasets.

17. Sarah is a researcher investigating the inherited and environmental factors that contribute to the development of PTSD. Her research would be most specifically classified as

   A. biology
   B. etiology
   C. cognitive psychology
   D. neuropsychiatry
   E. endocrinology

18. Tameka views an abstract painting at the museum and appreciates the richness of its reds, greens, blues, and yellows. Which of the following cell types enable Tameka's perception of these colors?

   A. Rod cells
   B. Hair cells
   C. Microvilli
   D. Cone cells
   E. Stereocilia

19. Pat's dog, Ringo, has learned to associate the word *treat* with being given a valued food item. Ringo's anticipatory excitement upon hearing Pat say the word *treat* represents which of the following?

   A. Unconditioned stimulus
   B. Conditioned stimulus
   C. Unconditioned response
   D. Conditioned response
   E. Positive reinforcement

20. Zendaya wants to recommend that her coworker visit her family's favorite restaurant, but she struggles to come up with the name of the restaurant. Which of the following cognitive processes is associated with Zendaya's inability to provide the name of the restaurant?

    A. Memory encoding
    B. Memory consolidation
    C. Memory retrieval
    D. Working memory
    E. Procedural memory

21. Tina has developed the ability to understand hypothetical statements, make her own hypotheses, explore abstract ideas, and pose abstract questions. She also has a keen sense of her own morality and her own ethics. According to Jean Piaget, Tina has reached the

    A. naturalistic stage
    B. sensorimotor stage
    C. preoperational stage
    D. concrete operational stage
    E. formal operational stage

22. The Rorschach inkblot test and the thematic apperception test (TAT) are both examples of

    A. projective measures
    B. prescriptive measures
    C. diagnostic measures
    D. interview methods
    E. self-report assessments

23. Hannah is a patient who witnessed the sudden death of her young daughter. She is now unable to recall any of the events from the days surrounding the death, and she even struggles to remember some basic details about her own life and her daughter's life. She has shown heightened distress since the event, including self-harming behaviors, and reports having flashback-like experiences despite not knowing their context. For which of the following disorders might a clinician want to evaluate Hannah?

    A. Dissociative identity disorder
    B. Dissociative amnesia
    C. Depersonalization disorder
    D. Conversion disorder
    E. Factitious disorder

24. Dhaval's car battery has died, and his neighbor Paul offers to jump-start Dhaval's car. Paul's decision to help Dhaval was partially informed by his expectation that he would likely need to ask his new neighbor for a favor in the future. Paul's justification for helping Dhaval is an example of which of the following?

    A. Socialization
    B. Persuasion
    C. Cultural influences
    D. Mere exposure effect
    E. Reciprocal altruism

ANSWER KEY AND EXPLANATIONS

1. C	6. B	11. E	16. D	21. E
2. D	7. C	12. A	17. B	22. A
3. E	8. A	13. C	18. D	23. B
4. C	9. B	14. D	19. D	24. E
5. B	10. C	15. D	20. C	

1. **The correct answer is C.** A major component of Freud's psycho-dynamic theory is that the mind is a physiological part of the body and that each person possesses a conscious, a subconscious, and an unconscious mind. Choices A and E are theorists who developed offshoots of psychoanalysis, and choices B and D are theorists whose ideas are unrelated to the development of psychoanalysis.

2. **The correct answer is D.** The highest level of Maslow's hierarchy of needs is self-actualization, which is achieved when an individual has a sense that they've reached their full potential. At the base of the hierarchy is physiological needs (choice E), followed by safety needs (choice C), social belonging (choice A), and self-esteem (choice B), eventually culminating in self-actualization.

3. **The correct answer is E.** Lateralization refers to the divergence in specialization between the right and left hemispheres of the cerebrum, in this case relating to the right hemisphere's function in understanding figurative and inferential meaning through language. Neuroplasticity, neurogenesis, synaptic pruning, and synaptogenesis are not illustrated by this example.

4. **The correct answer is C.** Optical illusions result in misinterpretation of visual stimuli because of the interplay between prior expectations and sensory input. Choices A and B represent bottom-up sensory processes, while choice D relates to the brain's interpretation of monocular visual cues. Choice E is incorrect as it lacks specificity.

5. **The correct answer is B.** The use of psychedelic substances leads to decreased activity in the brain's default mode network, which often shows atypical activation in individuals with mental health disorders such as PTSD. The salience and central executive networks (choices C, D, and E) relate to attention, cognition, and goal-oriented behaviors and are not believed to be central to the mechanisms of psychedelic therapy.

6. **The correct answer is B.** Drive-reduction theory relates to an individual's motivation to seek out food and water when experiencing hunger or thirst. Choices A, C, and D are theories of emotion rather than motivation, and choice E relates to one's experience of pain rather than hunger or thirst.

7. **The correct answer is C.** The imitation of behavior involves a cognitive process called modeling, which is learned through observation. The question does not state that this behavior was reinforced or punished, so choices A and B can be eliminated. Generalization and discrimination relate to classical conditioning, which does not account for the child's conscious imitation of the television character, so choices D and E are also incorrect.

8. **The correct answer is A.** Memory priming involves the shaping of present attentional resources based on past experiences. Selective attention is too broad, so choice B is incorrect. Choices C and D relate to creativity rather than memory and choice E is a mental shortcut used in decision making, so these options are also incorrect.

9. **The correct answer is B.** Also known as synaptogenesis, synaptic growth refers to the creation of new connections between neurons. While closely related, synaptic pruning (choice A) occurs after synaptic growth and is when neural connections are refined. Choices C, D, and E all refer to other concepts from developmental psychology.

10. **The correct answer is C.** Behavioral observation is more limited in its clinical applications than other personality assessment methods, eliminating choice D as an option. However, it is less prone to the introduction of bias than methods like interviews and self-report assessments. Choices A and B more accurately describe self-report assessments. Choice E more accurately describes factor analysis.

11. **The correct answer is E.** While antisocial personality disorder may be comorbid with certain types of anxiety disorders like agoraphobia (choice A) or social phobia (choice D), personality disorders are not automatically considered anxiety disorders.

12. **The correct answer is A.** The goal of CBT is to use talk therapy to help a person change thought and behavior patterns that inhibit their well-being. It is commonly used to treat depression and anxiety but has also shown efficacy in helping clinicians treat a variety of other physical and mental health concerns.

13. **The correct answer is C.** Compliance refers to the modification of one's behavior in response to direct requests or explicit social pressure. Conformity is driven by internal pressure to fit in, and obedience relates specifically to the demands of an authority figure, so choices A and B are incorrect. Attribution describes the ways individuals interpret and explain the behavior of others, so choices D and E can be eliminated.

14. **The correct answer is D.** The fundamental attribution error describes the tendency to overemphasize the impact of internal attributions on other people's behavior and to disregard the impact of external factors. Choice A is incorrect because actor-observer bias occurs when an individual sees others' actions or motives in a negative light when they would not do so for themselves in a similar scenario, but the question states that Meghan is always on time for work. Choices B, C, and E are incorrect because they imply association with stereotypes and prejudicial views, rather than attribution bias based on an observed event.

15. **The correct answer is D.** In research, a sample is a subset of individuals that participate in a study. Samples are considered representative when their characteristics accurately reflect those of the wider population, allowing the results of an experiment to generalize beyond the study participants. It is not possible to conduct research on an entire population, so choices A and B can be ruled out. Choice E is incorrect because normative samples, obtained in large-scale studies, serve as reference points whose characteristics are compared against a sample that participates in a given study. Choice C is not a type of sample.

16. **The correct answer is D.** Correlational studies are intended to find correlations between at least two datasets and are used in cases where creating an experiment would be unethical or impossible. For instance, an experiment to determine the impact of harmful drugs could not ethically be conducted, since asking subjects to take those drugs for experimental purposes would be unethical. However, analyzing datasets to determine the impact of self-reported drug use would allow researchers to look for correlations.

17. **The correct answer is B.** *Etiology* is a term used in many biological, psychological, and medical fields referring to research that is focused on the factors contributing to the origin of abnormal conditions and disease.

18. **The correct answer is D.** Embedded in the retina of the eye, cone cells are responsible for the perception of color. Rod cells are sensitive to the size, shape, brightness, and movement of an object, but not its color, so choice A is incorrect. The other choices are unrelated to visual perception.

19. **The correct answer is D.** Through repeated pairings of the word *treat* with the receipt of a rewarding food item, Ringo has learned the context and outcomes associated with that word. Anticipatory excitement is a response, not a stimulus, so choices A and B can be ruled out, and this response did not occur until after the word had been paired with the food item in previous experiences, so choice C can also be ruled out. While treats may be given as a reward during positive reinforcement training, the association between the word and the outcome involves classical conditioning, rather than operant conditioning, so choice E is also incorrect.

20. **The correct answer is C.** Memory retrieval refers to the process of bringing forth stored memories, such as the name of a familiar restaurant. Choices A and B are incorrect, as these processes must occur before retrieval. Choice D is incorrect because working memory is a limited-capacity system, which typically only stores information for 30 seconds or less. Choice E is also incorrect because procedural memory refers to the acquisition and retention of skills, rather than the recollection of facts like the name of a restaurant.

21. **The correct answer is E.** The formal operational stage is the final stage of development in Piaget's model of childhood development. The formal operational stage begins in the preadolescent years and lasts through adulthood; it is marked by the ability to hypothesize and understand hypothetical scenarios, develop and respond to abstract questions and thoughts, and engage in discourse on morality and ethics. Choices B, C, and D refer to earlier stages in Piaget's model. Choice A is not the name of any of Piaget's stages.

22. **The correct answer is A.** Projective measures differ from other personality assessment methods in that they are designed to determine how a person's personality operates at a subconscious level. Both the Rorschach inkblot test and the TAT are projective measures that use subconscious associations to evaluate personality. Choices B and C do not refer to existing assessment methods. Choices D and E refer to other types of personality assessment.

23. **The correct answer is B.** Of the choices given, Hannah's symptoms are most consistent with dissociative amnesia, which is characterized by an inability to remember events or autobiographical details that one would normally be able to remember, particularly surrounding traumatic events. Choices A and C are also dissociative disorders, but they are not consistent with Hannah's symptoms. Choices D and E are somatoform disorders.

24. **The correct answer is E.** Reciprocal altruism occurs when someone acts to benefit another individual, with the expectation that they may benefit from that individual's help in the future. Choices A and C are incorrect as they are too broad to describe Paul's justification for helping Dhaval. The question does not suggest that Dhaval used persuasion to convince Paul to help, but it does indicate that Dhaval is a new neighbor, so choices B and D are also incorrect.

INTERPRETING YOUR DIAGNOSTIC TEST RESULTS

Now that you've taken the diagnostic test to establish a baseline, it's time to interpret your score. The purpose of a diagnostic test is exactly what it sounds like—it diagnoses your strengths and weaknesses so you can make informed decisions about how you want to study going forward. While this diagnostic test is only about a quarter of the length of the approximately 95-question CLEP Introductory Psychology exam, the ratio of question types and the time allotted reflect the conditions of the full-length exam. CLEP uses a formula to convert your raw score into a scaled score ranging from 20 to 80, so your raw score doesn't translate exactly into your final score on the exam, but your performance on this diagnostic test can help you determine the areas where you might want to direct your focus when studying.

The CLEP Introductory Psychology exam covers 13 distinct testing categories, each of which are weighted differently.

Category	Percentage of Total Questions
History, approaches, and methods History of psychology, approaches (biological, behavioral, cognitive, humanistic, psychodynamic, biopsychosocial), research methods (experimental, clinical, correlational), ethics in research	11%–12%
Biological bases of behavior Endocrine system, etiology, functional organization of the nervous system, genetics, neuroanatomy, physiological techniques	8%–9%
Sensation and perception Attention, other senses (somesthesis, olfaction, gustation, vestibular system), perceptual development, perceptual processes, receptor processes (vision, audition), sensory mechanisms (thresholds, adaptation)	7%–8%
States of consciousness Hypnosis and meditation, psychoactive drug effects, sleep and dreaming	5%–6%
Motivation and emotion Biological bases, hunger, thirst, sexual desire, pain, social motivation, theories of emotion, theories of motivation	5%–6%
Learning Biological bases, classical conditioning, cognitive processes in learning, observational learning, operant conditioning	8%–9%
Cognition Intelligence and creativity, language, memory, thinking and problem solving	8%–9%
Developmental psychology across the lifespan Dimensions of development (physical, cognitive, social, moral), gender identity and sex roles, heredity-environment issues, research methods (longitudinal, cross-sectional), theories of development	8%–9%
Personality Assessment techniques, growth and adjustment, personality theories and approaches, self-concept and self-esteem	7%–8%
Psychological disorders and health Affective disorders, anxiety disorders, dissociative disorders, eating disorders, stress and coping, personality disorders, psychoses, somatoform disorders, theories of psychopathology	8%–9%
Treatment of psychological disorders Behavioral therapies, biological and drug therapies, cognitive therapies, community and preventive approaches, insight therapies (psychodynamic and humanistic approaches)	6%–7%

(continues)

(*Continued*)

Category	Percentage of Total Questions
Social psychology Aggression/antisocial behavior, attitudes and attitude change, attribution processes, conformity, compliance, obedience, discrimination, group dynamics, interpersonal attraction, prejudice, prosocial behavior, stereotypes	9%–10%
Statistics, tests, and measurement Descriptive statistics, inferential statistics, measurement of intelligence, reliability and validity, samples, populations, norms, types of tests	3%–4%

Let's look at your diagnostic test scores by category. Record your score for each category in the following chart.

MY DIAGNOSTIC TEST SCORES BY CATEGORY		
Category	**Question Number(s)**	**Raw Score**
History, approaches, and methods	1, 2, 16	_____ /3
Biological bases of behavior	3, 17	_____ /2
Sensation and perception	4, 18	_____ /2
States of consciousness	5	_____ /1
Motivation and emotion	6	_____ /1
Learning	7, 19	_____ /2
Cognition	8, 20	_____ /2
Developmental psychology across the lifespan	9, 21	_____ /2
Personality	10, 22	_____ /2
Psychological disorders and health	11, 23	_____ /2
Treatment of psychological disorders	12	_____ /1
Social psychology	13, 14, 24	_____ /3
Statistics, tests, and measurement	15	_____ /1
Total Raw Score		_____ /24
Full Test Raw Score Projection*		_____ /96**

* Multiply raw score by 4

** CLEP's full length exam is approximately 95 questions; this diagnostic will provide a rough estimate.

Admittedly, evaluating your diagnostic score comes with some limitations; you can only calculate a raw score (rather than a score weighted using CLEP's techniques) and the limited number of sample questions can only help you guess at which categories are a struggle for you. However, it gives you a broad snapshot of your strengths and potential growth areas as you prepare for your exam.

EVALUATING YOUR STRENGTHS AND AREAS FOR IMPROVEMENT

Now that you can see how you performed in each category, reflect on your strengths and areas for improvement.

- What went well for you during the diagnostic test? Which categories were easiest for you?
- What did you struggle with during the diagnostic test? Which categories were hardest for you?
- After your experience, what are some things you want to keep in mind as you study?

Let's look at an example of a hypothetical test taker's diagnostic test scores and self-evaluation as a guide to help you pinpoint your strengths and areas for improvement in the context of the scoring categories. If you really cannot identify a strength or space for improvement in a category, mark it as *not applicable* (n/a).

DIAGNOSTIC TEST SELF-EVALUATION EXAMPLE

Full Test Raw Score Goal: 67/96

Category	Correct Answers	Strengths	Areas for Improvement
History, approaches, and methods	2/3	I had a good working knowledge of methods.	I need a better understanding of important theories and theorists.
Biological bases of behavior	2/2	This was all very familiar to me.	I could do better at recognizing how biology relates to consciousness.
Sensation and perception	2/2	The biology parts made sense to me, like the parts about senses.	n/a
States of consciousness	0/1	n/a	I got confused by the terms.

(continues)

DIAGNOSTIC TEST SELF-EVALUATION EXAMPLE (*CONTINUED*)

Motivation and emotion	1/1	I was familiar with the terms.	I only guessed, so it might have just been a lucky guess—I should still study this category.
Learning	1/2	I understand conditioning well.	I could learn more about cognitive processes related to learning.
Cognition	1/2	I know a lot about memory.	The stuff on language was new to me.
Developmental psychology across the lifespan	0/2	I knew a lot of the terms, even if I didn't understand the questions about them.	All the theories and theorists were unfamiliar to me, so I had to guess a lot.
Personality	0/2	I understand many of the terms.	I kept confusing the different theories.
Psychological disorders and health	1/2	I know what a lot of the disorders are.	I missed a question on somatoform disorders.
Treatment of psychological disorders	0/1	Many of the terms were familiar.	This is completely new to me.
Social psychology	0/3	I was familiar with a lot of the terms.	I was totally lost—most of this is new to me, so I'll have to memorize a lot.
Statistics, tests, and methods	1/1	Statistical methods are something I've studied a lot in other classes.	I could still use help seeing how it relates to psychology.
Raw Score	**11/24**	**I understand the biology behind psychology pretty well. I also already know a lot of important terms.**	**I need to pay more attention to specific theories and philosophical ideas. I need to recognize how the biology stuff I do know relates to psychology.**
Full Test Raw Score Projection*	**44/96****		

* Multiply raw score by 4

** CLEP's full length exam is approximately 95 questions; this diagnostic will provide a rough estimate.

Now fill in your answers based on your diagnostic test results. Try to evaluate your strengths and areas for improvement in each category. If you need more space, feel free to jot notes in a notebook.

DIAGNOSTIC TEST SELF-EVALUATION

Full Test Raw Score Goal: _____ /96

Category	Correct Answers	Strengths	Areas for Improvement
History, approaches, and methods	_____ /3		
Biological bases of behavior	_____ /2		
Sensation and perception	_____ /2		
States of consciousness	_____ /1		
Motivation and emotion	_____ /1		
Learning	_____ /2		
Cognition	_____ /2		

(continues)

DIAGNOSTIC TEST SELF-EVALUATION (*CONTINUED*)			
Developmental psychology across the lifespan	_____ /2		
Personality	_____ /2		
Psychological disorders and health	_____ /2		
Treatment of psychological disorders	_____ /1		
Social psychology	_____ /3		
Statistics, tests, and methods	_____ /1		
Raw Score	_____ /24		
Full Test Raw Score Projection*	_____ /96**		

* Multiply raw score by 4

**CLEP's full length exam is approximately 95 questions; this diagnostic will provide a rough estimate.

Keep these reflections in mind as you set goals for yourself and create a study plan.

SETTING GOALS

Now that you've reflected on your diagnostic test experience, think about your goals. If you decided to take your exam tomorrow without any further preparation and you did things the exact same way, you would likely perform the same way you did on the diagnostic test. Since you are using this book, you likely have some time to prepare for the exam, which means you have ample opportunity to improve your performance.

As a CLEP test taker, your general goal is to maximize the number of questions you answer correctly so that you have the best chance of scoring high enough to earn credit. The American Council of Education (ACE) recommends a scaled score of 50 (on a scale of 20 to 80) as a credit-earning score for CLEP Introductory Psychology and most other CLEP exams. However, individual schools may require a higher score than ACE recommends. Be sure to verify that your institution(s) of choice accept(s) CLEP Introductory Psychology exams for credit, then find out the minimum credit-earning scaled score required. Please note that the process for calculating a scaled score from a raw score varies by test subject and test form. There is no universal way to determine whether your raw score will earn credit. However, the common guidance is that answering 70% of questions correctly (67/96 for the CLEP Introductory Psychology exam) will put you near the ACE-recommended score. That value can act as a general goal, but first prioritize building on your strengths and addressing the areas of improvement that you identified in your Diagnostic Test Self-Evaluation. From there, you can set a score goal that works for you and make a study plan to achieve it.

CREATING A STUDY PLAN

When creating a study plan, first determine how much time you have to devote to preparation. If you have an hour a day for several months, you'll probably approach things differently than someone who is trying to study as comprehensively as possible in two weeks. Figure out how much time you have and set a reasonable goal for how much studying you would like to do in that time. Then, divide up the amount of preparation time you have according to your study priorities. Only you can determine the best way to do this. However, your diagnostic test offers helpful clues about how to do this most effectively.

Determining What to Study

The hypothetical test taker achieved a raw score of 11/24 on their diagnostic test, which would translate to a raw score of 44/96 on a full-length exam. They are aiming for a raw score of 67, meaning they'll need to answer 23 more questions correctly on the full-length exam to achieve their goal. The test taker can now use this information to plan their study time.

They should start by looking at the four categories in which they performed best: biological bases of behavior; sensation and perception; motivation and emotion; and statistics, tests, and methods. It might seem like the test taker doesn't need to spend time studying these categories, but strong categories represent an opportunity to pick up extra points that can compensate for questions missed in difficult categories. Moreover, the test taker noted that for at least one of these categories (motivation and emotion), they likely do still need some study time. The test taker will want to focus more time on other categories, but they should still make at least some time to study their stronger categories, particularly regarding any areas for improvement they identified in their analysis.

Next, the test taker should consider the categories in which they had the lowest performance: in this case, that would be the five categories for which they scored 0 points (states of consciousness, developmental psychology across the lifespan, personality, treatment of psychological disorders, and social psychology). From there, they should identify which is weighted most significantly and select that as their highest priority category—our test taker would thus identify social psychology as their highest study priority and the others as secondary priorities. Even for categories that are weighted lower, the test taker has the most room to improve in areas where they struggled and should plan to spend a bit of extra time on those categories accordingly.

The test taker should continue to apply this analytical process to the remaining categories. They should consider how much room there is for improvement in each category and how they can use the strategies that will help them most. If they are unsure how a category should be weighted in their study plan, skimming the related content review chapters in this book can help in gauging how familiar they are with a particular subject.

Creating a Study Schedule

After the test taker has analyzed their diagnostic test results and prioritized their study plan by category, they can create a schedule. Let's say our test taker has 1 hour per weekday for 6 weeks to study for their exam. At the end of the 5 weeks, they plan to take a practice test (Chapter 13 in this book), saving time in the last week for any last-minute review based on the results of their practice test.

When you break it down, this test taker has 25 total hours to devote to studying before their practice test and 5 more available for review after the practice test. Accordingly, they might plan their time as follows:

History, approaches, and methods	2 Hours
Biological bases of behavior	1 Hour
Sensation and perception	1 Hour
States of consciousness	1.5 Hours
Motivation and emotion	1.5 Hours
Learning	1.5 Hours
Cognition	1.5 Hours
Developmental psychology across the lifespan	2.5 Hours
Personality	2.5 Hours
Psychological disorders and health	2 Hours
Treatment of psychological disorders	2 Hours
Social psychology	4 Hours
Statistics, tests, and methods	1 Hour
Review before practice test	1 Hour
Review after practice test	5 Hours

It's a good idea to approach plans flexibly and adjust as you progress. If the test taker felt confident that they had reviewed social psychology thoroughly after 3 hours of study and decided to spend a spare hour on other categories instead, that would still be a perfectly suitable plan. The test taker could even break down their study plan by day to stay on track, as in the following example.

		STUDY PLAN EXAMPLE			
Week	**Monday**	**Tuesday**	**Wednesday**	**Thursday**	**Friday**
1	History, approaches, and methods	States of consciousness	Learning	Cognition	Motivation and emotion
2	Developmental psychology across the lifespan	Personality	Psychological disorders and health	Treatment of psychological disorders	Social psychology
3	Treatment of psychological disorders	Social psychology	History, approaches, and methods	States of consciousness; learning	Developmental psychology across the lifespan; personality
4	Cognition; motivation and emotion	Psychological disorders and health	Social psychology	Statistics, tests, and methods	Personality
5	Social psychology	Developmental psychology across the lifespan	Biological bases of behavior	Sensation and perception	Review
6	Review concepts missed on the practice test				

Of course, you can allot your study hours in any way that makes sense for you—and not everyone will be able to plan their studying in such an orderly fashion. Nonetheless, creating a specific study calendar that dedicates time to different categories and for returning to them later for review is a good idea. It also is a good reminder that multiple repetitions correlate with a better chance of meeting your score goals. Plan to include variety and ample opportunity to review categories you have already studied. If you follow a clear study plan, then by the time you take your practice test, you will be thoroughly prepared to improve your score.

USING THIS BOOK

Remember that a CLEP exam isn't just about what you know but also how well you can remember foundational details across the entirety of the material covered in a semester-long course. The diagnostic test provides a snapshot of how you might perform on your CLEP exam, but it's not the entire picture—you also likely know which aspects of the subject matter you know better and which will require more review. Use your diagnostic test to form an initial study plan but recognize that you may need to adjust how you divide your study time as you review the 13 scoring categories covered on the exam. Each category is covered in Chapters 4–12. While some of these chapters are devoted to a single scoring category, others include information that is relevant for multiple scoring categories. For complex categories, like biological bases of behavior, relevant information may span multiple chapters. Use the introductory paragraphs at the beginning of each content chapter to help determine which scoring categories are covered by its contents.

As a reminder, the **bold key terms** throughout this book highlight important concepts that are likely to come up on your exam. Alongside the study plan you make based on your diagnostic test results, these bold key terms can help guide any research you may need to do beyond this guide to feel fully prepared for your CLEP exam. Information found in tables and charts should also be considered important, even if a term is not bolded within the chart. As with all CLEP exams, you may still encounter questions about more obscure topics than those presented in this guide, so utilize any other knowledge or resources you have as you work through the content categories. You can also find a wealth of supplementary materials to fill out your study plan—including full-length practice tests, videos, and interactive presentations—at **www.petersons.com/testprep/clep**.

Chapter 4

History, Approaches, and Methods

OVERVIEW

- History of Psychology
- Approaches to Psychology
- Research Methods
- Conclusion
- Readiness Check: History, Approaches, and Methods
- Test Yourself: History, Approaches, and Methods

This chapter covers a brief history of psychology from its origins as a matter of mythos and magic through its recognition as a discrete field of study. The perspectives of major theorists in the field and the methods of research that support psychology as a **soft science** with elements of **hard science** will also be explored. Questions related to the history, approaches, and methods of psychology will account for 11%–12% of the CLEP Introductory Psychology exam.

HISTORY OF PSYCHOLOGY

Psychology is the study of how the human mind functions. Psychologists also study human development and neural physiology as well as internal and external behaviors, motivations, interpersonal relationships, mental disorders, and more. At various times throughout its early history, psychology was viewed as inseparable from religion, as the work of spirits, as a simple matter of stimulus and response, or as a measure of morality. In many ancient cultures such as those of the Egyptians, Romans, Greeks, and Incans, people were so convinced that abnormal behavior was a sign of spiritual possession that they participated in a practice known as **trepanning**. Also called trepanation, trepanning involves creating an opening in the skull with either a specialized screw or a sharp blow from a rock with the goal of releasing evil spirits. In later cultures, there was no differentiation between the physiology of the brain and the mind.

René Descartes, a French philosopher and scientist active in the early 17th century, was one of the first to explore the concept of the mind as conceptually different from the body. Although Descartes thought the mind was contained in the heart, not the head, he endorsed a philosophy that "ideas" were nebulous and abstract rather than physical in nature. Descartes's concept was novel for the era, particularly because the Catholic Church controlled much of scientific study up to that point. At the time, the prevailing theory was that thoughts and feelings were given to individuals and monitored by God. To avoid being labeled a heretic, Descartes had to exercise caution in espousing his theory. The notion that an idea could exist independently of both the body and a deity challenged the church's views. It marked a vital turning point for the eventual development of psychology as a field of study.

One of the first attempts at using scientific psychological study methods was by **Franz Joseph Gall**, an Austrian scientist who developed the theory of **phrenology** in the late 18th century. Phrenology, which is now considered a **pseudoscience**, posited that the shape of a person's skull, along with certain facial features, defined their intelligence and personality traits. While the theory was eventually proven to be completely inaccurate, it was well regarded at the time and used to justify the status quo of racism and classism. Most notably, phrenology posited that one could identify "lower class" facial features and use them to show evidence of criminality. Phrenology has long since been dismissed, but it is an example of an early attempt to quantify personality and intellect with objective data.

During the 19th century, people experiencing mental illness were often sent to **asylums**. The worst asylums were devastatingly understaffed, prisonlike institutions where patients were neglected and subjected to what would now be considered torturous procedures—bloodletting and ice baths were both common treatments. Better conditions existed in **sanatoriums**, where wealthier patients typically received care. Because there was little research at the time to inform a unified system of diagnostics, the manner of care and the types of diagnoses varied greatly among institutions. Toward the middle of the 19th century, a movement arose calling for more humane treatment of people with mental illnesses. The movement asserted that patients should be allowed the freedom to move about the grounds of facilities and complete simple jobs. While conditions initially improved at some institutions, by the beginning of the 20th century, most asylums had reverted to a more institutional format in which patients still had severely limited rights.

Some of the challenge in recognizing the "mind" as something separate from but still connected to a person's physiology was the difficulty of establishing a basic **objective** method of testing that used the **scientific method** to produce standardized results. Even today, many psychological elements can only be measured through **subjective** testing. Examples of subjective testing include asking a person to self-report their pain level or observing a person's behaviors to determine their intensity. These measures are subjective because they rely primarily on **qualitative data** rather than **quantitative data**. As other sciences developed, psychological researchers and clinicians eventually developed their own methods to quantify data, meaning they figured out ways to translate objective and subjective results into measurable numbers. Today, psychologists use both types of data to evaluate the human mind and its functions.

APPROACHES TO PSYCHOLOGY

There are multiple ways to approach the study of the mind. Some focus more on the scientific and physical aspects, while others emphasize less tangible concepts and measurements. Because psychology is considered a soft science, its study is made up of theories rather than objective laws that govern hard sciences like chemistry and physics. Each approach has its value, and it is important to remember that human behavior, though often predictable, is also infinitely and individually variable. While more objective scientific measures are often necessary for studying the mind, the field of psychology is built on a series of dominant theories that integrate subjective analysis.

Psychodynamic Theory

Sigmund Freud was an Austrian neurologist who developed **psychodynamic theory** in opposition to his training as a physician, which focused on the mind as a physiological component of the body. Psychodynamic theory (also known as psychoanalytic theory) asserts that a person continues to be affected by childhood events throughout their adult life. According to Freud, each person possesses a **conscious**, a **subconscious**, and an **unconscious** mind. The conscious mind encompasses what a person is aware of from moment to moment—their thoughts and emotions as they experience them. The subconscious operates as storage for what a person has learned and experienced on a conscious level. The unconscious contains memories that a person is unaware of but that can still shape their actions and emotions.

Freud theorized that most of what we identify as fear, anxiety, and depression are a result of thoughts and emotions in the unconscious mind. Accordingly, part of psychodynamic therapy involves bringing those experiences back to the conscious mind to be analyzed. A practitioner of **hypnosis**, Freud often used this method to bring buried thoughts to light. He also posited that most of the unconscious mind is composed of memories made before the age of 5. One of his more controversial ideas involved what is known as the **Oedipus complex**, which is the idea that, almost from birth, young male children wish to be with their mothers romantically and that they are in masculine, even sexual, competition with their fathers. Later, Freudian psychologist **Carl Jung** proposed a similarly controversial theory called the **Electra complex**, which postulated a similar wish on the part of young female children to compete with their mothers for romantic attention from their fathers. Today, neither theory is widely used, and many (but not all) of Freud's other ideas have similarly been relegated to the field's history.

Adlerian Theory

After some of Freud's contributions to psychodynamic theory waned in popularity, a contemporary and former student of his named **Alfred Adler** added his own spin. Instead of focusing on early sexuality, **Adlerian theory** took a holistic view of personality, suggesting that different aspects of personality could be integrated to form a healthy psyche. Adler thought that feelings of inferiority versus superiority were the key to explaining the mind and that recognizing this internal struggle could help illuminate issues related to social justice.

Biological Theory

Biological theory uses the same systems and procedures to study psychology that are used in other biological fields. For example, to explain a person's reaction to a major stressor such as a physical assault or a car accident, biological theory asserts that biological mechanisms in the central nervous system contribute to **fight**, **flight**, **freeze**, or **fawn reactions**. While biological theory does assume that all humans have the same basic brain physiology, it makes allowances for varied responses due to individual differences in biochemical makeup and past experiences. Biological theory also postulates that trauma can cause physical changes to the brain, which, in turn, affect how an individual might respond to perceived threats.

Cognitive Approach

In the **cognitive approach**, the brain's physical structure is not considered as important as its less tangible mechanisms of thoughts, feelings, creativity, and intelligence. The mind is viewed like a computer—data goes in and gets processed and synthesized so that thoughts and feelings can occur. This concept is known as the **black box theory**, which states that the inner workings of the mind cannot be observed and therefore cannot be measured using biological methods. The causes of thoughts and feelings are considered unimportant to cognitive psychologists since they cannot be observed. Accordingly, cognitive psychology relies heavily on testing methods such as IQ tests and problem-solving exercises to extrapolate information about the mechanics of the inner workings of the mind instead.

Behavioral Approach

John B. Watson is considered the founder of the **behavioral approach** of psychology. Behavioral theory is based on the observation of a stimulus and a subject's response to it. The behavioral approach posits that humans and nonhuman animals can be studied by watching their behavior and then attempting to alter it with conditioning.

Classical and Operant Conditioning

One of Watson's best-known behavioral studies, the **Little Albert experiment**, involved an older infant pseudonymously called Albert. Initially, numerous tests were conducted to determine if Albert was an emotionally stable child. Albert was then deliberately given a phobia using **classical conditioning**. Classical conditioning involves the mental pairing of two stimuli, resulting in a learned association between them. The conditioned response operates below the conscious level. In Albert's case, he was placed on a blanket in the lab and given a white rat (positive stimulus) to play with. The child was initially not frightened of the rat and seemed to enjoy playing with it. However, Watson started pairing the appearance of the rat with a loud sound (neutral stimulus) that emanated from behind Albert, startling him. After several times, Albert began to associate the rat with the fear of the sound and would become distressed at just the sight of the rodent (conditioned response). Albert reportedly generalized this fear to any white, fluffy object and would cry and try to move away from it. While the experiment was successful in showing the efficacy of classical conditioning, it has since been regarded as an example of unethical and inhumane experimental design.

B. F. Skinner added another perspective to the behavioral approach, known as **operant conditioning**. Unlike classical conditioning, operant conditioning works at the conscious level and shapes behavior by offering consequences for targeted actions. We will cover the differences between classical and operant conditioning in greater depth in Chapter 8.

Reinforcement and Punishment

Another topic within the behavioral approach is reinforcement. **Positive reinforcement** encourages a desired behavior by offering a reward; for example, if a person is training their dog and gives them a treat when they sit after being instructed to do so, the treat (alongside any praise or encouragement the person gives) functions as positive reinforcement. By contrast, **negative reinforcement** encourages a behavior by removing something that a subject finds unpleasant; for example, if a child completes their homework before dinner and is then excused from doing the dishes, freedom from the chore counts as negative reinforcement intended to increase the likelihood that they will complete their homework before dinner in the future.

In contrast to reinforcement, which is meant to encourage a specific behavior, **punishment** is used to discourage a specific behavior. For example, if a student's phone is confiscated for texting in class, the goal of the punishment is to dissuade them from texting in class in the future. Punishment has been shown to be less effective at shaping behaviors than positive and negative reinforcement.

Humanistic Approach

Both a philosophy and psychological theory, the **humanistic approach** is the belief that people are inherently good and behave poorly not because they are "bad" but because they struggle. The goal of the humanistic approach is holistic, meaning it is intended to integrate all aspects of a person's experiences and personality. The end goal of this integration is **self-actualization**, a sense of true fulfillment that comes with having reached one's full potential. Humanistic psychology emerged as a mid–20th century response to both B. F. Skinner's behavioral research and Freud's psychodynamic theory. In the humanistic approach, a person in therapy is considered an equal partner in their treatment and is encouraged to participate. The theory focuses on a person's entire life rather than a specific age group, and individuals are encouraged to be mindful of their thoughts and behaviors so they may better understand themselves and their environment.

MASLOW'S HIERARCHY OF NEEDS

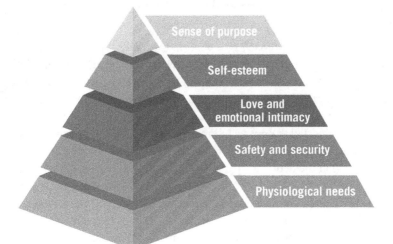

A prominent example of humanistic psychology is **Maslow's hierarchy of needs**, represented by a five-level pyramid that shows what a person needs to reach self-actualization. The base level represents physiological needs such as food and shelter. The second level is the need for safety and security, both of which are considered "basic" needs. The third and fourth levels represent psychological needs—level three is love and emotional intimacy, and level four is a sense of purpose and accomplishment. Lastly, at the top of the pyramid, the fifth level represents self-actualization: the feeling that one is achieving their full potential. Self-actualization is whatever that feeling means to a person, including leisure, creative endeavors, or a general sense of accomplishment. Humanistic psychologists see self-actualization as a goal to strive for since one cannot reach it unless all "lesser" needs are met first.

Biopsychosocial Approach

The **biopsychosocial approach** considers a person's biological predisposition to certain responses and disorders, their home and community environment, and their interior thoughts and feelings. Recognizing the intricate interplay of these factors allows for a deeper understanding of the origins of mental disorders and the underlying causes of behavior and feelings. This approach emphasizes how life experiences shape people differently and has the goal of finding a more reliable way to predict favorable outcomes for those treated according to this school of thought. The broad philosophical question that drives much of this approach is about "nature versus nurture" and which has the most impact—most biopsychosocial psychologists would posit that the answer lies somewhere in the middle.

The biopsychosocial approach is popular in the medical field because of its effectiveness in illuminating the ways that issues that are not caused by one another may nonetheless be related. For example, a patient with major depressive disorder and extensive liver damage may also have financial problems and a family history of addiction. While one of these elements is directly connected to another, all may be interrelated because patterns of correlation emerge across populations. In this example, a psychologist might note that the depressed person with a family history of addiction is much more likely to experience alcohol use disorder, which could be exacerbated by financial problems or existing liver issues. Someone struggling with alcoholism is more likely to make poor decisions regarding money and is also more likely to have liver problems. Recognizing the interconnectedness of these issues, a practitioner might therefore ask the patient about their history of alcohol use or any other interrelated concern. A potential biopsychosocial response to this situation would be to treat the depression with medication, provide counseling to improve coping skills and minimize drinking, and offer financial counseling or community services to help address related financial needs.

RESEARCH METHODS

A guiding principle behind psychological (and most other) scientific study is that **correlation** does not equal **causation**. When performing research in psychology, researchers are looking for connections (correlations) rather than causes—because while causes are incredibly difficult to prove, correlations can be ascertained by recognizing patterns.

A popular example used to differentiate the two is the metric that states that when sales of ice cream increase, so do shark attacks. Does eating ice cream attract shark attacks or do shark attacks make people hungry for ice cream? No, of course not—neither factor can be considered the cause of the other. However, there may be an explanation for why the two correlate, such as the fact that shark attacks are more likely to happen when people are at the beach, and people are more likely to both go to the beach and eat ice cream when the weather is warmer. The warm weather in this example is a type of factor known as a **confounding variable**, a possible cause for correlation that is not included in the design of an experiment. The relationship between shark attacks and ice cream sales is a **positive correlation** because both sets of data move in the same direction (increasing in this case, though it is also possible for a positive correlation to show a decreasing trend). A **negative correlation** occurs when the data presented moves in tandem but in opposite directions; for example, mitten sales increase as ice cream sales decrease.

Correlational Studies

Correlational studies seek to establish a relationship between two variables without determining causality, often because designing an experiment to determine cause would be unethical or impossible. Since causality is not a factor in correlational studies, the aim is to establish a relationship between at least two datasets. There is no variable being manipulated and no control group, which is why they are considered studies rather than proper experiments. For example, a correlational study involving the dangers of smoking marijuana while pregnant might have a group of pregnant subjects who self-report either smoking or not smoking. Researchers would then follow up to measure birth outcomes and measure them against the self-reported data. In this case, asserting that any behavior caused a certain outcome would be difficult, but analyzing trends among subjects may point to correlations that merit analysis. Correlational studies can also be conducted by analyzing datasets from existing sources.

The Experimental Method

Both psychologists and those in the broader medical field rely heavily on the **experimental method**. In this mode of study, researchers form a hypothesis and collect data from at least two groups of participants. They give one group (known as the **control group**) a **placebo** or do not intervene with the group, and they give the other group (known as the

experimental group) a particular treatment or manipulate another variable. These experiments are usually **blind experiments**, meaning that the participants do not know to which group they have been assigned. Sometimes, researchers prefer a **double-blind experiment**, meaning that the researchers also do not know which participants are in each group. Then, researchers compare the data via statistical analysis to see if a relationship between variables can be determined. For ethical reasons, some studies cannot be conducted in an experimental fashion. The previous example of a study on the effects of smoking marijuana while pregnant could not be done in a truly experimental manner because it would be unethical to intentionally give pregnant subjects marijuana when the effects of doing so are not yet known. As previously indicated, a correlational study that allows pregnant subjects to self-report their marijuana use is far more suitable.

There are two important aspects to consider when analyzing the results of research conducted using the experimental method: **internal validity** and **external validity**. Internal validity indicates the degree to which the intended target can be measured. It requires researchers to ask if the experiment could be replicated and, if so, whether it would produce the same or very similar results. For example, if an experiment is conducted but subsequent teams can't duplicate the result by following the same protocol, it lacks internal validity—a good indicator that it is not measuring the proper data. External validity, on the other hand, indicates how well the results of an experiment can be extrapolated to the "real world," where all variables can't be as easily controlled and confounding variables are sure to appear. Issues with external validity are common in research involving rodents or other nonhuman animals since results may differ drastically if the same experiments are conducted on human beings in a controlled environment, let alone human beings in the "real world." Good psychological research (or any research) must use sound and valid experimental design with internal and external validity.

Clinical Studies

Clinical studies rely heavily on **case studies**: individual write-ups on a patient's diagnosis, treatment, and prognosis. Clinical studies can offer specific information about patients and their symptomology and personal results, but since they do not include a control group or an experimental group, they are not true experiments, even if a variable (treatment type) is being manipulated within the study.

Ethical Research

Ethical research is a necessity in psychology and all other sciences. To conduct psychological research ethically, all participants must give their full consent. They may not know if they are in the control or experimental group, but they need to know about any possible outcomes resulting from receiving or not receiving treatment. Participants must not be put in harm's way regardless of their consent, and members of a control group must not be subjected to harm by being given a placebo. For example, if a participant in the control group for a new cancer drug receives a placebo for an experimental cancer treatment, they must also continue to receive standard cancer treatment, as going completely untreated would be detrimental to their health. Even in clinical studies, participants should be informed that their case may be shared (even anonymously) with other researchers and be asked for their consent.

CONCLUSION

The study of psychology has progressed from ancient practices like trepanation and beliefs attributing mental illness to negative spirits to the current network of qualitative and quantitative research methods that continue to illuminate the inner workings of the human mind. Approaches to the field are numerous and each approach contains strengths and weaknesses. Modern psychologists tend to blend methods—the currently dominant biopsychosocial method is one example—or choose methods suitable for their purposes. Similarly, each of the three main research methods in psychology—correlational studies, experiments, and clinical studies—have characteristics that make them suitable for different types of research, and researchers choose accordingly.

READINESS CHECK: HISTORY, APPROACHES, AND METHODS

- What is trepanning and how does it relate to ancient beliefs about psychology?
- How would you summarize René Descartes's philosophy of the mind? How did it differ from dominant ideas at the time?
- What is historically significant about the theory of phrenology and how did it benefit later research? Why was it proven to be a pseudoscience?

- What was the difference between an asylum and a sanatorium, and how did each relate to the conditions under which mental patients were typically treated in the 19th century?
- What are examples of a positive correlation and a negative correlation? Can you think of a confounding variable for your examples of each?
- What is the difference between qualitative and quantitative data, and why must psychology researchers rely on both?
- Can you summarize the following approaches to psychology and, if relevant, any key figures, studies, or experiments associated with them?
  - Psychodynamic theory
  - Adlerian theory
  - Biological theory
  - Cognitive approach
  - Behavioral approach
  - Humanistic approach
  - Biopsychosocial approach
- Can you summarize the following three major research methods and identify the types of studies that might be best suited for each?
  - Correlational studies
  - Experimental method
  - Clinical studies
- What are blind experiments and double-blind experiments? How does the definition of each relate to the difference between a control group and an experimental group?
- What does the phrase "correlation does not equal causation" mean?
- What are some of the important ethical concerns psychologists must consider when designing experiments and studies?

TEST YOURSELF: HISTORY, APPROACHES, AND METHODS

Directions: Each of the questions or incomplete statements below is followed by five suggested answers or completions. Select the one best answer for each. The Answer Key and Explanations will follow.

1. Which psychological approach is also considered a philosophical mindset and encourages therapy clients to actively participate in their treatment?

    A. Psychodynamic approach
    B. Humanistic approach
    C. Cognitive approach
    D. Biological approach
    E. Behavioral approach

2. In Freud's psychodynamic theory, what term describes a young boy feeling compelled to compete with his father for his mother's affection?

    A. Eldwood effect
    B. Uncanny effect
    C. Oedipus complex
    D. Milton explanation
    E. Electra complex

3. Which of the following questions relates to determining external validity?

    A. Can the results of the experiment be extrapolated to human subjects outside of lab settings?
    B. Can the results of the experiment be duplicated?
    C. Can the results of the experiment determine causality?
    D. Can the results of the experiment be trusted?
    E. What is the confounding variable in this study?

4. Anna is trying to stop biting her fingernails. If she can go a week without doing so, her mother will take her for a spa manicure as positive reinforcement. What is this type of system called?

A. Mechanical conditioning
B. Cognitive conditioning
C. Classical conditioning
D. Marginal conditioning
E. Operant conditioning

5. Who was the first prominent figure to assert that the mind was separate from the body?

A. Sigmund Freud
B. B. F. Skinner
C. John B. Watson
D. Franz Joseph Gall
E. René Descartes

Answer Key and Explanations

1. B	2. C	3. A	4. E	5. E

1. **The correct answer is B.** In the humanistic approach, humans are thought to be inherently good but prone to making poor or cruel choices because they are struggling to achieve self-actualization. Humanism emphasizes mindfulness about one's impulses and actions.

2. **The correct answer is C.** The Oedipus complex is the name Freud gave to his theory that young boys feel like they are in direct competition with their fathers for affection and intimacy from their mothers. Later, Carl Jung asserted that young girls similarly have an Electra complex (choice E) that puts them in competition with their mothers for affection and intimacy from their fathers.

3. **The correct answer is A.** External validity means that results can be applied outside of a controlled setting. Internal validity means that an experiment measured the proper dataset, and the results of the experiment could be replicated to produce the same or very similar results, as in choices B and D. Choices C and E refer to correlational studies.

4. **The correct answer is E.** Positive and negative reinforcement are typically related to operant conditioning. Operant conditioning involves making a choice about behavior, which is reinforced (with a positive or negative reward) or punished (to diminish a behavior). Operant conditioning contrasts with cognitive conditioning (choice B) wherein a connection is made between a neutral stimulus and a positive stimulus, resulting in an unconscious, conditioned response.

5. **The correct answer is E.** In the 16th century, Descartes felt that "ideas" were separate from the physical part of the mind. Due to the Catholic Church's power at the time, he had to write strategically so he wouldn't be considered a heretic for refuting the dominant belief that ideas came exclusively from God.

Chapter 5

Biological Bases of Behavior

OVERVIEW
- The Principles of Genetics
- The Etiology of Psychological Disorders
- The Nervous System
- The Endocrine System
- Conclusion
- Readiness Check: Biological Bases of Behavior
- Test Yourself: Biological Bases of Behavior

This chapter offers a comprehensive overview of the biology behind behavior, including genetics, the etiology of psychological disorders, the nervous system, and the endocrine system. Topics in this chapter primarily address the scoring category "Biological Bases of Behavior," which accounts for approximately 8% of the questions on the CLEP Introductory Psychology exam. Note, however, that the contents of Chapter 6 are also critical for addressing questions from this scoring category since sensation and perception are closely linked with the biological systems that govern behavior.

THE PRINCIPLES OF GENETICS

To understand how biology affects human behavior, it's helpful to start with **genetics**—the study of genes and heredity. **Deoxyribonucleic acid (DNA)** is a molecule that carries genetic instructions for the development, functioning, and reproduction of all living organisms. DNA consists of **nucleotides** and forms a double helix structure. **Ribonucleic acid (RNA)** is involved in **protein synthesis** and usually exists as a single-stranded structure.

Genes, which are segments of DNA, contain instructions that influence physical traits, biological functions, and one's susceptibility to certain diseases and **psychological disorders**. Each gene consists of different variant forms, called **alleles**, with one allele inherited from each parent. Located on chromosomes, alleles can be **dominant** or **recessive** and affect the expression of specific traits or disorders.

Chromosomes in cell nuclei determine physical traits. Humans have 23 pairs of chromosomes in each cell: 22 **autosomes** and 1 pair of **sex-determining chromosomes**. The **Y chromosome** is responsible for male-specific traits, while the **X chromosome** carries genes related to both male and female characteristics; females have two X chromosomes, and males have one X and one Y chromosome. Sometimes, people are born with **differences in sex development (DSD)** that result in chromosomal, gonadal, or anatomical anomalies. These conditions occur due to atypical genetic makeup and affect approximately 1 in 1,700 individuals.

Heritability gauges the genetic contribution to traits. Inheritance patterns include autosomal and **sex-linked traits**. Males, having only one X chromosome, express any gene variant on it, leading to a higher occurrence of X-linked disorders such as colorblindness and hemophilia A.

The **nature versus nurture debate** explores genetic and environmental influences on behavior. **Behavioral genetics** studies this dynamic, including **gene-environment interplay**. **Twin studies**, especially of **monozygotic twins** who share 100% of their genes, help assess genetic impact, with higher **concordance rates** indicating significant genetic contribution. Studies of **dizygotic twins**, who share 50% of their genes, provide insights into genetic and environmental factors simultaneously.

THE ETIOLOGY OF PSYCHOLOGICAL DISORDERS

In psychology, the study of the **etiology**—the causes and origins—of diseases or abnormal conditions plays a crucial role in comprehending different conditions and disorders, which generally arise from a combination of inherited genetic variants and environmental factors.

Inherited Psychological Disorders

Both **inherited factors** and **environmental factors** contribute significantly to psychological disorders, particularly when environmental factors affect how inherited factors are expressed. Psychological disorders usually result from the interaction of multiple genes; for instance, **depression** and anxiety have a **polygenic** basis. **Chromosomal duplications** can also lead to mental disorders such as **Down syndrome**, which disrupts typical brain and body development. Other psychological disorders, like **schizophrenia** and **bipolar disorder**, arise from **gene mutations** affecting neurotransmitter regulation or neural development.

Acquired Psychological Disorders

Environmental factors, including childhood experiences such as trauma or abuse, can have long-lasting effects on mental health. These **adverse childhood experiences (ACEs)** have been linked to an increased risk of developing various psychological disorders, including **post-traumatic stress disorder (PTSD)**, **anxiety disorders**, and depression.

PTSD is a psychological disorder that can develop after experiencing or witnessing a traumatic event. PTSD primarily stems from environmental factors, including exposure to severe stressors such as combat, natural disasters, or abuse. These traumatic experiences can cause lasting changes in brain function and structure, affecting an individual's ability to cope with stressful situations. Psychologists are also increasingly interested in the way numerous traumatic events over one's childhood can contribute to complex PTSD (CPTSD), which brings with it additional symptoms and comorbidities. Some clinicians use an **ACE score**—a measurement of how many ACEs an individual has experienced—to determine a person's risk level for CPTSD.

Life events such as loss or financial difficulties can trigger psychological disorders, especially when combined with genetic vulnerability. Social factors, like family dynamics and societal expectations, also contribute to psychological disorders. **Substance use disorders** are generally influenced by a combination of genetic predisposition and environmental factors like peer influence and traumatic experiences.

Understanding the complex relationship between inherited genetic factors and environmental factors is crucial to preventing, treating, and managing psychological disorders. Adopting a holistic approach that analyzes both influences promotes a comprehensive view of mental health care.

THE NERVOUS SYSTEM

Neurons are the building blocks of the **nervous system**, which is responsible for transmitting and processing information. To explore the complexities of the brain and its remarkable capabilities, it is important to understand neuron structure and how neurons communicate via electrical and chemical processes. The following table lists the various components of neurons and summarizes their characteristics and functions.

COMPONENTS OF NEURONS

Component	Characteristics/Functions
Axon	• Long, slender projection that extends from the soma and may vary in length • Carries electrical impulses away from the cell body • Transmits information to muscles, glands, and other neurons
Dendrite	• Branchlike structure that receives incoming signals from other neurons • Covered in tiny protrusions called dendritic spines that increase the surface area for synaptic connections • Integrates and relays electrochemical signals to the soma
Glia	• Also known as a glial cell • Nonneuronal cell that provides support and protection for neurons • Maintains chemical environment, insulates neurons, and assists in neuronal development and repair
Neurotransmitter	• Chemical substance that facilitates neural communication
Postsynaptic neuron	• "Receiving" neuron to which neurotransmitters bind to transmit signals across the synapses
Presynaptic neuron	• "Sending" neuron that releases neurotransmitters into the synaptic cleft
Soma	• Also known as the cell body • Serves as the core control center of the neuron • Integrates and generates signals from incoming stimuli • Houses the nucleus and other cellular machinery
Synapse	• Junction between neurons where neural communication occurs
Synaptic gap	• Small gap between neurons

Neurotransmission

Neurons communicate through the propagation of electrical signals. This process, called **neurotransmission**, involves both electrical and chemical elements.

When they are in a **resting state**, neurons are polarized (their interior is negatively charged compared with their exterior). The process of neurotransmission begins when the presynaptic neuron generates an electrical impulse, called an **action potential**. The action potential is associated with the influx of positively charged sodium ions across the axon terminal and the process of **depolarization**, whereby the electrical charge inside the neuron becomes less negative.

As the wave of depolarization travels down the length of the axon, the electrical signal triggers the opening of **voltage-gated ion channels**. **Calcium ions** then enter the axon terminal, and vesicles containing neurotransmitters fuse with the presynaptic membrane. Neurotransmitters are then released into the synaptic gap, where they bind to **receptors** on the postsynaptic neuron, initiating a response.

Some neurotransmitters are classified as **neurohormones**. These are chemical messengers released by neurons into the bloodstream, where they act as **hormones** that can affect distant target cells. Unlike traditional neurotransmitters, which act in a localized manner, neurohormones can have widespread effects throughout the body. Examples of neurohormones include **norepinephrine**, **epinephrine**, **oxytocin**, and **vasopressin**.

Substances that modify neuron activity and affect responsiveness to neurotransmitters are called **neuromodulators**. These molecules can alter the strength and efficacy of synaptic transmission and regulate neuronal excitability. Some neurotransmitters, including **dopamine**, **serotonin**, **acetylcholine (ACh)**, and **endorphins**, also act as neuromodulators.

The following tables outline the major hormones and neurotransmitters that will be important to know for the CLEP Introductory Psychology exam.

MAJOR HORMONES

Hormone	Target Tissues	Functions	Effects of Dysregulation
ACTH (adrenocorticotropic hormone)	Kidneys (adrenal cortex)	• Stimulates the synthesis and release of glucocorticoids, primarily cortisol, from the adrenal glands • Regulates metabolic activity and stress responses	• Excessive ACTH production can result in excessive cortisol production, leading to symptoms like weight gain, high blood pressure, and muscle weakness • Insufficient ACTH production can cause fatigue, weight loss, and low blood pressure

(continues)

MAJOR HORMONES (*CONTINUED*)

Hormone	Target Tissues	Functions	Effects of Dysregulation
FSH (follicle-stimulating hormone)	Gonads	• Stimulates the growth and production of gametes in both sexes	• High FSH levels may indicate ovarian failure or menopause in females and testicular failure or infertility in males
GH (growth hormone)	Muscles, bones	• Promotes the growth and development of bones, muscles, and other tissues in children and adolescents • Helps maintain muscle mass and bone density in adults	• Deficiency during childhood can lead to stunted growth and short stature • Excess GH in adults can cause the enlargement of facial features, hands, and feet
LH (luteinizing hormone)	Gonads	• Works in conjunction with FSH to regulate reproductive processes • Triggers ovulation and egg release in females • Stimulates testosterone production in the testes in males	• Reproductive issues
PRL (prolactin)	Mammary glands	• Stimulates reproductive development and promotes milk production after childbirth • Helps regulate the immune system	• Reproduction and fertility issues
TSH (thyroid-stimulating hormone)	Thyroid	• Stimulates and regulates the production and release of hormones from the thyroid gland • Stimulates the growth and function of the thyroid gland	• Low TSH levels are associated with hypothyroidism • High TSH levels are associated with hyperthyroidism

MAJOR NEUROTRANSMITTERS

Neurotransmitter	Characteristics/Functions	Effects of Dysregulation
ACh (acetylcholine)	• Primary neurotransmitter of the parasympathetic nervous system • Transmits signals between motor neurons and muscle fibers in the neuromuscular junction • Acts as both a neurotransmitter and neuromodulator, influencing arousal, memory, motivation, and attention	Neurodegenerative disease
Dopamine	• Neuromodulatory molecule with multiple biological functions • Plays a major role in reward-motivated behaviors since the anticipation of a reward increases dopamine • Contributes to voluntary movement, mood regulation, and cognition	ADHD, Parkinson's disease, schizophrenia
Epinephrine	• Also known as adrenaline • Acts primarily as a hormone but is also used by some neurons in the brain's medulla oblongata • Is also involved, like norepinephrine, in the sympathetic nervous system response, including pupil dilation	Hypertension, sleep disturbances, anxiety, decreased immunity
GABA (gamma-aminobutyric acid)	• Major inhibitory neurotransmitter in mammals that reduces neuronal excitability • May have regulatory roles in sleep-wake cycles • Reduces stress and anxiety when levels are high	Epilepsy, anxiety disorders
Glutamate	• Primary excitatory neurotransmitter in vertebrates • Plays an important role in synaptic plasticity, learning, memory, and synaptogenesis during brain development	Various neurobehavioral disorders, including autism and depression

(continues)

MAJOR NEUROTRANSMITTERS (*CONTINUED*)

Neurotransmitter	Characteristics/Functions	Effects of Dysregulation
Norepinephrine	• Also known as noradrenaline • Plays an important role in sympathetic nervous system response • Triggers, when released, an increase in heart rate and blood pressure; blood flow to the skeletal muscles; and the release of glucose from energy stores	Abnormal blood pressure and heart rate, low blood sugar, anxiety, depression, cognitive dysfunction
Serotonin	• Regulates mood, appetite, cognition, reward, learning, memory, and sleep • Plays an important role in social behavior, hierarchical organization, and regulation of aggression	Depression, anxiety, mood disorders

Movement and Reflexes

The **neuromuscular junction** is a vital link between nerve cells that helps signals from the nervous system reach muscles. This connection enables one to control body movements, including **voluntary muscle movement**. **Skeletal muscles**, also called voluntary muscles, are responsible for conscious movements like walking, running, lifting, and changing facial expressions. They consist of long, cylindrical cells called **muscle fibers**, which are bundled together to form muscle tissue.

At the neuromuscular junction, **motor neurons** originating in the spinal cord connect with muscle fibers by extending their long axons. These axons end in **synaptic terminals** that form bridges between motor neurons and muscle fibers. When an action potential reaches the synaptic terminal, it triggers the release of neurotransmitters such as acetylcholine, the primary neurotransmitter involved in the neuromuscular junction. Acetylcholine then binds to receptors on the muscle fiber, initiating a series of events that cause muscle contraction. This binding opens channels in the muscle membrane and allows the entry of positively charged ions, such as sodium, which in turn generates an electrical impulse that spreads along the muscle fiber and leads to its contraction.

After transmitting the signal, acetylcholine is broken down by the enzyme **acetylcholinesterase**, preventing continuous muscle contraction and allowing the muscle to relax in preparation for the next signal. The neuromuscular junction is a highly specialized connection, ensuring precise muscle contraction only upon receiving the appropriate signal from the nervous system. This specificity enables coordinated control over voluntary movements.

Reflexes, on the other hand, are rapid, involuntary responses to specific stimuli that safeguard the body and maintain **homeostasis**. Controlled by the spinal cord and lower parts of the brain, reflexes are automatic and do not require conscious thought, allowing quick reactions in potentially dangerous situations.

A reflex begins with a **stimulus**, which is any change in the environment that elicits a response. Stimuli can be external, like touch or a loud sound, or internal, such as pain or a change in body temperature. The second step involves receptors—specialized cells or nerve endings that detect the stimulus and convert it into an electrical signal. Different receptors detect different stimuli; for example, mechanoreceptors sense touch, while photoreceptors detect light. The third step includes **sensory (afferent) neurons** transmitting signals from the receptor to **interneurons (association neurons)**, which process and integrate information within the central nervous system.

REFLEX

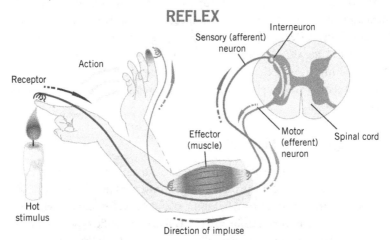

The fourth step in a reflex involves **motor (efferent) neurons** which transmit electrical impulses from the central nervous system to target muscles or **glands**, initiating the rapid and involuntary response in the fifth step: the appropriate **response**. The response is the immediate action or movement triggered by the reflex, occurring without conscious thought. For instance, accidentally touching a hot object will result in a reflex response—the quick withdrawing of the hand to prevent further injury.

Neurogenesis, Neuroplasticity, and Brain Development

Brain development begins in the womb, with neuron and neural connection formation starting as early as the first trimester. As the fetus grows, neurons multiply rapidly, forming the foundation of brain structure. This process, known as **neurogenesis**, continues after birth and is particularly active during infancy and early childhood, during which the brain refines its neural circuitry and optimizes functioning. Experiences and environmental stimuli shape the brain through **synaptic pruning**, wherein the brain refines neural circuits and strengthens those that are most relevant or frequently used.

Recent studies show ongoing neurogenesis throughout adulthood, mainly in the **hippocampus** and **olfactory bulb**. The hippocampus contributes to learning, memory, and emotional regulation, and the olfactory bulb processes smells. **Neuroplasticity**, or the brain's ability to reorganize itself by forming new neural connections, is crucial for adapting to changes, recovering from trauma, and acquiring skills across one's lifetime. Genetics, experiences, and learning all influence neuroplasticity.

Learning heavily depends on neuroplasticity because it involves the formation and strengthening of neural connections. This process, driven by neurotransmitters and synaptic modification, enhances neural communication and cognitive abilities. **Long-term potentiation (LTP)**, the lasting strengthening of synaptic connections between neurons, plays a vital role in consolidating and storing information for memory retrieval and knowledge acquisition.

Neuropsychiatric Medications

Neuropsychiatric medications target neurotransmitter systems by restoring balance to alleviate disorders. **Agonists** enhance or mimic the effects of neurotransmitters by binding to and activating them. **Selective serotonin reuptake inhibitors (SSRIs)** are a specific type of agonist that treats depression and anxiety disorders by blocking the reuptake of serotonin to increase overall serotonin levels. **Antagonists**, on the other hand, bind to and block the effects of neurotransmitters, thereby inhibiting their activity. **Neuroleptic drugs**, or antipsychotics, manage symptoms of schizophrenia and other psychotic disorders by acting as dopamine receptor antagonists. These drugs reduce dopamine activity to help control hallucinations, delusions, and other psychosis-related symptoms.

Divisions of the Nervous System

The nervous system is a complex network of specialized cells that coordinates and regulates the body's functions. It can be divided into the **central nervous system (CNS)** and the **peripheral nervous system (PNS)**. The CNS consists of the brain and the spinal cord, while the PNS refers to the nerves that branch out from the CNS. Further divisions within the PNS include the **somatic nervous system** and the **autonomic nervous system**.

The Somatic Nervous System

The somatic nervous system is responsible for the voluntary control of skeletal muscles and the relay of information to the CNS. It consists of **sensory neurons** that transmit information from **sensory receptors** (such as those for touch, pain, and temperature) to the spinal cord and brain. **Motor neurons** in the somatic nervous system also carry signals from the CNS to the skeletal muscles, enabling voluntary movements.

The Autonomic Nervous System

The autonomic nervous system controls involuntary functions and regulates internal organs, glands, and smooth muscles. It ensures the body's overall well-being by maintaining homeostasis and responding to stimuli. It is divided into the **sympathetic branch** and the **parasympathetic branch**, which work together to maintain overall balance, help the body adapt to different situations, allow for precise control of bodily functions, and ensure efficient responses to internal and external stimuli.

Commonly referred to as the "fight-or-flight" response, the sympathetic branch prepares the body for action by increasing heart rate, dilating airways, mobilizing stored energy, and redirecting blood flow to the muscles. It arises from the spinal cord and consists of a chain of ganglia running along both sides of the spinal column. Activated during times of stress, danger, or excitement, the sympathetic branch enables the body to respond quickly and efficiently.

The parasympathetic branch promotes relaxation, digestion, and energy conservation. It counters the effects of the sympathetic system by helping the body return to a state of rest and balance. The parasympathetic branch arises from the cranial nerves and the sacral region of the spinal cord. It reduces heart rate, constricts airways, stimulates digestion, and conserves energy.

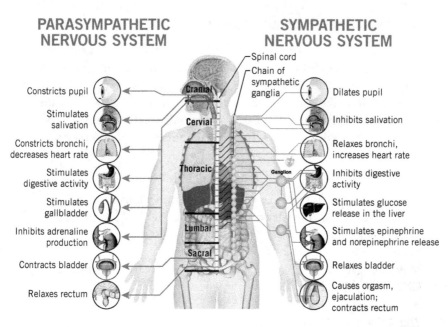

Major Structures of the Brain

The human brain is the organ that governs thoughts, emotions, and behaviors. Comprised of several interconnected structures, this extraordinarily complex organ guides human behavior based on predictions generated in response to previous experiences.

MEDIAN SECTION OF THE BRAIN

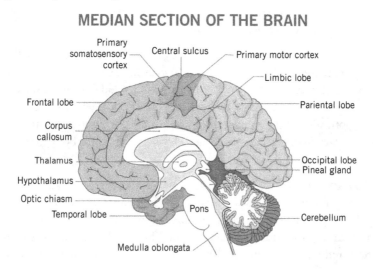

The Brainstem

The **brainstem** serves as a bridge between the cerebellum and the spinal cord, connecting the brain to the rest of the body. The regions of the brainstem are outlined in the table that follows.

REGIONS OF THE BRAINSTEM

Region	Characteristics/Functions
Medulla oblongata	• Often referred to simply as the medulla • Located at the base of the brainstem • Controls essential functions like breathing, heart rate, and blood pressure • Serves as a pathway for sensory information traveling between the brain and spinal cord • Damage to the medulla can cause respiratory and cardiovascular problems
Midbrain	• Located above the pons • Relays sensory and motor information to higher brain regions • Contains structures (like substantia nigra and the red nucleus) involved in movement control • Assists with processing visual and auditory information • Maintains attention and arousal • Damage to the midbrain can cause a wide array of movement issues, as well as difficulty with visual processing, hearing, and memory
Pons	• Located above the medulla • Serves as a relay center that connects and facilitates communication between parts of the brain • Influences sleep, arousal, facial expressions, and the coordination of movements, especially in the eye and facial muscles • Damage to the pons can result in difficultly controlling the muscles of the head, including those responsible for producing speech and swallowing
Reticular formation	• Network of nuclei scattered throughout the brainstem • Regulates arousal and consciousness • Filters sensory information to promote focus on relevant stimuli • Damage to the reticular formation can cause cognitive and behavioral impairments, including sleep and attentiveness difficulties

The Cerebellum

The **cerebellum** is located at the back of the brain underneath the cerebral hemispheres. Despite its small size, this structure contains more than 50% of the brain's neurons and plays a vital role in one's ability to move smoothly and maintain equilibrium. It receives and integrates information from sensory systems—such as the inner ear, muscles, and joints—to coordinate movements. Traditionally, it has been associated with motor coordination and balance, but modern research has suggested that the cerebellum also subtly influences human cognition by contributing to language processing and emotion regulation.

The Limbic System

The **limbic system** is vital in shaping and regulating human behavior, emotion, memory, and motivation. The structures of the limbic system are outlined in the table that follows.

STRUCTURES OF THE LIMBIC SYSTEM

Structure	Characteristics/Functions
Amygdala	• Pair of almond-shaped structures within the temporal lobes • Processes emotions, particularly fear and aggression • Recognizes and regulates emotional stimuli • Helps form emotional memories and modulate social behavior
Entorhinal cortex	• Situated adjacent to the hippocampus • Interfaces between the hippocampus and other brain regions • Helps with spatial navigation and integrates information from sensory systems
Hippocampus	• Seahorse-shaped structure adjacent to the amygdala • Supports learning and memory processes • Forms and consolidates new memories, particularly episodic memories that involve specific events or experiences • Contributes to spatial navigation and mentally mapping surroundings
Hypothalamus	• Located beneath the thalamus • Acts as a central regulator in the brain • Maintains homeostasis by controlling bodily functions like temperature, hunger, thirst, and sexual desire • Releases hormones, such as GnRH and CRH, which influence social behavior, stress responses, and emotions
Orbitofrontal cortex	• Region of the prefrontal cortex located just above the eyes • Involved in decision making, impulse control, and the integration of emotions and social information • Assists with the assessment of rewards and punishments to modulate human behavior • Damage can lead to impairments in decision making, emotion regulation, and social behavior

STRUCTURES OF THE LIMBIC SYSTEM (*CONTINUED*)

Structure	Characteristics/Functions
Piriform cortex	• Located within the olfactory system (sense of smell) • Processes and interprets smells to recognize and distinguish between different odors • Triggers memories associated with specific smells
Thalamus	• Located above the hypothalamus • Serves as the brain's relay station • Receives sensory information and routes it to the appropriate brain region for processing • Influences one's perception of the world by filtering and prioritizing sensory input • Plays a role in attention, alertness, and consciousness

The Cerebrum

The **cerebrum** is responsible for higher-order functions such as perception, cognition, language, and voluntary movement. The outermost portion of the cerebrum is called the **cerebral cortex**, which is densely packed with neuronal cell bodies. The key regions of the cerebrum, including its four lobes, are outlined in the table that follows.

STRUCTURES OF THE CEREBRUM

Structure	Characteristics/Functions
Corpus callosum	• Bundle of nerve fibers that facilitates communication between the brain's hemispheres • Allows for coordination between hemispheres
Frontal lobe	• Located at the front of the brain • Supports executive functions, decision making, impulse control, and planning • Houses the primary motor cortex, which assists in planning and coordinating movements
Gustatory cortex	• Located in the insula • Processes and interprets tastes
Occipital lobe	• Located at the back of the brain • Houses the primary visual cortex, where visual information is received and processed • Contains secondary and tertiary visual cortex areas for analyzing and interpreting visual stimuli to enhance visual perception
Olfactory cortex	• Located in the temporal lobe • Processes and interprets smells

(continues)

STRUCTURES OF THE CEREBRUM (*CONTINUED*)

Structure	Characteristics/Functions
Parietal lobe	• Located behind the frontal lobe • Processes sensory information from the body, including touch, temperature, and proprioception • Contains the primary somatosensory cortex, which receives and interprets sensory signals
Temporal lobe	• Located on the sides of the brain • Supports auditory processing and language comprehension • Involved in memory formation and retrieval • Houses the primary auditory cortex, which receives and interprets auditory information

Lateralization of the brain's hemispheres refers to the specialization of certain functions in each hemisphere. While both hemispheres contribute to various cognitive processes, certain functions are predominantly associated with one hemisphere over the other.

Studies conducted on individuals whose corpus callosum had been severed, often to prevent the frequency and severity of epileptic seizures, have shed light on some of the important differences between the functions of the brain's two hemispheres. The "big-picture-oriented" **right hemisphere** is often associated with creativity, spatial awareness, and emotion processing. It excels in visual-spatial tasks, facial recognition, and the processing of nonverbal cues. The more "detail-oriented" **left hemisphere** of the brain is often referred to as the language-dominant hemisphere because of its association with language processing, comprehension, analytical thinking, and logical reasoning. However, in approximately 15% of people, including most left-handed people, the right hemisphere contains the brain's language-dominant structures.

THE ENDOCRINE SYSTEM

The **endocrine system** is a network of glands that secrete hormones into the bloodstream. These hormones act as chemical messengers, traveling throughout the body to target cells and organs. Unlike the nervous system, which uses electrical signals and neurotransmitters for quick communication, the endocrine system works more slowly but has longer-lasting effects on the body.

Hormones

Hormones and neurotransmitters both help cells communicate, but they work differently. Neurotransmitters are chemicals released by neurons that affect nearby cells in a specific area, typically across synapses. On the other hand, hormones are made by **endocrine glands** and get released into the bloodstream, where they travel to cells and organs throughout the body. Hormones form complex networks, influence various body processes, and interact with the nervous system, immune system, and other bodily systems. Imbalanced hormone levels can affect mood, emotions, cognitive function, and overall well-being. Understanding these roles provides valuable insights into the complexities of human behavior and mental health.

Neuroendocrine Structures

The human body's neuroendocrine structures work together to facilitate seamless communication between the nervous system and the endocrine system. Neuroendocrine structures—the pineal gland, hypothalamus, and pituitary gland—are involved in numerous physiological processes, including sleep-wake cycles, growth, metabolism, and reproductive functions.

Pineal Gland

The pineal gland in the brain secretes melatonin, a hormone involved in regulating sleep-wake cycles and the body's circadian rhythm. Melatonin levels rise during periods of darkness to promote sleep and decrease during daylight hours to promote wakefulness.

Hypothalamus

The **hypothalamus**, located in the brain, serves as a crucial link between the nervous and endocrine systems. It controls the release of hormones from the **pituitary gland** through targeted production of inhibiting hormones. The hypothalamus also plays a role in regulating body temperature, hunger, thirst, and circadian rhythms.

MAJOR HORMONES SYNTHESIZED IN THE HYPOTHALAMUS

Hormone	Target Tissues	Functions
CRH (corticotropin-releasing hormone)	Pituitary gland	• Stimulates the release of ACTH from the pituitary gland to trigger the release of cortisol from the adrenal glands • Modulates mood, appetite, and immune function
Dopamine	System-wide effects	• Influences the release of prolactin from the pituitary gland • Regulates the menstrual cycle and fertility in females • Synthesizes in the midbrain and the kidneys' adrenal medulla
GnRH (gonadotropin-releasing hormone)	Pituitary gland	• Regulates the release of LH and FSH from the pituitary gland, which are critical for normal reproductive function
Oxytocin	CNS, mammary glands, uterus	• Serves various female reproductive functions, such as regulating breastfeeding and uterine contractions during labor • Contributes to social bonding and promotes trust and attachment toward "in-group" members while exacerbating negative attitudes toward those perceived as "out-group" members
Vasopressin	System-wide effects	• Regulates water balance and blood pressure

Pituitary Gland

The pituitary gland, often referred to as the "master gland," is divided into two parts: the **anterior pituitary** and the **posterior pituitary**. The anterior pituitary synthesizes and releases several hormones, including **growth hormone (GH)**, **prolactin (PRL)**, **thyroid-stimulating hormone (TSH)**, **adrenocorticotropic hormone (ACTH)**, **follicle-stimulating hormone (FSH)**, and **luteinizing hormone (LH)**. These hormones have diverse effects on the body, such as regulating growth, metabolism, reproductive functions, and the activity of other endocrine glands. The posterior pituitary stores and releases hormones including oxytocin and vasopressin, also known as the antidiuretic hormone (ADH).

MAJOR HORMONES SYNTHESIZED IN THE PITUITARY GLAND

Hormone	Target Tissues	Functions	Effects of Dysregulation
ACTH (adrenocorticotropic hormone)	Kidneys (adrenal cortex)	• Stimulates the synthesis and release of glucocorticoids, primarily cortisol, from the adrenal glands • Regulates metabolic activity and stress responses	• Excessive ACTH production can result in excessive cortisol production, leading to symptoms like weight gain, high blood pressure, and muscle weakness. • Insufficient ACTH production can cause fatigue, weight loss, and low blood pressure.
FSH (follicle-stimulating hormone)	Gonads	• Stimulates growth and production of gametes in both sexes	• High FSH levels may indicate ovarian failure or menopause in females and testicular failure or infertility in males.
GH (growth hormone)	Muscles, bones	• Promotes the growth and development of bones, muscles, and other tissues in children and adolescents • Helps maintain muscle mass and bone density in adults	• Deficiency during childhood can lead to stunted growth and short stature. • Excess GH in adults can cause the enlargement of facial features, hands, and feet.
LH (luteinizing hormone)	Gonads	• Works in conjunction with FSH to regulate reproductive processes • Triggers ovulation and egg release in females • Stimulates testosterone production in the testes in males	• LH dysregulation may indicate reproductive issues.
PRL (prolactin)	Mammary glands	• Stimulates reproductive development and promotes milk production after childbirth • Helps regulate the immune system	• Dysregulation can cause reproduction and fertility issues.

(continues)

MAJOR HORMONES SYNTHESIZED IN THE PITUITARY GLAND
(*CONTINUED*)

Hormone	Target Tissues	Functions	Effects of Dysregulation
TSH (thyroid-stimulating hormone)	Thyroid	• Stimulates and regulates the production and release of hormones from the thyroid gland • Stimulates the growth and function of the thyroid gland	• Low TSH levels are associated with hypothyroidism. • Excessive TSH levels are associated with hyperthyroidism.

The HPA Axis

The **hypothalamic-pituitary-adrenal (HPA) axis** is a complex neuroendocrine system that manages the body's stress response and ensures homeostasis. It involves the hypothalamus, pituitary gland, and **adrenal glands** working together to regulate the release of **cortisol**—a key **glucocorticoid** stress hormone affecting the body's **stress response** and other physiological processes.

Initiated when the hypothalamus detects stress, the HPA axis releases CRH, prompting the pituitary gland to release ACTH. ACTH then travels to the adrenal glands, specifically the adrenal cortex, stimulating cortisol production. **Cortisol** aids the body's stress response by increasing blood sugar, suppressing the immune system, and altering metabolism. The HPA axis maintains cortisol levels with a diurnal rhythm—higher in the morning for wakefulness and gradually decreasing through the day to prepare for sleep.

The HPA axis's crucial role includes preventing dysregulation and abnormal cortisol levels, which are linked to health issues like chronic stress, anxiety, depression, and immune dysfunction. Operating through a **negative feedback mechanism**, the HPA axis inhibits the release of CRH and ACTH when cortisol levels rise to prevent excessive production. Although cortisol acts as an immunosuppressant to prevent overactivity, chronically elevated levels of stress or physiological conditions can lead to immunosuppression, increasing susceptibility to illness.

Other Endocrine Structures

While many endocrine structures are located within the brain, multiple important endocrine structures are located outside of the brain. These structures—the adrenal glands, thyroid and parathyroid glands, pancreas, and gonads (ovaries and testes)—have important roles in regulating bodily functions and supporting homeostasis.

ENDOCRINE SYSTEM

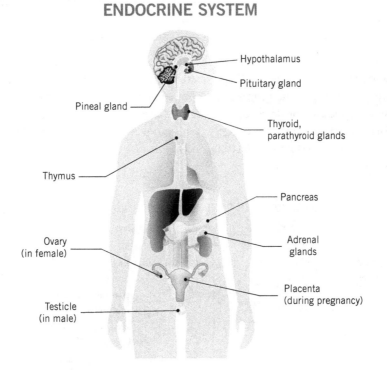

The adrenal glands, situated on top of the **kidneys**, produce several hormones, including cortisol, epinephrine (adrenaline), and norepinephrine (noradrenaline). Cortisol helps regulate stress responses, metabolism, and immune function, while adrenaline and noradrenaline trigger the fight-or-flight response, preparing the body for emergencies.

The **thyroid gland**, located in the neck, produces **thyroid hormones**, including **thyroxine (T4)** and **triiodothyronine (T3)**. These hormones regulate metabolism, growth, development, body temperature, and energy levels, playing a key role in maintaining homeostasis. Located near the thyroid gland, the **parathyroid glands** secrete parathyroid hormone (PTH), which helps regulate calcium levels in the blood, influencing bone health and muscle function.

The **pancreas** produces insulin and glucagon, which play vital roles in regulating blood sugar levels. **Insulin** promotes the uptake and storage of glucose, and **glucagon** stimulates the release of stored glucose into the bloodstream.

Hormones also play a significant role in reproductive processes and sexual behavior. **Estrogen** and **progesterone** in females and **testosterone** in males influence sexual development, libido, and fertility. Imbalances in these hormones can affect mood, sexual desire, and reproductive health.

The major **sex hormones** are present in both sexes in different amounts and are required for normal reproductive function. In females, the **ovaries** produce estrogen and progesterone. These hormones regulate the menstrual cycle and the development of female **secondary sexual characteristics**. In males, the **testes** produce testosterone, which is responsible for male sexual development, fertility, and the development of secondary sexual characteristics.

MAJOR HORMONES SYNTHESIZED OUTSIDE THE BRAIN

Hormone	Site of Synthesis	Target Tissues	Functions
Epinephrine (adrenaline)	Kidneys (adrenal medulla), medulla oblongata of the brain	Muscles, lungs, heart, blood vessels	• Prepares the body for the sympathetic nervous system response by increasing heart rate, blood pressure, and energy availability • Helps regulate blood flow and airway diameter
Estrogen	Gonads, kidneys (adrenal cortex), adipose tissue, placenta (in females)	Brain, bone marrow, female reproductive structures	• Is the primary female sex hormone and is also present in males in smaller quantities • Participates in the maturation of the uterus, breast development, and menstrual cycle regulation • Helps maintain bone health • Is behaviorally associated with communication, aggression, sexual arousal, learning, and memory
Glucocorticoids	Kidneys (adrenal cortex)	Liver, muscles, adipose tissues, pancreas, bone marrow	• Regulates metabolism, glucose levels, stress response, immune response, and the suppression of inflammation

MAJOR HORMONES SYNTHESIZED OUTSIDE THE BRAIN (*CONTINUED*)

Hormone	Site of Synthesis	Target Tissues	Functions
Insulin	Pancreas (beta cells of the islets of Langerhans)	Liver, skeletal muscles, adipose tissue	• Helps cells take in glucose from the bloodstream and promotes its storage as glycogen in the liver and muscles • Inhibits the breakdown of stored glucose • Promotes the synthesis of fats and proteins
Norepinephrine (noradrenaline)	Kidneys (adrenal medulla), sympathetic NS fibers	System-wide effects; blood vessels are a primary target	• Is crucial to the sympathetic nervous system response • Releases stored energy • Helps regulate blood pressure, heart rate, mood stability, focus, alertness, and other bodily functions
Progesterone	Gonads, kidneys (adrenal cortex)	CNS, cardiovascular system, female reproductive organs	• Stimulates breast development and prepares the uterus for pregnancy in females • Regulates the menstrual cycle and aids milk production in females • Acts as a precursor to testosterone in males
Testosterone	Gonads, kidneys (adrenal cortex)	Hair follicles, muscles, male reproductive organs	• Acts as the primary male sex hormone, but also present in females in smaller quantities • Initiates the development of male reproductive organs • Promotes the development of male secondary sexual characteristics like increased muscle mass, facial hair growth, and deepening of the voice • Plays a role in mood regulation, bone density, and libido
Thyroxine (T4)	Thyroid	Nearly all organ systems	• Regulates metabolism, growth, and development • Helps maintain body temperature, heart rate, and energy levels

CONCLUSION

Understanding the interplay between the nervous and endocrine systems is crucial for understanding their respective roles in determining behavior, propensity to certain disorders, and other biological factors. In the next chapter, we'll continue to build on these topics as we discuss how biology influences sensation and perception to shape an individual's perspective on the world.

READINESS CHECK: BIOLOGICAL BASES OF BEHAVIOR

To check how well you understand the concepts covered in this chapter, review the following questions. If you have trouble answering any of them, consider reading through this chapter again and reviewing the key terms before moving on to the next chapter.

- Can you define the following terms?
  - Gene
  - Allele
  - Chromosome
  - Neuron
  - Reflex
  - Stimulus
  - Neurogenesis
  - Neuroplasticity
- Can you discuss the following concepts?
  - Sex-linked traits
  - Behavioral genetics
  - Long-term potentiation and memory
  - Neuropsychiatric medications
  - Lateralization of the brain
  - HPA axis and the physiology of the stress response
- How is the etiology of psychological disorders influenced by both inherited and environmental factors?
- What are the major divisions of the nervous system and their functions?
- What are the major structures of the human brain and their functions?
- How do neurons communicate with each other and what are the functions of the major molecules involved in neurotransmission?
- How do neurotransmitters and hormones differ? Which molecules function as both a neurotransmitter and a hormone?
- What are the major glands, hormones, and structures of the endocrine system and their functions?

TEST YOURSELF: BIOLOGICAL BASES OF BEHAVIOR

Directions: Each of the questions or incomplete statements below is followed by five suggested answers or completions. Select the one best answer for each. The Answer Key and Explanations will follow.

1. Which of the following disorders is least likely to be caused by environmental factors?

    A. Down syndrome
    B. Post-traumatic stress disorder (PTSD)
    C. Depression
    D. Anxiety
    E. Substance use disorder

2. Which of the following substances acts both as a hormone and a neurotransmitter?

    A. Acetylcholine (ACh)
    B. Norepinephrine
    C. Prolactin (PRL)
    D. Gamma-aminobutyric acid (GABA)
    E. Cortisol

3. Damage to which part of the brain is most likely to cause issues with memory formation?

    A. Medulla oblongata
    B. Frontal lobe
    C. Orbitofrontal cortex
    D. Hippocampus
    E. Prefrontal cortex

4. Felicia's doctor is concerned about her stress levels and decides to run a hormone test for Felicia. Which of the following hormones would be expected to show elevated levels in a patient experiencing chronic stress?

    A. Cortisol
    B. Luteinizing hormone (LH)
    C. Vasopressin
    D. Oxytocin
    E. Serotonin

5. James is interested in studying the effect of genetics on a particular psychological disorder and decides to conduct a twin study using multiple pairs of monozygotic twins. Which of the following best explains why James would choose this option?

A. Since monozygotic twins share 50% of their genetic material, studying them provides insights into both environmental and genetic factors that contribute to psychological disorders.

B. It is easier to isolate environmental factors when two people come from the same family.

C. Since monozygotic twins share 100% of their genetic material, high concordance rates between them suggest a strong correlation between genetic disorders and certain psychological conditions.

D. It is easier to isolate genetic factors when people share most of their genetic material.

E. Since dizygotic twins share 100% of their genetic material, high concordance rates between them suggest a strong correlation between genetic disorders and certain psychological conditions.

Answer Key and Explanations

1. A	2. B	3. D	4. A	5. C

1. **The correct answer is A.** While environmental factors can exacerbate or change the expression of any number of psychological disorders, Down syndrome is caused by genetic factors—namely, a chromosomal duplication. All the others may have some genetic basis but are more likely than Down syndrome to be caused by environmental factors.

2. **The correct answer is B.** Norepinephrine (choice B) acts as a hormone by traveling in the bloodstream and causing a target tissue, blood vessels, to constrict. Additionally, norepinephrine is involved in the transmission of nerve signals, acting as a neurotransmitter. Acetylcholine (choice A) and GABA (choice D) only function as neurotransmitters, and prolactin (choice C) only functions as a hormone.

3. **The correct answer is D.** The hippocampus is the site of long-term potentiation in the brain, so damage to the hippocampus is likely to cause issues with the formation of new memories. Damage to structures in the brain's cerebrum (choices B, C, and E) may result in cognitive dysfunction, and damage to the medulla oblongata (choice A) can have major effects on the body's ability to maintain homeostasis and regulate the cardiovascular and respiratory systems.

4. **The correct answer is A.** Cortisol is the primary hormone associated with stress, so a person with chronic stress is likely to show elevated cortisol levels. None of the other hormones are specifically associated with chronic stress.

5. **The correct answer is C.** While dizygotic twins share 50% of their genetic material, monozygotic twins share 100%—choice A can immediately be eliminated. Choices B and D are both too vague to be correct, and choice E falsely conflates the term *dizygotic* with *monozygotic*, leaving choice C, which correctly asserts that because monozygotic twins are genetically identical, it's possible to identify concordances that point to likely genetic bases for psychological conditions.

Chapter 6

Sensation and Perception

OVERVIEW
- Sensation
- Transduction
- Perception
- Conclusion
- Readiness Check: Sensation and Perception
- Test Yourself: Sensation and Perception

This chapter offers an overview of the biological mechanisms of sensation and perception. Building on the biological topics discussed in Chapter 5, this chapter reviews sensation and perception, subjects addressed by approximately 8% of CLEP Introductory Psychology exam questions.

SENSATION

The human sensory system allows people to perceive and experience environments through an intricate interplay of receptors, sensory organs, cells, and regions of the brain.

Sensation is the process of detecting and receiving sensory information through sensory organs. Within the senses lie specialized mechanisms to detect stimuli. Each sense possesses unique sensory organs that capture specific **stimuli** types. For instance, the eyes detect light, the ears detect sound waves, the nose detects odors, the tongue detects taste, and the skin detects touch and temperature.

Receptor processes convert external stimuli into neural signals that can be transmitted to the brain. Specialized **receptor cells** within each sensory organ are responsible for this conversion. In the case of the eyes, photoreceptor cells, known as rods and cones, transform light into electrical signals. Similarly, hair cells within ears convert sound waves into neural impulses.

TRANSDUCTION

Transduction is the conversion of one form of energy into another. In human sensation and perception, this involves converting external stimuli into electrical signals that the nervous system can comprehend. Transduction occurs within the receptor cells of each sensory organ. For example, mechanoreceptors within the skin convert mechanical pressure or vibration into neural signals.

PERCEPTION

Perception entails interpreting and organizing sensory inputs in the brain, ultimately resulting in a person's conscious experience of the external world. Perceptual processes include attention, pattern recognition, and the integration of sensory information with past experiences and knowledge.

Perceptual processes help humans identify sounds, interpret smells, taste flavors, and feel textures. **Psychophysics** is a field of study that explores the relationship between physical stimuli and the psychological responses they elicit. It delves into how humans perceive and interpret sensory information, bridging the gap between the physical external world and a person's subjective perceptual experiences. Importantly, a person's perception of the world is *not* a direct reflection of the external environment but rather a result of complex processes in the brain that involve both top-down and bottom-up processing working to shape their unique perception of reality.

Bottom-up processing involves analyzing incoming sensory stimuli without relying heavily on prior knowledge or expectations. In other words, bottom-up processing begins with raw sensory data and works up to higher-level cognitive processes. By contrast, **top-down processing** involves using prior knowledge, expectations, and cognitive processes to make sense of incoming sensory information. While bottom-up processing provides raw sensory information, it is often incomplete and ambiguous. Top-down processing helps to fill in the gaps and provide meaning and context to raw sensory data. These tandem mental processes allow people to develop a coherent and meaningful understanding of the world.

One example of how these processing mechanisms interact is the perception of faces. When humans see a face, they use bottom-up processing to analyze visual perceptions of features such as the arrangement of eyes, nose, and mouth. However, they use top-down processing to recognize that the face belongs to a specific individual. Prior knowledge and memory of other faces provide the necessary context for the perceived visual information.

Sensory information in the environment is only perceivable once a particular threshold is reached. The **sensory threshold** refers to the level of intensity at which a stimulus becomes detectable by one's sensory system. It determines the minimum amount of stimulation required for an individual to perceive a sensation. The **absolute threshold** represents the lowest level of intensity at which a stimulus can be detected at least 50% of the time. The absolute threshold varies across different sensory modalities and individuals: for sight, it may be the faintest perceivable light, and for hearing, it could be the quietest perceivable sound.

The **difference threshold**, also known as the **just noticeable difference (JND)**, signifies the slightest detectable difference between two stimuli. It measures the minimum change required for an individual to perceive a distinction between two sensory experiences. The difference threshold is influenced by factors such as the nature of the stimulus, individual sensitivity, and the initial intensity of the stimulus. According to **Weber's law**, proposed by **Ernst Heinrich Weber** in the mid-19th century, the size of the difference threshold is proportionate to the intensity of the stimulus. The theory suggests that humans are more sensitive to changes in low-intensity stimuli than high-intensity stimuli. For instance, humans are more likely to detect a 10% change in the weight of a small object than a proportional change in a larger one.

Sight

Sight, or **vision**, is the primary sense for simian primates, including humans. Vision is the perception and interpretation of light, which is essential for understanding the environment. In the **retina**, electromagnetic waves in the visible light spectrum stimulate **photoreceptors**, **rods**, and **cones**, initiating the visual process. Cones enable color vision and detail, and rods are sensitive to low light and movement. Electrical signals travel via **optic nerves**, the **optic chiasm**, and the **thalamus** to reach the **primary visual cortex** for processes of perception and recognition.

Primates generally have **trichromatic vision** and can perceive a wide range of colors. **Color deficiency**, also known as color blindness, affects a portion of the population and includes conditions like **protanopia** (inability to perceive red) and **deuteranopia** (inability to perceive green). **Tritanopia**, a reduced sensitivity to blue light, is extremely rare.

With forward-facing eyes and binocular vision, the human visual system provides a three-dimensional perception of the world. **Depth perception** is the ability to perceive distance and three-dimensional objects in the environment. The brain relies on various cues to create a sense of depth. There are two main types of depth cues: binocular and monocular. **Binocular depth cues** suggest depth by comparing two slightly different images received by each eye. The differences in perception are known as **retinal disparity**, and binocular depth cues help the brain calculate the distance and depth of objects by analyzing the differences between the images. **Monocular depth cues** are those provided by the perceptions of just one eye. These cues, shown in the graphic below, allow the perception of depth and distance even when using a single eye to view a scene.

MONOCULAR DEPTH CUES

| Occlusion | Relative size | Distance to horizon | Linear perspective |

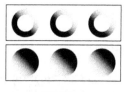

| Texture gradient | Casting shadows | Shading |

Despite its complexity, human vision has limitations. The human visual field is about 180 degrees, narrower than that of animals with laterally positioned eyes. Human vision is less sensitive in low light, lacks ultraviolet or infrared perception, and has a **blind spot** due to the **optic disc**. The brain compensates for the blind spot by "filling in" missing information to create seamless perception. Perceptual illusions, like **optical illusions**, reveal the intricate interplay between sensory input and cognitive processing. Evolution has shaped human perception to prioritize essential information for survival over fully accurate representations of physical reality.

Hearing

Hearing, or **audition**, is associated with the sensation and perception of **sound**. The stimuli for audition are **sound waves**, which are variations in air pressure caused by vibrating objects. The **cochlea** is a spiral-shaped inner ear structure containing specialized auditory receptor cells called **cochlear hair cells**, which are responsible for converting mechanical vibrations into electrical signals. These hair cells are connected to auditory nerve fibers and are arranged according to their responsiveness to different sound frequencies, allowing the perception of a wide range of pitches. The electrical signals generated by the hair cells are transmitted to the brainstem via the auditory nerve. From there, the information is relayed to the thalamus and the **auditory cortex**, where sound perception and recognition occur.

Smell

Smell, or **olfaction**, allows the perception and discernment of various scents in the environment. **Volatile** molecules in the air stimulate smell. These molecules enter the nasal cavity and bind to **olfactory receptors**, specialized neurons embedded in the **olfactory epithelium** within the nasal cavity. Olfactory receptors contain receptor proteins that bind to specific odorant molecules. Once triggered, olfactory information is transmitted as electrical signals via the **olfactory nerve fibers** to the **olfactory bulb** located at the base of the brain. From there, the information is relayed to the **olfactory cortex**, which perceives and recognizes odor. The olfactory system is unique as it is the only sensory system that bypasses the thalamus and directly connects to the olfactory cortex. This direct pathway allows for the rapid and instinctive perception of smell.

Taste

Taste, or **gustation**, is the perception and differentiation of flavors. The stimuli for taste are chemical substances dissolved in saliva. These substances interact with taste receptors clustered into **taste buds** located on the tongue, palate, and throat. Taste buds consist of 10 to 50 taste receptor cells with protrusions called **microvilli**, or gustatory hairs, which extend into **taste pores** and make contact with the substances in saliva. When taste receptor cells are stimulated, they send electrical signals to the brain, resulting in taste perception.

Different types of taste receptors are responsible for detecting sweet, sour, salty, bitter, and umami (savory) tastes. A common myth suggests that taste buds located on different parts of the tongue are responsible for the perception of different tastes; however, taste buds can sense all tastes, regardless of their location. Once taste receptors are activated, the information is transmitted via **cranial nerves** to the brainstem, specifically the **gustatory nucleus** of the medulla. From there, the information is relayed to the **thalamus** and then to the **gustatory cortex**, where taste perception and recognition occur.

Touch

The sense of touch, or **cutaneous mechanoreception**, has two major divisions: crude touch and fine, discriminative touch. **Crude touch** is the perception of nonlocalized touch and mechanical pressure changes on the skin's surface. The receptors involved in crude touch are free nerve endings distributed throughout the skin. Crude touch signals are transmitted through the **spinothalamic tract**, which ascends through the spinal cord to the thalamus. From the thalamus, the information is relayed to specific regions of the somatosensory cortex for further processing.

Discriminative touch, or fine touch, is the perception of fine details, textures, and spatial localization and involves **mechanoreceptors** such as Merkel cells, Meissner's corpuscles, and Pacinian corpuscles. These receptors are sensitive to mechanical stimuli and contribute to the sensation of texture and shape. Discriminative touch information is transmitted through the **dorsal column–medial lemniscus pathway (DCML)**. The signals ascend through the spinal cord to the thalamus and then to the **somatosensory cortex** for further processing. Different regions within the somatosensory cortex specialize in processing specific aspects of discriminative touch, such as texture or spatial localization.

Somatosensation

Traditionally, it has been understood that humans have the five senses discussed so far, but they actually have many more. **Somatosensation** is a complex sensory system involved in the perception and interpretation of various sensations from the body. Biologists consider cutaneous mechanoreception an aspect of somatosensation, but other elements include **proprioception, thermoception, nociception,** and **pain**.

Proprioception

Proprioception allows a person to sense movement and their body's position. The stimuli for proprioception are the stretch and tension within muscles, tendons, and joints, all of which contain **proprioceptor cells**, including muscle spindles, Golgi tendon organs, and joint receptors. Proprioceptor cells provide information about muscle length, muscle tension, and joint position. Muscle spindles, for example, are specialized sensory receptors within the muscle fibers that detect changes in muscle length. When a muscle stretches or contracts, the sensory endings within the muscle spindles generate electrical impulses. Sensory nerves transmit proprioceptive information to the spinal cord. The information then ascends to the brainstem, cerebellum, and somatosensory cortex via the DCML pathway for conscious perception and fine-tuning of motor control.

Thermoception

Thermoception is the perception of temperature changes, and it is facilitated by specialized nerve endings in the skin and mucous membranes called **thermoreceptors**. These receptors detect temperature changes through **ion channels** sensitive to specific temperature ranges. Thermoception signals are transmitted through the spinothalamic tract. The thermoreceptor neurons synapse in the spinal cord and ascend to the thalamus, where they are relayed to the somatosensory cortex for perception. The somatosensory cortex and the insular cortex process thermoceptive information. These regions integrate temperature signals with other sensory inputs to provide a comprehensive perception of temperature.

Nociception and Pain

Nociception refers to the initial detection and transmission of noxious stimuli by nociceptors. It is a physiological process that activates sensory nerves and transmits signals to the central nervous system. Nociception does not necessarily equate to pain perception but serves as an important initial warning system. **Nociceptors** detect potentially damaging or noxious stimuli, such as extreme temperatures, mechanical pressure, or chemical irritants. These specialized nerve endings are found throughout the body, particularly in the skin, muscles, and organs.

When nociceptors activate, they transmit electrical signals through nerve fibers known as **A delta fibers** and **C fibers**. A delta fibers have thick, myelinated axons that rapidly relay information about stimuli in the environment related to cold, pressure, and sharp, acute pain. C fibers are unmyelinated, with thinner axons, and are primarily associated with sensations of warmth, aching, itching, and cramping. The signals carried by A delta fibers and C fibers travel to the spinal cord where neurotransmitters like **substance P** are released, amplifying nociceptive signals. From the spinal cord, nociceptive signals ascend to the brain through the spinothalamic tract. The thalamus acts as a relay station that directs information to various regions of the brain, including the somatosensory cortex, limbic system, and prefrontal cortex, which contribute to the perception and emotional aspects of pain.

Pain perception is the conscious experience of pain and involves the interpretation and processing of nociceptive signals in the brain. While pain is a complex and essential aspect of sensory experience that conveys potential harm or injury, it is a subjective and multidimensional experience influenced by various factors, including past experiences, emotions, and cognitive processes.

Balance

The **vestibular** sense enables perception of the body's balance, equilibrium, and spatial orientation. Its stimuli are the movements and position of one's head and body, including changes in linear acceleration and rotational movements. The vestibular system includes specialized **hair cells** located within the vestibular organs of the **inner ear**, namely the **utricle**, **saccule**, and **semicircular canals**. These hair cells respond to changes in head position and movement. The hair cells within the vestibular system possess tiny projections called **stereocilia**. When the head moves or changes position, the movement of fluid within the inner ear causes the stereocilia to bend, leading to electrical signals transmitted to the brain. Information from the vestibular organs is transmitted via the **vestibular nerve to** the brainstem, cerebellum, and **vestibular cortex**. These pathways contribute to one's perception of balance, spatial orientation, and coordination.

CONCLUSION

Crafted over millions of years, the sensory system is a remarkable triumph of evolution, empowering humanity to perceive and comprehend the world in all its complexity. Through the interplay of receptors, cells, sensory organs, and brain regions, physical stimuli are woven into the composite tapestry of human experience. From the visual spectacles captured by the eyes and the nuanced subtleties of taste and smell to the sophisticated coordination of the visual, vestibular, and proprioceptive systems to maintain balance, each sense assumes a distinctive role in shaping the perception of reality.

READINESS CHECK: SENSATION AND PERCEPTION

To check how well you understand the concepts covered in this chapter, review the following questions. If you have trouble answering any of them, consider reading through this chapter again and reviewing the key terms before moving on to the next chapter.

- Can you differentiate between sensation, transduction, and perception?
- What is the role of receptors in detecting sensations?
- What are stimuli and how do they relate to sensation?
- What is the difference between bottom-up processing and top-down processing?
- What is Weber's law and how does it relate to sensation and perception?
- What role does interpretation play in perception?
- Can you recall the body parts, processes, and roles of the following senses?
  - Sight (vision)
  - Hearing (audition)
  - Smell (olfaction)
  - Taste (gustation)
  - Touch (cutaneous mechanoreception)
  - Somatosensation: proprioception, thermoception, nociception, and pain
  - Balance (vestibular)

TEST YOURSELF: SENSATION AND PERCEPTION

Directions: Each of the questions or incomplete statements below is followed by five suggested answers or completions. Select the one best answer for each. The Answer Key and Explanations will follow.

---

1. Which of the following processes describes conversion of external stimuli into electrical signals that the nervous system can comprehend?

   A. Sensation
   B. Transduction
   C. Mechanoreception
   D. Nociception
   E. Somatosensation

2. Of the following, one's conscious perception of pain is most closely linked with

   A. proprioception
   B. thermoception
   C. nociception
   D. cutaneous mechanoreception
   E. balance

3. Which of the following senses bypasses the thalamus when sending signals to the brain?

   A. Smell
   B. Sight
   C. Hearing
   D. Taste
   E. Touch

4. Which of the following terms can be defined as a sense that allows a person to perceive movement and the position of their body?

   A. Somatosensation
   B. Balance
   C. Gustation
   D. Proprioception
   E. Nociception

5. Fill in the blanks: Psychophysics explores the relationship between
_____ stimuli and the _____ responses they elicit.

A. physical, physiological
B. physical, psychological
C. emotional, physiological
D. emotional, psychological
E. physical, psychosocial

Answer Key and Explanations

1. B	2. C	3. A	4. D	5. B

1. **The correct answer is B.** Transduction is the process of converting physical stimuli from one's environment into electrical signals that can be categorized and comprehended by the nervous system. Choices A, C, D, and E involve the sensation of stimuli, which are not perceived until they've undergone transduction.

2. **The correct answer is C.** Nociception is the transmission of electrical signals through A delta fibers and C fibers, both of which help in the perception of certain types of pain. Each of the choices may relate to pain, but of the choices, nociception is most closely linked to the way humans perceive pain.

3. **The correct answer is A.** The olfactory system, which governs the sense of smell, is unique as the only sensory system that bypasses the thalamus and directly connects to the olfactory cortex.

4. **The correct answer is D.** Proprioception is the sense that allows one to perceive movement and the position of the body. It is one aspect of somatosensation (choice A). Balance (choice B) is a more specific version of spatial awareness that concerns the body's equilibrium and orientation, whereas gustation (choice C) relates to taste, and nociception (choice E) relates to noxious stimuli and is unrelated to the body's ability to perceive movement and position.

5. **The correct answer is B.** Psychophysics explores the relationship between physical stimuli and the psychological responses they elicit.

Chapter 7

States of Consciousness, Motivation, and Emotion

OVERVIEW

- Sleep and Dreaming
- The Study of Consciousness
- Altered States of Consciousness
- Motivation and Addiction
- Primitive Instincts
- Emotion
- Conclusion
- Readiness Check: States of Consciousness, Motivation, and Emotion
- Test Yourself: States of Consciousness, Motivation, and Emotion

While the last two chapters considered how biology affects human behavior, this chapter offers an overview of the biology underlying the conscious human mind. Exploring topics like sleeping, dreaming, consciousness, instinctual behavior, emotion, and motivation sheds light on the impact of biology on overall human experience. This information is addressed by approximately 10%–12% of the CLEP Introductory Psychology exam.

SLEEP AND DREAMING

The psychology and neurobiology underlying sleep and dreaming reveal important insights into human psychology. Sleep serves restoration, memory consolidation, and emotional regulation functions, while dreaming provides a window into one's inner experiences during sleep.

Sleep

Characterized by reduced sensory awareness and decreased motor activity, sleep is an essential part of daily life. Sleep consists of two significant stages: **non-rapid eye movement (NREM) sleep** and **rapid eye movement (REM)** sleep.

The functions of NREM and REM sleep are distinct and complementary. NREM sleep is associated with physical restoration and rejuvenation, while REM sleep is associated with mental and emotional processes. Both stages are necessary for a healthy sleep cycle and overall well-being. Disruptions or imbalances in NREM and REM sleep can have significant effects on human health. Sleep disorders, such as insomnia or sleep apnea, can disrupt the natural progression of sleep stages, leading to daytime fatigue, impaired cognitive function, and mood disturbances. REM sleep behavior disorder (RBD) is a condition in which the muscle paralysis that typically occurs during REM sleep is absent, causing individuals to physically act out their dreams. This disorder can risk injury to oneself or others.

NREM Sleep

Also known as quiet sleep, NREM sleep is the initial stage of the sleep cycle. It can be further divided into three distinct stages: **N1, N2,** and **N3.**

STAGES OF NREM SLEEP

Stage	Characteristics/Functions
N1	• Lightest stage of sleep • Typically lasts a few minutes • Sleeper experiences a sense of drifting in and out and is easily awakened • Brain wave activity slows, showing mixed frequencies
N2	• Accounts for half of the entire sleep cycle • Decreased body temperature and heart rate • Brain waves are mostly slow, low-frequency Theta waves
N3	• Also known as deep sleep or slow-wave sleep • Brain waves at their slowest (Delta waves) • Facilitates restorative functions such as tissue repair, growth, immune system strengthening

REM Sleep

REM sleep is the stage of sleep where most dreaming occurs. It is characterized by rapid eye movements, muscle paralysis, and brain wave activity similar to wakeful states. REM sleep usually occurs about 90 minutes after falling asleep and recurs in cycles throughout the night. During REM sleep, the brain becomes highly active, resembling the wakeful state. This stage is crucial for cognitive functions, emotional processing, and memory consolidation. It is believed that REM sleep plays a role in learning and creativity and regulates mood and emotions.

Dreaming

Dreaming occurs primarily during REM sleep. Dreams are vivid, sensory experiences that often involve complex narratives, emotions, and visual imagery. The psychology of dreaming has been the subject of various theories and interpretations, including the **psychoanalytic theory** of **Sigmund Freud**, who suggested that dreams represent unconscious desires and symbolic meanings.

In recent years, interest in the role of dreaming in creativity and problem solving has been growing. Some researchers propose that dreams can help individuals generate new ideas, insights, and solutions to complex problems. This perspective highlights the creative potential of dreaming and its ability to facilitate novel connections and associations in an individual's thinking.

One important theory is the **neurocognitive theory of dreaming**, put forward by **Mark Solms** in the early 2000s. This theory suggests that dreaming is a complex cognitive process that serves a purpose. Solms argues that dreams are not meaningless or random; they reflect unconscious desires, fears, anxieties, and emotions. He believes that dreams play a role in emotional regulation, memory consolidation, and problem solving. According to this theory, dreams provide a window into one's innermost thoughts and emotions.

Threat simulation theory of dreaming, proposed by **Antti Revonsuo** in 2000, suggests that dreams help the brain practice and prepare for potential threats and dangers. According to this theory, dreaming involves the simulation of threatening situations, which allows one to rehearse and develop strategies to deal with them. This theory highlights the adaptive function of dreaming and its role in preparing individuals for real-life challenges.

THE STUDY OF CONSCIOUSNESS

The exploration of **consciousness** has long captivated the fields of psychology and neuroscience. In essence, consciousness refers to a person's awareness of themselves and the world around them. It encompasses a vast array of mental processes, such as perception, attention, memory, and introspection. Although psychologists deliberate on how to precisely define conscious phenomena, there are a few generally agreed-upon perspectives that shed light on the concept of consciousness.

In his influential 1974 essay, "What Is It Like to Be a Bat?," **Thomas Nagel** argues that conscious mental states arise when there is a subjective experience unique to individuals, regardless of species. This concept suggests that every living being has their own distinct way of perceiving the world. Nagel critiques reductionist approaches to consciousness, asserting that science can never truly explain what it feels like to be a bat. He maintains that the only form of consciousness one can ever fully comprehend is their own subjective experience. While Nagel's stance on the limitations of **scientific materialism** remains a topic of ongoing discussion, the idea that conscious phenomena encompass a fundamentally subjective experience has gained widespread acceptance across various academic disciplines.

Philosophical Perspectives

The study of the **philosophy of mind** seeks to understand the nature of the mind, consciousness, and mental processes. Psychology, with its focus on human behavior and mental processes, and **neuroscience**, with its exploration of the brain and its functions, have both provided valuable insights and perspectives on the philosophy of mind.

Dualism versus Monism

The **mind-body problem** is a core topic of discussion that probes the complex relationship between the mind and body. It raises questions such as whether the mind and body are distinct entities and, if so, how they interact causally. One of the most well-known theories addressing this issue is **dualism**, often associated with philosopher **René Descartes**. Dualism posits that consciousness is fundamentally separate from the physical body and brain. According to this theory, consciousness is a nonphysical entity that exists independent of the material world. Dualism also suggests a divide between mind and matter, with consciousness being a property of the mind or soul. However, dualism has faced criticism and sparked debates due to its challenges in explaining the interaction between the immaterial mind and the physical brain.

In contrast to dualism, **monism**, sometimes called nonduality, proposes that consciousness is an inherent property of the physical world. One prominent form of monism is **materialism**, also called physicalism. Materialists argue that consciousness can be fully explained by the physical processes of the brain and nervous system. According to this view, conscious experience emerges from the complex interactions of neurons, electrical signals, and biochemical processes.

Cognitive Psychology

Cognitive psychology has shed light on fundamental questions in the philosophy of mind. By conducting experiments and observations, cognitive psychologists explore different aspects of consciousness, including attention, awareness, and self-perception. Additionally, psychology has contributed to the study of the philosophy of mind through its exploration of mental disorders and abnormal psychology. By studying abnormal mental states, psychologists have gained insights into the normal functioning of the mind and the mechanisms underlying mental processes.

Neuroscience

Neuroscience, on the other hand, has brought a biological perspective to the philosophy of mind. By examining the structure and function of the brain, neuroscientists have provided a foundation for analyzing the physical basis of mental processes. Advances in **neuroimaging techniques**, such as **functional magnetic resonance imaging (fMRI)**, have allowed researchers to observe brain activity and correlate it with different mental states and processes. Neuroscience has contributed to the philosophy of mind by addressing questions about the relationship between the physical brain and the nonphysical concept of the mind. For instance, the discovery of **mirror neurons**, which are neurons that fire both when an individual performs an action and when they observe someone else performing the same action, has sparked debates about the nature of empathy, imitation, and understanding of others' mental states. This research has implications for philosophical discussions about the nature of consciousness, the self, and social cognition.

ALTERED STATES OF CONSCIOUSNESS

The study of **altered states of consciousness (ASCs)** has captivated scientists, as it provides valuable insights into the intricacies of human perception, cognition, and subjective experience. An altered state of consciousness is any condition in which an individual's thoughts, feelings, or perceptions deviate from their usual waking state. Altered states can be caused by various means that may or may not involve the use of psychoactive substances.

Nonpharmacological Altered States

Nonpharmacological altered states of consciousness include a wide range of experiences that do not involve the use of drugs or medications. These states can be induced by various factors, including pathological conditions, physical and physiological activities, psychological practices, and even spontaneous occurrences.

Pathologically altered states of consciousness arise from medical conditions such as epilepsy and brain damage. **Epilepsy** is a neurological disorder characterized by recurrent **seizures**, which can lead to altered perceptions, sensations, and consciousness. During a seizure, individuals may experience unusual sensory perceptions, loss of awareness, and even hallucinations. Similarly, brain damage resulting from traumatic injuries or diseases can lead to altered states of consciousness, affecting cognitive functions, memory, and awareness.

Physical and physiological factors can also induce altered states of consciousness. **Fasting**, for example, is a practice that involves abstaining from food for a certain period. Some individuals may experience altered mental states through prolonged fasting, including increased focus, clarity, and even spiritual experiences. Another physical factor that can induce an altered state is sexual activity. During sexual arousal and orgasm, individuals may experience intense pleasure and altered states of consciousness characterized by heightened sensations and altered perceptions.

Psychological influences, such as **music**, **meditation**, and **hypnosis**, have long been recognized for their ability to induce altered states of consciousness. Music, with its rhythmic patterns and emotional content, can evoke powerful emotional and sensory experiences, leading to altered states of consciousness characterized by relaxation, emotional release, and even transcendence. Meditation, on the other hand, involves focused attention and mindfulness that can lead to a state of deep relaxation, heightened awareness, and altered perceptions of time and self. Hypnosis, a state of heightened suggestibility, can induce altered states of consciousness in which individuals may experience increased focus, relaxation, and a heightened sense of imagination.

Spontaneous altered states of consciousness can also occur without any deliberate effort or external influence. **Daydreaming**, for example, is a common spontaneous altered state wherein individuals lose themselves in a series of thoughts, fantasies, and imaginary scenarios. Daydreaming often involves detachment from the immediate environment and a temporary shift in attention. **Near-death experiences (NDEs)** are another example of spontaneous altered states. NDEs occur in individuals who have had a close brush with death and often involve a range of extraordinary experiences, such as feelings of peace, out-of-body sensations, and encounters with light or deceased loved ones. For those with mental disorders or trauma, **dissociation** and **psychoses** can also lead to altered states of consciousness.

Pharmacological Altered States

Pharmacological altered states of consciousness are achieved using **psychoactive drugs**, which have been the subject of extensive research in psychology and medicine. These substances alter brain function and behavior, leading to a variety of effects that can present differently in different individuals. In most cases, overdosing on these drugs can cause serious health complications or be life threatening, which is one of many reasons that addiction poses a health risk.

Stimulants are a class of drugs that increase alertness, attention, and energy levels. They stimulate the **central nervous system**, resulting in increased heart rate, blood pressure, and metabolism. Common examples of stimulants include nicotine, amphetamines, cocaine, and caffeine. The effects of stimulants can include increased focus, euphoria, and a temporary energy boost. Prolonged use of stimulants can lead to addiction, insomnia, and even psychosis.

Depressants have the opposite effect of stimulants. They slow down the central nervous system, leading to relaxation, sedation, and reduced inhibition. Depressants include drugs such as alcohol, barbiturates, and benzodiazepines. While the initial effects of depressants can induce feelings of calmness and relaxation, excessive or prolonged use can result in slowed breathing, impaired judgment, and addiction.

Opioids are a category of drugs that are derived from or mimic the effects of opium. They include substances such as heroin, morphine, and prescription pain medications like oxycodone. Opioids are powerful pain relievers that can induce feelings of euphoria and relaxation. Opioids are highly addictive, however, and their misuse can lead to respiratory depression, overdose, and death.

Cannabinoids, found in marijuana and synthetic cannabinoids, primarily affect the brain and produce psychoactive effects. They bind to **cannabinoid receptors** and alter the release of neurotransmitters, resulting in changes in mood, perception, and cognition. The effects of cannabinoids can include relaxation, euphoria, altered perception of time, and increased appetite. The long-term effects of marijuana use are still being studied, but excessive use of cannabinoids has immediate effects like the impairment of memory, coordination, and motivation.

Hallucinogens, including psychedelics, are a class of drugs that alter perception, thoughts, and feelings. Hallucinogens can induce vivid sensory experiences, distortions of time and space, and profound introspection. The effects of hallucinogens are highly subjective and can vary from person to person. They can also have profound psychological effects and may cause intense emotional and spiritual experiences. The use of hallucinogens can also lead to anxiety, panic, and in some cases, long-lasting psychological effects.

Psilocybin mushrooms and lysergic acid diethylamide (LSD) are examples of **psychedelic substances** that alter perception, mood, and cognition. They bind to **serotonin** receptors in the brain, particularly the **5-HT2A receptor**, leading to profound changes in sensory experiences, emotions, and thoughts. These substances can induce experiences described as mystical or spiritual and have been studied for their potential therapeutic effects in certain mental health conditions, such as **post-traumatic stress disorder (PTSD)**. Studies using psychedelics have revealed altered patterns of brain activity and connectivity, including increased communication between brain regions that do not typically interact. For example, the **default mode network**, involved in **self-referential thinking**, becomes less active, while connectivity between the visual cortex and other brain regions increases, leading to visual hallucinations. Psychologists believe that these neurobiological changes underlie the unique subjective experiences reported during psychedelic "trips" and provide key insights that have driven continued research on the potential therapeutic benefits of psychedelic substances that are administered in controlled settings.

The neurobiological effects of these psychoactive drugs highlight the complex interactions between these substances and the brain. Understanding these mechanisms is crucial for comprehending the risks and potential therapeutic uses of these drugs. Further research in this field could contribute to the development of effective interventions, harm-reduction strategies, and novel treatment approaches for individuals negatively affected by substance use.

MOTIVATION AND ADDICTION

Motivation can be described as the internal processes that initiate, guide, and sustain behavior toward achieving a desired outcome. It is a fundamental aspect of human behavior, driving individuals to pursue goals, engage in activities, and strive for success.

Biology of Motivation

The brain's reward system—a complex network of brain regions that are involved in experiencing pleasure and reinforcement—is primarily centered around the mesolimbic dopamine pathway. This pathway involves the release of dopamine, the key chemical component underlying motivation, reward, and reinforcement. The anticipation and pursuit of rewards activate this pathway, reinforcing behavior and driving motivation. The prefrontal cortex, a key brain region involved in executive functions and decision making, also plays a crucial role in motivation. This part of the brain is involved in evaluating potential rewards, planning and executing goal-directed behavior, and inhibiting impulsive responses. The prefrontal cortex interacts with the reward system to regulate motivation and guide behavior toward the achievement of long-term goals.

Motivation is influenced by cognitive processes like goal setting, self-efficacy, and expectancy. Specific, challenging goals enhance motivation; self-efficacy boosts confidence; and expectancy shapes motivation by influencing the perceived likelihood of success.

Emotions such as desire, excitement, or fear can significantly impact motivation by influencing the value placed on a particular outcome and the emotional salience of the goal. For example, a desire for social connection may motivate social activities, while fear of failure drives harder work to avoid negative outcomes. Social motivation consists of processes and mechanisms that influence one's desire to engage in social interactions.

Values, influenced by internal and external factors, help shape motivation. Intrinsic motivation is driven by inherent satisfaction or enjoyment, while extrinsic motivation involves external rewards or avoiding punishment.

For instance, someone may be intrinsically motivated to listen to their favorite music but extrinsically motivated to get to work on time.

Numerous motivation theories highlight cognitive, emotional, social, and value-based factors. Some of the primary theories of motivation include Maslow's hierarchy of needs, three needs theory, social exchange theory, and expectancy-value theory.

THEORIES OF MOTIVATION

Theory	Origin	Description
Maslow's hierarchy of needs	Abraham Maslow, 1943	• Motivation is influenced by a hierarchy of needs wherein foundational needs must be met before an individual can move on to the next level. • The hierarchy is often illustrated as a pyramid (see page 53).
Three needs theory (achievement motivation theory)	David McClelland, 1960s	• People have three basic needs: achievement, affiliation, and power. • Needs are learned through social experiences and vary in strength among individuals.
Social exchange theory	Claude Lévi-Strauss, 1960s	• Individuals are motivated to seek social connections and engage in reciprocal relationships. • Reciprocal relationships help people obtain social support, companionship, and other tangible or intangible benefits.
Expectancy-value theory	Martin Fishbein and Icek Ajzen, 1970s	• Motivation is influenced by the expectation of achieving a goal and the value attached to that goal. • Individuals engage in behaviors that they believe will lead to desirable outcomes they value.
Self-determination theory	Edward Deci and Richard Ryan, mid-1980s	• Intrinsic and extrinsic factors drive motivation. • Individuals are motivated when they feel a sense of autonomy, competence, and relatedness. • Satisfied individuals are intrinsically motivated to engage in behaviors that promote personal growth and well-being.

Addiction

At its core, **addiction** hijacks the brain's reward system to attune it to a particular type of reward governed by physical or psychological dependence. The mesolimbic dopamine pathway includes the **ventral tegmental area (VTA)** and the **nucleus accumbens (NAc)**, both of which play key roles in motivation and addiction.

When a person engages in pleasurable activities or consumes addictive substances such as drugs, alcohol, or nicotine, the brain releases dopamine in the NAc. This dopamine surge creates a sense of pleasure and reinforces the behavior, creating a desire for repeated engagement in the activity or substance. Over time, the brain adapts to this repeated dopamine release and develops **tolerance**, requiring higher levels of the substance or behavior to achieve the same pleasurable effect.

In addiction, the brain undergoes changes significant enough to develop physical or psychological dependence on the source of dopamine. One such change is the remodeling of neural circuits involved in reward processing. **Chronic drug use** or engagement in addictive behaviors leads to neuroadaptations that alter the sensitivity of dopamine receptors, reducing the pleasurable effects of natural rewards and increasing the drive for drugs or addictive behaviors.

Genetics and individual differences also play a role in **addiction vulnerability**. Certain genetic variations can influence an individual's susceptibility to addiction by affecting the function of neurotransmitters, receptors, and other molecules involved in reward processing and impulse control. Understanding the neurobiology of addiction has significant implications for prevention and treatment strategies. Targeting the brain's reward system and the neural circuits involved in addiction can help researchers develop medications and behavioral interventions to reduce cravings, promote abstinence, and restore normal brain function.

PRIMITIVE INSTINCTS

Primitive instincts like **hunger, thirst, sexual desire**, and **pain** exert significant influence over human behavior. Deeply embedded in human evolution, these instincts continue to shape the thoughts, feelings, and actions of all animals, including humans. They are indispensable for survival and have been steering human behaviors and decision-making processes throughout history. While multiple brain regions are involved in these instincts, the **hypothalamus** especially influences hunger, thirst, and sexual desire.

Hunger

Hunger is a physiological and psychological condition that propels individuals to pursue and consume food. Hunger can be understood through the framework of the **drive-reduction theory**, proposed in 1943 by Yale psychologist **Clark Hull**. This theory posits that depletion of the body's energy reserves triggers hunger, which in turn motivates individuals to partake in behaviors that restore their **energy equilibrium** and **homeostasis**. Psychological and environmental factors such as food availability, cultural influences, and learned food associations also contribute to the sensation of hunger.

The orchestration of hunger involves an interaction between different brain regions, hormones, and neurotransmitters. Within the hypothalamus, there are specialized cell clusters known as the **arcuate nucleus** and the **paraventricular nucleus** that control **appetite**. The release of **neuropeptides** is orchestrated by various signals from the body, such as circulating hormones and nutrients. The hormone **ghrelin**, produced by the stomach, acts on the hypothalamus to stimulate appetite. **Leptin**, a hormone released by adipose tissue, acts on the hypothalamus to suppress appetite and increase energy expenditure. These hormonal signals assist in regulating food intake by providing feedback to the brain about the body's energy status.

Thirst

Thirst compels individuals to search for and consume water. Like hunger, drive-reduction theory can explain a person's reaction to thirst from a psychological standpoint. When the body lacks hydration, thirst is activated as a mechanism to restore fluid balance. Changes in the body's fluid balance and osmolarity primarily trigger the sensation of thirst. **Osmoreceptors**, specialized cells in the hypothalamus, detect these changes and stimulate the feeling of thirst when the body becomes dehydrated or the blood becomes more concentrated. Once the sensation of thirst is activated, the brain sends signals to various regions responsible for water balance regulation. The hypothalamus then releases **vasopressin**, also known as antidiuretic hormone (ADH), which acts on the kidneys to conserve water and reduce urine output.

Sexual Desire

Sexual desire and behavior are influenced by a combination of psychological and neurobiological factors. Sexual motivation is one of the most contested drives among psychologists, so there are numerous theories to explore it; however, most theories boil down to either evolutionary or sociocultural factors. **Evolutionary theory** suggests that sexual desire is driven by the desire to reproduce and pass on genetic material. **Sociocultural factors**, such as social norms, values, and personal experiences, also shape sexual desire and behavior.

From a neurobiological perspective, sexual desire and behavior are regulated by a complex interplay of brain regions, hormones, and neurotransmitters. Within the hypothalamus, specialized clusters of cells called the **sexually dimorphic nucleus (SDN)** and the **preoptic area (POA)** contribute to sexual desire. The SDN, larger in males than in females, likely contributes to observed differences in sexual behavior between the sexes. The POA, on the other hand, is involved in the release of hormones such as **gonadotropin-releasing hormone (GnRH)**, stimulating the release of **luteinizing hormone (LH)** and **follicle-stimulating hormone (FSH)** from the **pituitary gland**. These hormones are essential for regulating reproductive function.

Other brain regions also play roles in sexual behavior. The **amygdala**, for example, processes emotions and can influence sexual arousal and attraction. The prefrontal cortex, responsible for decision making and impulse control, can also modulate sexual behavior. Hormones such as **testosterone** and **estrogen** influence sexual desire and behavior. Testosterone, primarily produced in the testes in males and the ovaries in females, is associated with libido and sexual motivation. Estrogen, primarily produced in the gonads, also influences sexual desire and the achievement of orgasm. Neurotransmitters, including dopamine, serotonin, and **oxytocin**, are also involved in the regulation of sexual motivation and pleasure.

The neurobiology of sex encompasses diverse expressions of human sexuality. Research indicates that **sexual orientation**—whether **heterosexual, homosexual, bisexual, asexual**, or any other designation—has a **neurobiological basis**. Structural and functional differences in certain brain regions have been found between individuals with different sexual orientations, suggesting a biological foundation for human sexuality and gender identity.

Pain

Pain is a multifaceted experience that combines sensory and emotional elements and functions as a signal of harm or injury. It can be influenced by various factors, including one's thoughts, feelings, and past experiences. According to the **gate control theory of pain**, the perception of pain is regulated by neural mechanisms that can either heighten or reduce pain signals.

The **transmission of pain signals** from the body to the central nervous system involves a series of intricate steps. When **nociceptors**, specialized nerve fibers involved in the sensation of potentially harmful stimuli, are activated, they release neurotransmitters such as **substance P** and **glutamate**, which carry pain signals to the **spinal cord**. The spinal cord is a crucial gateway for pain signals to reach the brain. It contains specialized neurons that receive and transmit these signals to higher brain centers. The transmission of pain signals can be modified at the spinal cord level through a process known as **gate control**. This mechanism involves the interplay of various inhibitory and excitatory signals that can either enhance or suppress the transmission of pain signals.

Once pain signals reach the brain, they are processed and integrated into several regions, including the **thalamus**, **somatosensory cortex**, and structures within the **limbic system**. The thalamus acts as a relay station, directing pain signals to specific areas of the brain for further processing. The somatosensory cortex is responsible for perceiving the location, intensity, and quality of pain. Meanwhile, structures in the limbic system contribute to the affective and emotional aspects of pain.

Chronic pain, which persists beyond the normal healing time, is a complex condition that involves changes in the neurobiology of pain. Prolonged exposure to pain can lead to alterations in the central nervous system, including sensitization of pain pathways and changes in neurotransmitter activity. These neuroplastic changes can contribute to the persistence and amplification of pain, even in the absence of ongoing tissue damage.

EMOTION

Emotions are an integral part of human experience, influencing each person's thoughts, behaviors, and overall well-being. Emotions are influenced by cognitive processes, such as **appraisal** and **interpretation**, as well as by a network of brain regions and neurotransmitters. Emotions are often described as **multicomponent processes** involving subjective experience, physiological arousal, expressive behaviors, and cognitive appraisal. Psychologists have proposed various theories of emotion; some of the most impactful include the James-Lange theory, Cannon-Bard theory, appraisal theory, and two-factor theory.

THEORIES OF EMOTION

Theory	Origin	Description
James-Lange theory	**William James** and **Carl Lange**, late 19th century	• Human bodies react to a stimulus before experiencing the corresponding emotion. • Emotion is dependent on the physical responses that precede it (e.g., trembling or elevated heart rate occur prior to feelings of fear).
Cannon-Bard theory	**Walter Cannon** and **Philip Bard**, early 20th century	• Physiological responses and emotional experiences occur independently and simultaneously (e.g., confronted with a threatening situation, a person's heart may race while they simultaneously feel fear).
Appraisal theory	**Magda Arnold** and **Richard Lazarus**, 1950s; ideological roots in ancient Greek philosophy (e.g., Aristotle and Plato)	• Emotions are influenced by one's evaluation and interpretation of a given situation. • Individual perception may vary, even in responses to an identical situation (e.g., one person experiences fear and another experiences anticipation and joy on a roller coaster ride).
Two-factor theory (Schachter-Singer theory)	**Stanley Schachter** and **Jerome Singer**, 1962	• Emotions are the result of both physiological arousal and cognitive interpretation (e.g., a rapid heartbeat and sweaty palms may be interpreted as excitement on a roller coaster ride but as fear during a home break-in).

Biology of Emotion

Emotions are influenced by the interplay of brain regions, neurotransmitters, and neural circuits. The amygdala, a key structure in the limbic system, plays a central role in processing and regulating emotions. It is involved in the detection and evaluation of emotional stimuli, particularly those related to **fear** and **threats**. The **prefrontal cortex** helps modulate emotional responses, inhibit impulsive behavior, and engage in cognitive reappraisal.

Neurotransmitters, such as serotonin, dopamine, and **norepinephrine**, also play a significant role in emotion. Serotonin regulates mood, happiness, and well-being. Dopamine is associated with reward and motivation, and norepinephrine is involved in the body's stress response. Imbalances in these neurotransmitters can contribute to **depression**, **anxiety disorders**, or **bipolar disorder**.

Furthermore, the **autonomic nervous system (ANS)** plays a vital role in the physiological component of emotion. The ANS is responsible for regulating bodily functions, such as heart rate, blood pressure, and sweating, which are associated with emotional arousal. The **sympathetic branch** of the ANS is activated during the "fight-or-flight" response, leading to increased physiological arousal during intense emotions. The **parasympathetic branch**, on the other hand, helps regulate and restore the body to a calm state after an emotional episode.

CONCLUSION

The study of consciousness, altered states, motivation, and emotion is interconnected, providing valuable insights into the human mind. By investigating these areas, psychologists can begin to unravel the mysteries of the mind and gain a deeper understanding of human behavior, cognition, and the nature of subjective experiences. This knowledge can be applied to various fields, including clinical psychology, education, organizational behavior, and therapy.

READINESS CHECK: STATES OF CONSCIOUSNESS, MOTIVATION, AND EMOTION

To check how well you understand the concepts covered in this chapter, review the following questions. If you have trouble answering any of them, consider reading through this chapter again and reviewing the key terms before moving on to the next chapter.

- Can you define the following terms?
    - Consciousness
    - Scientific materialism
    - The mind-body problem
    - Default mode network

- Can you discuss the following concepts?
  - NREM versus REM sleep
  - Philosophical dualism versus monism
  - Altered states of consciousness
  - The biology of emotion
  - The biology of motivation
  - Intrinsic versus extrinsic motivation
  - Social motivation
- Can you explain the following theories?
  - Neurocognitive theory of dreaming
  - Threat simulation theory of dreaming
  - Drive-reduction theory
  - Gate control theory of pain
  - Theories of emotion (appraisal, James-Lange, Cannon-Bard, and Schachter-Singer)
  - Theories of motivation (Maslow's hierarchy, three needs, expectancy value, self-determination, and social exchange)
- What methods and techniques are used to gain insight into the mechanisms underlying the brain's mental processes?
- Can you provide examples of altered states of consciousness?
- What are the major drug classes, and how do they influence human physiology and behavior?
- Can you explain addiction and the biological variables that influence one's susceptibility to addictive substances?

TEST YOURSELF: STATES OF CONSCIOUSNESS, MOTIVATION, AND EMOTION

Directions: Each of the questions or incomplete statements below is followed by five suggested answers or completions. Select the one best answer for each. The Answer Key and Explanations will follow.

1. Which of the following statements is true about REM sleep?

   A. It is divided into three distinct stages.
   B. It is the initial stage of the sleep cycle.
   C. It typically lasts for a few minutes.
   D. It is the stage during which most dreaming occurs.
   E. It is characterized by decreased sensory awareness.

2. Dualism is a philosophical perspective that suggests which of the following?

   A. Consciousness will one day be fully explained as a physical property of the brain.
   B. Consciousness is an inherent property of the physical world.
   C. The mind and body are distinct, separate entities.
   D. The mind and body have no causal interactions between them.
   E. Consciousness emerges from the interactions between neurons.

3. Which of the following altered states of consciousness (ASCs) involve a state of heightened imagination and suggestibility?

   A. Meditation
   B. Fasting
   C. Daydreaming
   D. Near-death experiences
   E. Hypnosis

4. Addiction is most closely associated with which of the following neurotransmitter systems?

   A. Serotonin
   B. Gamma-aminobutyric acid (GABA)
   C. Epinephrine
   D. Norepinephrine
   E. Dopamine

5. Andre and his sister Pamela visit an amusement park and experience an increase in their blood pressure, heart rate, and alertness while riding the largest roller coaster. While Andre described the experience as terrifying and negative, Pamela described the experience as thrilling and positive. Which of the following best explains the differences in their subjective experience of the same ride?

A. James-Lange theory

B. Cannon-Bard theory

C. Schachter-Singer two-factor theory

D. Appraisal theory of emotion

E. Expectancy-value theory

Answer Key and Explanations

1. D	2. C	3. E	4. E	5. C

1. **The correct answer is D.** REM sleep is the stage during which most dreaming occurs and lasts for approximately 90 minutes. NREM sleep occurs before REM sleep and is divided into three distinct stages (N1, N2, and N3). Both REM and NREM sleep are characterized by a decrease in sensory awareness and motor activity.

2. **The correct answer is C.** Dualism is the view that the mind and body are distinct, separate entities. Scientific materialism, a form of monism, views consciousness as the result of interactions between neurons and typically posits that one day, consciousness will be explained by physical science. The causality of interactions between the brain and body is a topic of ongoing discussion in both monistic and dualistic schools of philosophic thought.

3. **The correct answer is E.** While other ASCs, such as daydreaming, are also associated with heightened states of imagination, hypnosis is the only one of these ASCs associated with a state of heightened suggestibility.

4. **The correct answer is E.** All addictions involve modification to the brain's dopamine circuits. Other neurotransmitter levels may also fluctuate in response to an individual engaging with certain drugs or behaviors, but every form of addiction involves the hijacking of dopamine-releasing circuits in the brain.

5. **The correct answer is C.** The Schachter-Singer two-factor theory of emotion highlights the role of subjective cognitive interpretation in the processing of emotions, explaining how both Pamela and Andre could show similar physiological responses while experiencing different emotions. The James-Lange and Cannon-Bard theories of emotion focus on the sequence of physiological and emotional responses, rather than the variation in cognitive interpretation of experiences. Self-determination theory and expectancy-value theory are theories related to motivation, rather than emotion.

Chapter 8

Cognition and Learning

OVERVIEW
- Cognition
- Attention and Memory
- Learning
- Language
- Conclusion
- Readiness Check: Cognition and Learning
- Test Yourself: Cognition and Learning

Learning involves gaining knowledge, skills, attitudes, or behaviors through experience and blending new information with what is already known to apply that knowledge in new situations. Cognitive processes, on the other hand, are the mental activities that come into play during the acquisition, processing, storage, and use of information. Learning and cognition both lie at the foundation of knowledge acquisition, enabling people to build skills over time and adjust to an ever-changing environment. As scoring categories, learning and cognition are each the subject of about 8%–9% of the questions, meaning that topics from this chapter account for approximately 16%–18% of the CLEP Introductory Psychology exam.

COGNITION

Cognition involves mental processes that facilitate information acquisition, storage, and utilization. It includes numerous functions like **perception, attention, memory, language, problem solving**, and decision making. Through extensive and ongoing research, psychologists and cognitive scientists explore the complexities of human thought, reasoning, and comprehension. **Thinking**, a core cognitive process, involves manipulating and transforming information to solve problems, make decisions, and generate ideas. Thoughts go beyond sensory experiences, encompassing abstract mental attitudes like intentions and judgments.

Cognitive psychologists study the intricacies of thought, investigating both mental processes and strategies for problem solving and decision making to understand the underlying mechanisms that drive human cognition. As a field, **cognitive psychology** delves into expertise and creativity and seeks to understand how individuals develop domain-specific knowledge and generate innovative ideas.

Biology of Cognition

Alongside psychology, **neurobiology** offers valuable insights into the intricate neural mechanisms behind cognition and thinking. Advancements in **neuroimaging techniques**, such as **functional magnetic resonance imaging (fMRI)** and **electroencephalography (EEG)**, allow researchers to pinpoint the specific brain regions and networks involved in cognitive processes.

COGNITIVE FUNCTIONS OF BRAIN REGIONS

Brain Region	Role in Cognition
Basal ganglia	• Contribute to cognitive processes like habit formation, reward processing, and decision making; subcortical structures also called basal nuclei • Facilitate the selection and execution of appropriate actions based on learned associations and goals • Regulate motor control
Hippocampus	• Plays a key role in memory formation as the site of long-term potentiation • Aids in spatial navigation
Parietal cortex	• Allows for spatial cognition, attention, and working memory • Helps individuals orient themselves in space, manipulate information in working memory, and allocate attentional resources
Prefrontal cortex	• Aids executive functions like planning, decision making, and problem solving • Facilitates higher-order cognitive processes, including working memory, attentional control, and cognitive flexibility
Temporal cortex	• Regulates emotions, processes sensory experiences and language • Aids in the encoding, retrieval, and comprehension of memories

Neural networks are vital for cognition and thinking. They consist of both local and long-range connections and enable the integration and coordination of information across different brain regions. The **default mode network**, active during rest, is involved in **self-referential thinking**, introspection, and mind wandering. Other networks, such as the **salience network** and the **central executive network**, are responsible for attentional control, cognitive control, and goal-directed thinking.

Metacognition

Metacognition enables individuals to monitor and control their own thinking processes, such as by actively engaging in their own learning, setting goals, self-monitoring progress, and making strategy adjustments. Metacognition has two main components: **metacognitive knowledge** and **metacognitive regulation**. Metacognitive knowledge pertains to understanding how one learns, the strategies available, and self-assessment. Metacognitive regulation involves planning, monitoring, and evaluating cognitive activities.

A key benefit of metacognition is improved learning efficiency. When individuals are aware of their own thinking processes, they can identify difficulties, correct errors, and take appropriate steps to improve their understanding. For example, a student who recognizes their knowledge gaps is better equipped to seek additional information or request clarification than a student who is unaware of what they don't know.

Metacognition is closely linked to **self-regulated learning**, where individuals take charge of their learning by setting goals, planning learning activities, monitoring their progress, and making adjustments. Self-regulated learners proactively engage in their learning, positively influencing their own learning outcomes. Research consistently shows that these learners are typically more motivated, persistent, and successful in their learning endeavors.

Problem Solving

Problem solving is a complex cognitive process that involves various functions such as perception, attention, memory, reasoning, and decision making. Psychologists have developed different models and theories to explain problem solving, including the **problem-solving cycle** and the **information-processing approach**.

The problem-solving cycle includes stages like identifying the problem(s), generating potential solutions, evaluating solutions, selecting the best solution(s), and implementing the chosen solution(s). This model highlights the dynamic, iterative nature of problem solving, emphasizing the need for flexibility and adaptation.

The information-processing approach focuses on acquiring, organizing, and manipulating information. It emphasizes the role of working memory, long-term memory, and attention. In this approach, individuals draw upon their existing knowledge and experiences to identify relevant information, generate hypotheses, and evaluate potential solutions.

Cognitive biases and mental shortcuts called **heuristics**, used to simplify perceived problems, also play a role in problem solving. Biases such as **confirmation bias**, the tendency to favor information that confirms one's preexisting beliefs, and **anchoring bias**, the tendency to prefer the first information received, influence decision making and lead to suboptimal choices. The **availability heuristic** is a mental shortcut that leads individuals to make decisions based on readily available examples, information, or recent experiences, even when recent experiences may not accurately reflect current risk. Understanding these tendencies is important for improving decision-making and problem-solving skills.

All the brain's structures play a role in problem solving, but the **anterior cingulate cortex (ACC)** is particularly important for monitoring and detecting potential errors or conflicts during problem solving, aiding in one's ability to evaluate and adjust approaches and strategies.

Intelligence and Creativity

Various psychological and neurobiological factors shape intelligence and creativity. While **intelligence** primarily focuses on cognitive abilities, **creativity** involves a combination of cognitive processes, personality traits, and **motivation**.

Intelligence is broadly defined as the capacity to acquire and apply knowledge, solve problems, reason, and adapt. It encompasses a range of cognitive processes, including memory, attention, perception, and problem solving. Psychologists have developed various theories and models for analyzing intelligence, with the **intelligence quotient (IQ) test** being a well-known, though imperfect, example for measuring intelligence.

The psychology of intelligence explores how individuals acquire and process information, make decisions, and solve problems. Cognitive psychologists examine factors such as working memory, attentional control, and cognitive flexibility, which play crucial roles in problem solving and decision making. They also examine intelligence in relation to other constructs like personality traits and emotional intelligence. Research indicates a correlation between high intelligence and academic achievement, job performance, and success in various domains.

Creativity involves generating novel and valuable ideas, solutions, or products through both **divergent thinking**, the ability to generate multiple and diverse ideas, and **convergent thinking**, the ability to select and refine ideas to produce high-quality outcomes. Psychologists have developed various tests and measures, like the **Torrance Tests of Creative Thinking**, to assess creativity.

The psychology of creativity focuses on cognitive processes and personality traits that contribute to creative thinking, including cognitive flexibility, associative thinking, and the ability to overcome **functional fixedness** (the tendency to see objects and ideas only in their usual function). Creativity is also influenced by motivation, intrinsic interest, and one's willingness to take risks.

Exploring the psychology underlying intelligence and creativity provides insights into how these constructs are facilitated and how they contribute to human achievement and progress. This understanding can aid in developing strategies to enhance intelligence and foster creativity, leading to advancements in various fields of human endeavor.

ATTENTION AND MEMORY

The bidirectional relationship between attention and memory is influenced by multiple variables. Attention facilitates memory by selectively directing focus toward relevant stimuli, aiding the **encoding** and **consolidation** of information. When an individual pays attention to something, they allocate cognitive resources to processing and encoding it, increasing the likelihood of it being stored in memory. **Selective attention** prioritizes certain information based on relevance or significance.

Attention is crucial for memory **retrieval**. **Retrieval inhibition** prevents interference from competing memories and enhances the accuracy of recollection by filtering irrelevant details to retrieve relevant information more effectively. **Memory priming**, influenced by an individual's past experiences and knowledge, shapes attentional biases and determines one's present focus. For example, if an individual has a strong memory associated with a particular place, their attention may be drawn to similar environments or cues that remind them of that memory.

Attention and memory are vital for learning, and the interaction between attention and memory extends beyond individual experiences. When an individual directs their attention toward new information, they engage in cognitive processing that facilitates its encoding and subsequent integration into their existing knowledge base. The more actively one processes information, the more likely it is to be consolidated and retained in memory.

Attention

Attention involves selectively allocating cognitive resources to relevant stimuli or tasks, concentrating on specific information while disregarding irrelevant input. Attention can be directed externally toward sensory input (e.g., visual or auditory stimuli) or internally toward thoughts, memories, or mental processes. There are several theories that attempt to explain the dynamics of attention; three of the most common are early selection theory, late selection theory, and the spotlight model.

THEORIES OF ATTENTION

Theory	Description
Early selection theory	Attention operates as a filter during an early stage of information processing, allowing only selected stimuli to reach conscious awareness.
Late selection theory	All stimuli are processed to some extent; attention determines which stimuli receive conscious awareness and further processing.
Spotlight model	Attention operates like a spotlight by selectively illuminating a specific area of focus while leaving the rest in the periphery.

One important aspect of the **attention spotlight** is its limited capacity. Attentional resources are finite since people cannot attend to every detail simultaneously. Instead, one must selectively focus on the most relevant or salient information. Selective attention helps filter out irrelevant or less important stimuli to facilitate concentration.

Neurobiologically, the brain's **attentional system** is distributed across various regions, including the **prefrontal cortex**, **parietal cortex**, and

superior colliculus. These regions work in concert to regulate attention and coordinate information processing. **Neurotransmitter** levels also influence attention; **dopamine** enhances one's attention and focus, and the release of **norepinephrine** increases vigilance, alertness, and readiness to respond to stimuli.

Attention deficit hyperactivity disorder (ADHD) disrupts the attention spotlight. While most individuals can control and direct their attention effectively, individuals with ADHD struggle to maintain focused attention. Their attention spotlight may be more diffuse and less able to filter out distractions, leading to difficulty staying on task and completing activities. They may also struggle to inhibit impulsive behaviors and regulate their activity levels. Treatment for ADHD typically involves a combination of behavioral interventions and medication. Behavioral interventions aim to help individuals with ADHD develop strategies for managing their attention and impulsivity. Medicinal interventions, such as stimulant medications, may improve attention and reduce hyperactivity in individuals with ADHD by increasing dopamine levels.

Research in cognitive psychology emphasizes attention's crucial role in learning. Studies have shown that attentional processes, such as selective attention and **divided attention**, impact learning outcomes. This research has led to the development of strategies to help people improve attention and enhance learning, such as providing clear instructions, reducing distractions, and engaging learners through active participation.

Memory

Memory is the cognitive process responsible for encoding, storing, and retrieving information and experiences. It enables individuals to retain and recall past events, knowledge, and skills. Memory can be divided into three main stages: encoding, consolidation, and retrieval. During encoding, information is transformed into a format that can be stored in the brain. Consolidation strengthens and stabilizes encoded information, making it more resistant to forgetting. Finally, retrieval is the process of accessing and bringing forth stored information when needed.

One key aspect of memory encoding is **sensory memory**, which is the initial stage of memory processing. Sensory memory is a brief and transient form of memory that allows individuals to retain sensory information from their environment for a short period. It is divided into different modalities, such as **iconic memory** (visual sensory memory) and **echoic memory** (auditory sensory memory).

Short-Term Memory

From sensory memory, information deemed important is transferred to short-term memory. **Short-term memory**, also known as **working memory**, is a limited-capacity memory system that temporarily holds and manipulates information. It allows individuals to retain and work with information for a brief period, typically up to 30 seconds.

Implicit Long-Term Memory

Implicit long-term memory, also known as **nondeclarative long-term memory**, refers to the retention and retrieval of information without conscious awareness. It influences one's thoughts, behaviors, and emotions and can manifest in various forms, including **priming**, **emotional memory**, and **procedural memory**.

Priming. Priming involves the influence of a stimulus on subsequent processing and behavior, even when that influence happens unconsciously. For instance, if a person is presented with a series of words that includes *yellow*, they may later be more likely to recognize or conjure words related to the color yellow.

Central to **classical conditioning**, priming occurs because initial exposure activates related concepts and associations in memory, making them more accessible. Priming can occur in various domains, such as **semantic priming**, where words related in meaning facilitate processing (e.g., *doctor* priming *nurse*), as well as **perceptual priming**, where prior exposure to a visual or auditory stimulus enhances recognition or identification of similar stimuli (e.g., the sound of a bird priming the identification of a picture of a dove).

Emotional Memory. Emotional memory refers to the storage and retrieval of memories associated with emotional experiences. Emotional events are often remembered more intensely and vividly than neutral events and, in turn, influence one's emotions, decision making, and responses to future situations. The formation and storage of emotional memories are facilitated by the **amygdala**, which receives sensory information and assigns emotional significance to stimuli.

Procedural Memory. Procedural memory involves acquiring and retaining skills to facilitate the smooth execution of motor and cognitive tasks. It allows individuals to perform certain tasks, such as riding a bicycle or playing a musical instrument, without consciously thinking about the specific steps involved. The **cerebellum** contributes to the acquisition and retention of procedural memory, while the **basal ganglia** receive input from the cerebrum and relay information back to the motor cortex, facilitating the automation of learned motor skills.

Explicit Long-Term Memory

Explicit long-term memory, also known as **declarative long-term memory**, refers to the conscious recollection of facts, events, and experiences. It involves the deliberate retrieval of information that can be expressed verbally and is further divided into **semantic memory** and **episodic memory**.

Semantic Memory. Semantic memory refers to one's knowledge and understanding of general facts, concepts, and meanings. It allows individuals to recall facts and other information about the world. Semantic memory is involved in language comprehension, problem solving, and decision making.

Episodic Memory. Episodic memory refers to one's ability to recall specific events and personal experiences, such as remembering a family vacation or a birthday celebration. It enables the conscious recollection of contextual details, including time, place, emotions, and sensory information. **Mental time travel**, which refers to the ability to both consciously reexperience past events in the present and imagine potential future scenarios, is made possible by episodic memory.

LEARNING

Psychology has made significant contributions to the collective understanding of cognitive processes in learning. Psychologists have conducted experiments to investigate how individuals perceive, attend to, interpret, and remember information, providing numerous insights into the cognitive processes involved in learning. One prominent theory is the **information-processing approach**, which suggests that cognitive processes involve encoding, storage, and retrieval of information.

Biology of Learning

The biology of learning focuses on **neurons**, **synapses**, and **neurotransmitters** to explain the mechanisms underlying the acquisition and retention of knowledge. The following table details some key concepts related to biological aspects of learning.

KEY CONCEPTS: BIOLOGY OF LEARNING

Term	Definitions/Characteristics/Functions
Neuroplasticity	• Refers to the brain's ability to reorganize itself by forming new neural connections and modifying existing ones • Allows the brain to adapt and change in response to experiences • Occurs through synaptic plasticity and neurogenesis
Synaptic plasticity	• Refers to the process by which the strength and efficiency of connections between neurons (synapses) are modified • Involves changing the structure and function of synapses to transmit information more effectively • Can be divided into two primary forms: long-term potentiation (LTP) and long-term depression (LTD)
Long-term potentiation (LTP)	• Enhances synaptic strength between neurons to increase the efficiency of neural communication • Leads to the strengthening of the synapse with a postsynaptic neuron from the activation of a presynaptic neuron
Long-term depression (LTD)	• Weakens synaptic connections between neurons • Refines and tunes neural circuits to eliminate unnecessary or unwanted connections • Shapes neuronal networks to optimize information processing
Neurogenesis	• Refers to the process of generating new neurons in certain regions of the brain, particularly the hippocampus • Occurs primarily in early development but continues throughout adulthood in the olfactory system and hippocampus • Provides new neurons that can integrate into existing neural networks and participate in learning processes

Multiple neurotransmitters play vital roles in the neurobiology of learning. **Glutamate** is involved in long-term potentiation (LTP), facilitating the enhancement of synaptic strength. Dopamine reinforces behaviors that lead to positive outcomes, thereby promoting learning and the formation of new memories. Dopamine release during rewarding experiences enhances the encoding and consolidation of information, making it more likely to be retained in long-term memory.

Types of Learning

Classical conditioning, **operant conditioning**, and **observational learning** are three distinct types of learning that influence how individuals acquire new knowledge, skills, and behaviors.

Classical Conditioning

Classical conditioning, as famously demonstrated by **Ivan Pavlov** with his experiments on dogs, involves several key components. The **unconditioned stimulus (UCS)** is a stimulus that naturally elicits a specific response, such as food leading to salivation in Pavlov's experiments. The **unconditioned response (UCR)** is the innate response to the UCS, such as salivation. The **conditioned stimulus (CS)** is a neutral stimulus that, through repeated pairing with the UCS, comes to elicit a **conditioned response (CR)**. The conditioned response is the learned response to the CS, which is similar or identical to the UCR.

Psychologists have identified multiple aspects of classical conditioning. **Acquisition** refers to the initial learning phase when the CS and UCS are paired, leading to the formation of an association. **Extinction** occurs when the CS is presented repeatedly without the UCS, resulting in the weakening or disappearance of the conditioned response. **Generalization** refers to the tendency to respond to stimuli that are like the CS, while **discrimination** involves distinguishing between the CS and other similar stimuli.

Operant Conditioning

Operant conditioning, also known as instrumental conditioning, was extensively studied by **B. F. Skinner**. Skinner's research focused on understanding how behaviors are shaped and maintained through the consequences they produce. Unlike classical conditioning, which involves association between stimuli, operant conditioning focuses on the relationship between behaviors and their outcomes.

In operant conditioning, behaviors are strengthened or weakened based on the consequences that follow them. **Reinforcement** refers to the process of increasing the likelihood of a behavior occurring, while **punishment** refers to the process of decreasing the likelihood of a behavior occurring. Reinforcement can be positive, through the addition of a desirable stimulus, or negative, through the removal of an aversive stimulus. **Positive reinforcement**, such as praising a child for completing their homework, may increase the likelihood of the child doing their homework in the future. **Negative reinforcement** increases the likelihood of a behavior occurring by removing an aversive stimulus; for instance, a loud and particularly unpleasant alarm might negatively reinforce a person getting out of bed before it goes off.

Punishment decreases the likelihood of a behavior occurring by providing an aversive consequence. **Positive punishment** involves the addition of an aversive stimulus. For example, placing a child in time-out for their misbehavior may decrease the likelihood of them engaging in that behavior again. **Negative punishment** decreases the likelihood of a behavior occurring by removing a desirable stimulus. For instance, taking away a teenager's phone for breaking curfew may decrease the likelihood of them breaking curfew in the future.

Observational Learning

Observational learning, proposed by **Albert Bandura**, involves learning by observing others and imitating their behaviors. Also known as social learning or vicarious learning, observational learning emphasizes the roles of **observation** and **imitation** in learning and behavior. Through observation, individuals can acquire new skills, knowledge, and attitudes without direct reinforcement or personal experience.

Observational learning involves learning through imitation and occurs through a cognitive process called **modeling**. Individuals observe and imitate the behaviors of others, and their behavior is shaped by the consequences they observe. For instance, if a younger sibling recognizes that their older sibling is praised for helping around the house, they may consequentially learn that helping around the house results in parental praise. This learning process can occur through both **live models** (people physically present) and **symbolic models** (such as those portrayed in the media).

Bandura outlined four key processes involved in observational learning: attention, **retention**, **reproduction**, and motivation. In the context of observational learning, attention refers to the individual's focus on the model's behavior and is influenced by factors such as the model's appeal or attractiveness to the observer, the relevance of the behavior, and the observer's level of interest. Retention involves encoding and storing observed behavior in memory, and reproduction involves physically imitating the behavior observed. Finally, motivation refers to the observer's drive to imitate the behavior. Motivation can be influenced by the consequences the model experiences, as well as the observer's own expectations of reinforcement.

LANGUAGE

Language is broadly defined as a system of communication that uses symbols (words) and rules (grammar) to convey meaning. Unlike communication, which is present in many species, language is believed to be a uniquely human ability that allows for the expression of thoughts, emotions, and intentions. Psychologists and **linguists** have extensively studied language to understand its structure, acquisition, and processing. Language production involves generating and organizing thoughts into linguistic structures, considering factors such as grammar, syntax, and pragmatics.

Biology of Language

Neurobiology provides insights into the neural mechanisms underlying language. Advances in neuroimaging techniques have allowed researchers to identify key brain regions involved in language processing. Studies have identified a network of brain regions called the **language network**, which includes **Broca's area**, **Wernicke's area**, and the **arcuate fasciculus**.

Broca's area, located in the frontal lobe, is involved in speech production and syntax processing. Damage to this area can result in expressive speech difficulties, known as **Broca's aphasia**. Wernicke's area, located in the temporal lobe, is involved in language comprehension and semantic processing. Damage to this area can lead to receptive language difficulties, known as **Wernicke's aphasia**. The arcuate fasciculus is a tract of axons that connects neurons of the Broca's and Wernicke's areas, facilitating the transfer of information between these regions.

Research has shown that for most individuals, the **left hemisphere** of the brain plays a dominant role in language processing. This lateralization of language functions is known as the **left hemisphere dominance hypothesis**. However, there is evidence to suggest that the **right hemisphere** also contributes to certain aspects of language processing, such as discourse comprehension and **prosody**: the patterns of stress and intonation in different languages.

Theories of Language

Language acquisition starts at a young age, and children learn to understand and speak their native language through a combination of **innate predispositions** and **environmental input**. Psychologists and linguists have extensively studied language to understand its structure, acquisition, and processing, resulting in numerous theories on how people develop language.

The **behaviorist theory**, proposed by **B. F. Skinner**, suggests that language is learned through conditioning and reinforcement. According to this theory, children acquire language by imitating and being rewarded for correct language usage. However, this theory fails to explain how children acquire complex language structures and understand novel sentences.

The **nativist theory**, proposed by linguist **Noam Chomsky**, posits that language acquisition is innate and governed by a **language acquisition device (LAD)**. Chomsky argued that children are born with a **universal grammar** that enables them to acquire language rapidly and effortlessly. This theory highlights the importance of the underlying cognitive mechanisms and innate language structures in language development.

Another approach called **connectionism** suggests that language processing and production involve the activation and interaction of distributed neural networks in the brain. The term connectionism was coined in the 1930s by **Edward Thorndike**, and this approach to language processing was further developed by American neuropsychologist **Warren Sturgis McCulloch** and logician **Walter Harry Pitts** during the 1950s. According to this perspective, language acquisition and processing occur through the strengthening and weakening of connections between neurons.

CONCLUSION

The intertwined processes of cognition and learning play a fundamental role in shaping human experience, contributing to the development of civilizations across the globe. The harmonious collaboration between attention and memory enables individuals to achieve their goals and exert influence over the world around them. Through the power of thinking, people can process information, solve problems, derive meaning from their encounters, and generate innovative ideas.

Unconsciously, classical conditioning molds human behavior, allowing individuals to adaptively respond to various stimuli. Meanwhile, conscious forms of learning, such as operant conditioning and observational learning, facilitate the ongoing enhancement of the principles that govern civilization. Language, a sophisticated and unique form of communication in humans, serves as the vehicle for transmitting creative and revolutionary solutions to the challenges faced by humanity.

READINESS CHECK: COGNITION AND LEARNING

To check how well you understand the concepts covered in this chapter, review the following questions. If you have trouble answering any of them, consider reading through this chapter again and reviewing the key terms before moving on to the next chapter.

- Can you define the following terms?
  - Cognition
  - Thinking
  - Default mode network
  - Attention
  - Attention deficit hyperactivity disorder (ADHD)
  - Synaptic plasticity
- Can you discuss the following concepts?
  - Metacognition
  - Problem solving
  - Cognitive biases and heuristics
  - Intelligence
  - Creativity
  - Short-term memory
  - Emotional versus procedural memories
  - Semantic versus episodic memories
- Can you explain the following theories?
  - Early selection theory of attention
  - Late selection theory of attention
  - Spotlight model of attention
  - Information-processing model of learning
  - Behaviorist theory of language
  - Nativist theory of language
  - Connectionism

- Can you explain the main brain regions associated with cognition and learning?
- Can you describe the three main stages involved in memory and the order in which they occur?
- How does long-term potentiation differ from long-term depression?
- Can you provide examples of and define secondary forms of memory related to implicit and explicit long-term memory?
- What are the similarities and differences between classical conditioning, operant conditioning, and observational learning?

TEST YOURSELF: COGNITION AND LEARNING

Directions: Each of the questions or incomplete statements below is followed by five suggested answers or completions. Select the one best answer for each. The Answer Key and Explanations will follow.

---

1. Of the following choices, the feature of the brain most involved in self-referential thought is the

   A. salience network
   B. default mode network
   C. central executive network
   D. hippocampus
   E. prefrontal cortex

2. After an argument with his friend, Steven searches the internet for more information. During his search for sources to send his friend, Steven selects sources consistent with his original position, disregarding any sources that contain conflicting information. Which of the following tendencies best describes Steven's behavior?

   A. Confirmation bias
   B. Anchoring bias
   C. Availability heuristic
   D. Problem-solving heuristic
   E. Convergent-thinking bias

3. Which of the following cognitive processes involves an individual's ability to access information stored as a memory?

   A. Encoding
   B. Consolidation
   C. Perceptual priming
   D. Semantic priming
   E. Retrieval

4. After discovering that she has been stealing candy from her sister, Janella's parents decide to discourage this behavior by taking away Janella's favorite toy for one week. This consequence could be described as

A. positive reinforcement
B. negative reinforcement
C. positive punishment
D. negative punishment
E. neutral punishment

5. Damage to which of the following brain regions would be most likely to result in an individual having trouble with their production of speech?

A. The temporal lobe
B. Wernicke's area
C. Broca's area
D. The somatosensory cortex
E. The gustatory cortex

Answer Key and Explanations

1. B	2. A	3. E	4. D	5. C

1. **The correct answer is B.** The default mode network is a collection of different structures in the brain, whose coordinated activity has been shown to relate to self-referential thought and introspection. Choices D and E are too specific, and choices A and C are related to goal-directed thinking and cognitive control rather than self-referential thought.

2. **The correct answer is A.** Confirmation bias refers to the tendency to favor information that confirms one's preexisting beliefs. Choices B and C involve biases and heuristics related to the time and order of learned information. Choices D and E are not recognized as biases or heuristics.

3. **The correct answer is E.** The recollection of memories that have been stored in the brain involves memory retrieval. Choices A and B involve the storage and stabilization of memories. Choices C and D relate to priming, a form of implicit learning, rather than memory.

4. **The correct answer is D.** The consequence Janella's parents impose involves removing something Janella desires (a negative punishment), rather than adding a new aversive stimulus such as a time-out (positive punishment). Janella's parents wish to decrease the frequency of her undesirable behavior, which involves punishment rather than reinforcement, so choices A and B can be disregarded. Punishment does not have a recognized neutral form, so choice E can also be eliminated.

5. **The correct answer is C.** Broca's area is associated with speech production and syntax processing. Wernicke's area is associated with language comprehension and semantic processing rather than the production of speech, so choice B is incorrect. Choices A, D, and E are also incorrect, as Broca's area is in the brain's frontal lobe.

Chapter 9

Developmental Psychology across the Lifespan

OVERVIEW

- Dimensions of Development
- Theories of Development
- Heredity and Environment
- Gender Identity and Sex Roles
- Research Methods for Developmental Psychology
- Conclusion
- Readiness Check: Developmental Psychology across the Lifespan
- Test Yourself: Developmental Psychology across the Lifespan

Developmental psychology, also known as "lifetime psychology," covers each stage of a person's psychological growth from the prenatal stage through the geriatric years. There are numerous theories about what constitutes a developmental milestone and when most people will or should reach each milestone, especially as they leave childhood and become adults. This chapter covers the basic components of human physical, cognitive, moral, and social development; the theories of development that concern each type; and the research methods that developmental psychologists have used to collect data and study development. These concepts and others from developmental psychology will account for 8%–9% of the CLEP Introductory Psychology exam.

DIMENSIONS OF DEVELOPMENT

Physical development in infancy and early childhood tends to happen in stages: most babies roll before they can pull themselves up to a seat, crawl before they walk, and develop **gross motor skills** before they can hone **fine motor skills**. Gross motor skills include balance and the movements of larger muscle groups, including actions like walking, running, skipping, and throwing a ball. Fine motor skills involve small muscle groups and more intense coordination, including actions like holding a pencil to write, fastening buttons, or eating with utensils. Every stage of muscle development provides the basis for the next stage.

Between the ages of 3 and 8, children typically experience a burst of development in both gross and fine motor skills. In this time, children may progress from being unsteady on their feet and unable to write legibly to being able to climb, dress, write, draw, and feed themselves. Many factors can negatively affect physical development, including poor nutrition, preverbal trauma, birth injury, pollutants in the environment, and a stressful home environment. While **developmental milestones** are now considered to be normative ranges rather than strict deadlines, they are useful guidelines because some disabilities do not become apparent until a child misses one or more milestones. The Centers for Disease Control and Prevention and the American Academy of Pediatrics publish milestone guidelines for physical development that are generally accepted around the world.

Interaction with the environment helps fuel the bursts of growth that young children go through. In terms of brain physiology, children go through periods of both **synaptic growth** and **synaptic pruning**. Synaptic growth, also called synaptogenesis, refers to the formation of new connections between neurons, which begins early in brain development. While the formation of new synapses occurs throughout the lifespan, this process peaks when children are approximately 2 years old. This surge in synaptic growth is then followed by a more extended phase of synaptic pruning. During this time, the brain rids itself of unused connections and forms new, more efficient **neural pathways**. Although synaptic pruning persists into early adulthood, it reaches its peak during childhood. By the age of 10, approximately half of the synapses initially present in the brain at 2 years old have been pruned. Compared with adults' brains, children's brains have heightened **neural plasticity**, which gives them the ability to restructure their connections in response to novel information or injuries like seizures or traumatic brain injuries.

THEORIES OF DEVELOPMENT

Development can describe both physical and psychological processes, which occur in tandem as a person grows and matures. There are numerous theories about how this development occurs; this section will address some of the most dominant theories of development in psychology.

Jean Piaget's Stages of Childhood Development

Jean Piaget was a Swiss psychologist and philosopher of the 20th century who used **naturalistic observation** to study the cognitive development of young children. In naturalistic observation, psychologists conduct research by watching subjects without interfering. As he watched his own children, Piaget discovered that they made the same types of errors and achievements around the same ages and that childhood development seemed to progress in a systematic, linear fashion. He then developed a series of simple tests to confirm his hypothesis on childhood development and expanded his research to a much larger **sample size** of participants across a range of ages.

PIAGET'S STAGES OF CHILDHOOD DEVELOPMENT

	Stage	Approximate Age Range	Key Milestones
1	Sensorimotor	Infant to 2 years	Habituation, development of gross and fine motor skills, use of imagination
2	Preoperational	2 to 7 years	Understanding of basic abstract concepts, use of mental representations, object permanence
3	Concrete operational	7 to 11 years	Conservation, reversibility
4	Formal operational	11 years through adulthood	Understanding of hypotheticals, formation of hypotheses, exploration of advanced abstract concepts

Sensorimotor Stage

According to Piaget, the first stage of development is the **sensorimotor stage**, which occurs from birth to around age 2. An enormous amount of growth takes place in the first two years of life. Initially, babies move and learn primarily through reflexes and have trouble organizing different sensory information into a single, organized concept. However, infants as young as 3 months old exhibit signs of **habituation**, or the diminished impact of a familiar sight or item. For instance, children at this age may lose interest in toys that once fascinated them or grow disinterested in physical environments they see habitually. Because interest positively correlates with development, mental stimulation is paramount at this stage, even if infants don't appear to notice much.

As young children continue to take an interest in their environment and interact with caregivers, they become motivated to explore. They go through growth spurts, refine gross and fine motor skills, and eventually develop the ability to integrate sensory information, communicate verbally, and complete more complex and voluntary tasks. Additionally, most children can use their imaginations to "play pretend" by the end of the sensorimotor stage.

Preoperational Stage

The **preoperational stage** lasts from about ages 2 to 7. During this period, children develop the ability to understand more abstract concepts. They also learn to use mental representations to conceive of objects. As a result, they develop **object permanence**, meaning they can recognize that things and people still exist even when they can't see or hear them. Toddlers begin to understand that they are separate from their caregivers and have their own identities, though they often struggle with recognizing that others may have different wants or points of view. They also begin to conceptually understand identity. For example, a toddler can recognize that their father is still their father if he shaves off his beard—the change may upset them, but they can ultimately recognize the continuity of his identity both with and without the beard.

Concrete Operational Stage

In the preadolescent years from about ages 7 to 11, children enter the **concrete operational stage**. During this time, they improve their ability to categorize objects and begin to recognize that two things that seem different can still fall under the same category. Spatial skills and abstract problem-solving skills improve during this period as well.

One example of improved categorization and spatial skills is **conservation**, wherein a child can group two disparate-seeming objects or ideas together. For example, a child of this age can recognize that the same amount of liquid may appear different in two differently shaped containers. As the concrete operational stage progresses, children grow more skilled at focusing on different dimensions (objects) at the same time and understand the concept of **reversibility** (i.e., an object can change and then return to its original form).

Formal Operational Stage

Finally, during the preadolescent years children enter the **formal operational stage**, which lasts through their teen years and into adulthood. At this point, they develop the ability to hypothesize, understand hypotheticals, and understand more abstract questions, such as those concerning morality and ethics.

Erik Erikson's Stages of Psychosocial Development

Erik Erikson also studied childhood in his research on human social development. Erikson's work differed from Piaget's in that it focused less on how humans develop abstract abilities and more on the ways they develop healthy egos and build relationships with others. Erikson described multiple **psychosocial development stages** that continue throughout a person's lifespan. Each stage involves a crisis that must be resolved before the person can move forward with their ego intact. As his research progressed, Erikson relaxed his original definitions of the time frames in which each crisis had to be resolved, but regardless of the timing, he noted that successful resolution of a crisis tended to foster certain personal virtues. Failure to resolve a given crisis tended to inhibit a person from moving forward to the next crisis and stage of development, resulting in **maldevelopment** that could lead to unhappiness and interpersonal dysfunction.

ERIKSON'S STAGES OF PSYCHOSOCIAL DEVELOPMENT

	Crisis	Approximate Age Range	Associated Virtue	Result of Positive Development	Result of Maldevelopment
1	Trust vs. mistrust	Birth to 18 months	Hope	Sense of security, trust in caregiver(s)	Mistrust, withdrawal, anxiety
2	Autonomy vs. shame and doubt	18 months to 3 years	Will	Sense of independence and identity	Compulsion, sense of inadequacy, fear of new people and experiences
3	Initiative vs. guilt	3 to 6 years	Purpose	Initiative, awareness of boundaries, ability to form and execute plans	Self-doubt, guilt, lack of initiative

(continues)

ERIKSON'S STAGES OF PSYCHOSOCIAL DEVELOPMENT (*CONTINUED*)

	Crisis	Approximate Age Range	Associated Virtue	Result of Positive Development	Result of Maldevelopment
4	Industry vs. inferiority	7 to 11 years	Competence	Confidence, competence in completing tasks	Sense of inferiority or inadequacy, diminished self-confidence
5	Identity vs. role confusion	12 to 18 years	Fidelity	Identification of personal beliefs and values, long-term goal setting, stronger sense of self	Role confusion/ identity crises, increase in rebellious behavior, sense of feeling "lost"
6	Intimacy vs. isolation	19 to 29 years	Love	Greater capacity for intimacy, ability to form mutually dependent bonds, stronger commitment to platonic and romantic relationships	Isolation, depression, sense of estrangement
7	Generativity vs. stagnation	30 to 64 years	Care	Feeling that one matters and contributes meaningfully to society	Sense of stagnation, feelings of emptiness, stifled personal growth, self-absorption
8	Ego integrity vs. despair	65+ years	Wisdom	Acceptance of the life one has led, integrated sense of self	Despair, sense of failure, bitterness, increased fear of death

Stage 1: Trust versus Mistrust

Erikson's first stage, which covers infancy from birth to about 18 months of age, is the crisis of **trust versus mistrust**. To develop trust, an infant must know that their basic needs will be met. These basic needs include nourishment and shelter as well as social needs, such as the need for affection. If an infant is provided with a secure environment and responsive caregiver(s), they will be able to move more easily through the crisis of trust versus mistrust, resulting in the development of the virtue of hope. Conversely, an infant who lives in an insecure environment or who cannot rely on their caregiver(s) is likely to experience withdrawal, anxiety, and mistrust.

Stage 2: Autonomy versus Shame and Doubt

From ages 18 months to 3 years, a period also known as toddlerhood, children undergo the crisis of **autonomy versus shame and doubt**. As toddlers, children learn that they are capable of independent action. They develop a sense of their own independent identity and begin to recognize how many tasks they are capable of handling on their own. Encouragement and support in the development of independence are crucial to children at this stage. The result of support through this crisis is the development of the virtue of will, while maldevelopment at this stage can contribute to compulsion, feelings of inadequacy, fear of new experiences, or doubt in one's ability to function as an independent being.

Stage 3: Initiative versus Guilt

Stage three, which lasts from ages 3 to 6, is characterized by the crisis of **initiative versus guilt**. The objective during this stage is for children to learn to create and maintain boundaries while also developing their own initiative and fostering their own interests. Children become more attuned to when their boundaries have been overstepped and may recognize the guilt or disappointment that comes with being unsuccessful at a task they initiated. Play is central to this stage in that it helps children build relationships with others and begin to recognize their own likes and dislikes. Children who are supported through this stage develop a sense of purpose alongside crucial skills like forming and executing plans and expressing desires and needs. However, children who are not supported at this stage tend to develop self-doubt or guilt and may be reluctant to initiate certain activities.

Stage 4: Industry versus Inferiority

From ages 7 to 11, school-age children must resolve the crisis of **industry versus inferiority**. During this stage, they learn to feel confident when they are competent at a task and, by contrast, tend to develop a sense of inferiority if they cannot complete a task competently. Accordingly, successful support through this stage tends to result in children developing the virtue of competence. Children who are not supported through this stage or who receive significant criticism or negative feedback as they develop these skills tend to experience diminished self-confidence and a general feeling of inadequacy.

Stage 5: Identity versus Role Confusion

In the preteen years from ages 12 through 18, a period known as **adoles-cence**, young people must face the crisis of **identity versus role confu-sion**, during which they experiment with different identities in pursuit of one they can call their own. Prior to this stage, children mostly absorb the values and perspectives of those around them, but at this stage, they begin to make sense of what they know about the world in terms of what they know about themselves. This time of concentrated exploration helps adolescents develop a strong sense of self as they grow into adults. They are likely to start identifying beliefs and values they hold dear and setting long-term goals, fostering the virtue of fidelity. However, when adolescents are restricted in their exploration of themselves and the world, they tend to experience role confusion, which sometimes manifests as an **identity crisis**. Unresolved identity issues correlate with a lack of direction in adulthood and an increased tendency toward rebellious behaviors.

Stage 6: Intimacy versus Isolation

In early adulthood, from ages 19 through 29, young adults must overcome the crisis of **intimacy versus isolation**. It is during this stage that most people first learn to develop more intimate platonic and romantic rela-tionships. As they develop close, reciprocal bonds, young adults become more comfortable sharing who they are with other people and tend to welcome forms of **mutual dependency**. During this stage, young adults tend to develop a greater capacity for being open with others, commit-ting to relationships, and making personal sacrifices and compromises to support healthy relationships. Those who are successful in navigating this crisis develop the virtue of love, whereas those who struggle to form close and meaningful relationships may suffer from isolation, which can lead to depression and a sense of estrangement from the rest of the world.

Stage 7: Generativity versus Stagnation

In middle age, which Erikson identified as the range from ages 30 to 64, adults must navigate the crisis of **generativity versus stagnation**. During this period, most adults want to build a life that supports their future visions, and they do so by pursuing career opportunities, investing time and effort in their families, or deciding what kinds of contributions they wish to make to society. Generativity corresponds with a feeling that one is contributing meaningfully to the world and tends to accompany increased concern for others and mindfulness about future generations.

When people do not feel like they matter or are contributing meaningfully to the world, they tend to experience a sense of stagnation, which may be accompanied by feelings of emptiness as well as a tendency toward self-absorption or stifled personal growth.

Stage 8: Ego Integrity versus Despair

Beginning around age 65, people enter Erikson's final stage of psycho-social development, which is characterized by the crisis of **ego integrity versus despair**. Those who feel that they have been successful in bringing their life meaning and finding purpose tend to experience ego integrity and acceptance of the life they lead. Others, noting regrets about the life they've lived, tend to experience despair or a sense of failure, which can result in bitterness, overwhelming disappointment, and an increased fear of death.

Lawrence Kohlberg's Stages of Moral Development

While both Piaget and Erikson provide useful ways of thinking about how humans develop, the theories of **Lawrence Kohlberg** add nuance by considering how people develop a sense of morality as they grow. Kohlberg's **moral development theory** outlines the ways in which individuals develop a personal code of ethics. In Kohlberg's theory, there are three stages of moral reasoning with two levels each.

KOHLBERG'S STAGES OF MORAL DEVELOPMENT

	Stage	Approximate Age Range	Level of Moral Reasoning
1	Preconventional	3 to 7 years	1: Avoiding punishment
			2: Self-interest
2	Conventional	8 to 13 years	1: Good boy/good girl orientation
			2: Law-and-order mentality
3	Postconventional	14 years to adulthood	1: Obedience to social contract
			2: Recognition of universal principles

Preconventional Stage

The first stage, from ages 3 to 7, starts with **avoiding punishment** at the first level, then continues to a focus on **self-interest**. For example, as individuation from caregiver(s) occurs, a child may find themselves at odds with what those around them want and opt to pursue their own desires when they can. Their moral development at this stage is still focused on the contrast between reward and punishment; their moral reasoning has not yet moved beyond the need to protect their own interests and avoid getting in trouble.

Conventional Stage

Between ages 8 and 13, a child transitions to moral reasoning based on an external sense of ethics. At the first level, a child may follow a code of conduct that Kohlberg referred to as the **good boy/good girl orientation**, wherein they behave well to get accolades, not because of a specific desire to be moral. This stage is a natural outgrowth of the prior stage's focus on reward and punishment. As they move through the conventional stage, children transition toward a **law-and-order mentality**. At this level, they are very rule-oriented and may have trouble questioning those rules or making exceptions for special circumstances.

Postconventional Stage

From age 14 through adulthood, most people tend to start following a personal code of ethics that governs their moral reasoning—they do what they think is right simply because it is what they think is the correct course of action. At the first level, adolescents tend to obey the **social contract**, meaning they recognize rules as social agreements that can be changed and negotiated depending on the circumstances that surround them. Eventually, they move toward moral reasoning characterized by abstract **universal principles**. At this point, people tend to have an understanding that certain questions of ethics, morality, or justice go beyond clear-cut rules. For instance, a person might recognize that stealing food while starving is ultimately different than shoplifting luxury goods that one could easily afford, regardless of whether they believe that stealing is universally wrong.

HEREDITY AND ENVIRONMENT

The genetic and biological factors that relate to heredity and environment are addressed in Chapter 5, but environmental factors in both the home and the community can also inhibit or enhance a person's development across their lifespan. Any number of factors outside a person's control—socioeconomic status, race or ethnicity, access to food, and the degree of security a person feels in their home environment, for example—can all affect development.

Attachment Theory

Attachment theory, a concept made popular by **Mary Ainsworth**, is a way of describing the relationship patterns that develop between an infant or young child and their caregiver(s). Attachment theory combines aspects of psychosocial development with analysis of the social and physical environment in which a young child develops. These patterns can have lifelong consequences, and attachment is almost exclusively determined by the caregiver's responsiveness to their child's needs and the security of the home environment, though a child's individual temperament does play a role in their interactions.

Ideally, children will develop a **secure attachment style**. Children who trust and feel comfortable with their caregiver(s) and who can reliably expect that their needs will be met tend to explore freely with their caregiver(s) present. While temperaments vary, securely attached individuals tend to be friendly to strangers while also maintaining healthy boundaries. When these needs for secure attachment go unmet, the result is an **insecure attachment style**. Many psychologists believe that as children with insecure attachment styles move into adulthood, they may struggle to establish secure relationships with others, which is why it can be useful for adults to examine how their childhood development may relate to their attachment style.

There are three types of insecure attachment, all of which can indicate dysfunction, neglect, or even abuse on the part of the caregiver(s) in early childhood. The first is an **anxious-ambivalent attachment style**, which is typically developed by children with unreliable caregivers. Children with an anxious-ambivalent attachment style explore very little when their caregivers are in the room and tend to be wary of strangers. They may show little interest in their caregivers but become extremely distressed and angry when they leave. When their caregivers return, these children again show little interest.

The next type is an **anxious-avoidant attachment style**, generally developed by children with neglectful caregivers. These children show little interest if their caregivers depart and again when they return, perhaps showing hesitant interest before turning away. These children also do not show much interest in exploring and tend to ignore strangers.

The third type is a **disorganized attachment style**, which is frequently developed by children who experience abuse, trauma, or mental illness in association with their primary caregiver. These children may exhibit bizarre behaviors, such as scooting backward away from their caregivers, approaching strangers with interest before falling to the floor, or making strange movements when their caregivers depart or return.

These attachment styles influence relationship formation and, like many other factors in development psychology, can have long-lasting effects on the way people relate to others throughout their lives.

Trauma, Abuse, and Poverty

One major factor that can contribute to and perpetuate mental illness, poverty, and/or relational dysfunction is **generational trauma**. Generational trauma occurs when a traumatic event causes familial, cultural, and/or economic distress that results in symptoms of dysfunction and mental illness that trickle down from generation to generation. For example, a person who has a physically abusive parent may be more likely to abuse their own children since they haven't learned healthier coping mechanisms or parenting techniques. They may genuinely not realize that what they're doing is abusive, perhaps because it is not quite as physically cruel as what they themselves experienced and had modeled for them, or because they abuse their children in a different way than their parents did, perhaps through emotional or verbal abuse instead of physical abuse. Those second-generation abused children will, in turn, be much more likely to abuse their own children for the same reasons, and the pattern can continue for many generations. When psychologists speak of **cycle breakers**, they are referring to individuals who recognize these cyclical tendencies as generational trauma and work hard to change their behaviors and end the cycle.

Poverty itself is a risk factor for mental illness and abuse. Low-income communities tend to have more pollutants, higher crime rates, fewer job opportunities, and less effective public schools. Because low-income communities tend to have larger populations of color, generational trauma is also an issue in which systemic racism is magnified. They are also often located in food deserts, meaning that low-income families are more likely to have limited access to nutritious foods. All these factors can contribute to insecurity that can cause or exacerbate mental health issues. Impoverished parents are also more likely to suffer from substance use disorders. As a result of the increased risk factors for those raised in poverty, a common form of abuse in impoverished homes is **parentification**, wherein children are forced to take on adult caregiving roles in the family, whether it be tending to the physical needs of their siblings or acting as an emotional confidant for a parent. This type of abuse is not exclusive to those in poverty, but the environmental factors that correlate with poverty tend to make it much more common in low-income populations. Any one of these issues can hinder a person's development, but taken together, along with the stress of experiencing poverty, it is clear why poverty is a risk factor for mental illness and abuse.

GENDER IDENTITY AND SEX ROLES

To examine the role of **gender identity** and **sex roles** in developmental psychology, one must first recognize the distinction between sex and gender. While the two terms are often used synonymously in colloquial contexts, scientists define **sex** as a biological concept that corresponds with the types of reproductive organs an individual is born with and **gender** as a **social construct**, meaning it is an idea created by society rather than a biological fact. Today, psychologists typically recognize three distinct sexes (male, female, and intersex) and a multitude of gender identities, including **cisgender**, **transgender**, **nonbinary**, and many more. Cisgender identities are those that have traditionally been assigned at birth to male and female babies based on biological sex.

Children become aware of their sex at a young age, often asking innocent questions about their genitals and why they look different than those of their parents or siblings. From a young age, children are aware of their physicality, but their conception of gender comes later, initially in the form of modeling by parents and other adults. Between the ages of 2 and 3, children may not necessarily identify with their like-sexed parents, perhaps even engaging in activities or making statements that do not align with the gender prescribed for them at birth. For example, a young boy might want to dress like his older sister or express a desire to be a mother when he grows up. However, during early childhood, children tend to embrace gender in a performative way, learning the unspoken social rules of gender from family, peers, and media. Despite the performance of gender expectations, sexual and gender development tends to remain latent during the elementary school years.

As they enter adolescence, children typically choose to either embrace or, if their environment allows it, discard their gender identity. Just as Erikson outlined in his theory of the identity versus role confusion crisis, exploring gender and one's relationship to it is an important part of developing identity for adolescents. Today, most psychologists note that young people who are permitted to find their own level of comfort with gender tend to have better outcomes in adult marriages and partnerships than those who are forced into rigid gender roles, and they tend to report a greater degree of satisfaction in their intimate platonic and romantic relationships.

Sigmund Freud's Stages of Psychosexual Development

Sigmund Freud based much of his work on what he called the five stages of **psychosexual development**. While much of this theory was later refuted by his colleagues, Freud's concepts are still used to discuss the process of sexual maturation, and his concept of psychosexual development provides necessary context to the psychoanalytic theory for which he remains well known. Freud believed that maladaptive psychosexual development relates to symptoms of hysteria and neuroticism, both of which are now considered outdated terms for anxiety disorders. He asserted that unsuccessfully transitioning through the five stages of psychosexual development could cause a disruption of the **ego** (the conscious mind) as it tries to reconcile the desires of the **id** (the urge to satisfy basic needs and wants without scruples) and the **superego** (the "better self," which retains a sense of morality and rules).

Freud described the first psychosexual stage as the **oral stage**—as expected, the focus at this stage is on the mouth. At this stage, the id remains in control. According to Freud, disruption during the oral stage of development contributes to dependence on others, aggression, and an oral fixation, which he claimed contributed to maladaptive behaviors like thumb-sucking, overeating, and smoking. The ego then develops during the **anal stage**. During this time, the primary focus is on expelling or withholding feces. Disruption at this stage can result in obsession, meanness, and a tendency to be overly tidy or overly messy. Freud characterized the next stage as the **phallic stage**, during which the genitals are used for self-pleasure. An issue that causes a person to be "stuck" in this stage can result in self-absorption, vanity, and a dysfunctional relationship with their family. During the next stage, **latency**, the superego develops and there is little to no **libido**, which Freud characterized as an individual's psychosexual energy and a force that drives human behavior. The final stage of psychosexual development, the **genital stage**, occurs when a person has fully matured and sex organs can be used for intercourse.

Unlike Erikson's views on social development, which remain prominent among psychologists, researchers are increasingly skeptical of Freud's theories about psychosexual development. Nonetheless, they have played a significant role in the history of developmental psychology.

RESEARCH METHODS FOR DEVELOPMENTAL PSYCHOLOGY

There are two main forms of research for studying psychology across the lifespan: **longitudinal research** and **cross-sectional research**.

In longitudinal studies, researchers follow a single cohort of subjects for years, checking in at appointed times corresponding with various stages throughout their lives. Researchers benefit from using the same **sample** of participants over a long period because they get thorough background information and interviews and can adjust for **confounding variables**. The drawbacks to longitudinal studies include participant attrition (meaning some participants drop out of the study before its completion) and the length of time it takes to conduct research.

In contrast to long-form research in longitudinal studies, cross-sectional research is quicker and incorporates various age groups simultaneously. The challenge with this type of research is that there will be more difficulty finding confounding variables, and data procured from different samples of participants tends to be less reliable.

CONCLUSION

It is important for students of psychology to understand childhood and lifetime development so that they can develop an understanding of how people can take good care of themselves, their loved ones, and their communities. Understanding the unique needs of each age group across the lifespan assists psychology practitioners in developing methods that contribute to a more equitable society. Developmental psychology covers a range of theories regarding social, sexual, moral, physical, and cognitive development, making it a microcosm of the kinds of social issues that come up often in the field of psychology. Fostering a deeper understanding of developmental psychology can help psychologists recognize and treat potential dysfunctions with lifelong effects and can assist researchers with identifying emergent psychological issues.

READINESS CHECK: DEVELOPMENTAL PSYCHOLOGY ACROSS THE LIFESPAN

To check how well you understand the concepts covered in this chapter, review the following questions. If you have trouble answering any of them, consider reading through this chapter again and reviewing the key terms before moving on to the next chapter.

- What is the difference between gross and fine motor skills and when do they develop?
- How does the concept of milestones relate to developmental psychology? How have different theorists conceived developmental milestones?
- If you needed to design a study to research the physical education needs of elementary school children in different grades, which design would you use and why?
- Can you name each of Jean Piaget's four stages of childhood development and describe the traits or tendencies of each stage?
- Can you name each of Erik Erikson's eight stages of psychosocial development and describe the traits or tendencies of each stage?
- How do Piaget's, Erikson's, and Kohlberg's models of development account for those who deviate from expected development paths, if at all?
- What is the difference between sex and gender and how do each relate to developmental psychology?
- What are the tenets of Sigmund Freud's theory of psychosexual stages and how are these theories regarded today?
- What is generational trauma and how does it affect a person's development? How do other environmental risk factors like poverty and access to food affect development?
- What is the difference between secure and insecure attachment styles and what are the three forms of insecure attachment that Mary Ainsworth identified?
- What is the difference between longitudinal research and cross-sectional research? What are the benefits and drawbacks of each?

TEST YOURSELF: DEVELOPMENTAL PSYCHOLOGY ACROSS THE LIFESPAN

Directions: Each of the questions or incomplete statements below is followed by five suggested answers or completions. Select the one best answer for each. The Answer Key and Explanations will follow.

1. Which pattern of attachment indicates an unreliable caregiver?

   A. Ambivalent-anxious attachment
   B. Secure attachment
   C. Disorganized attachment
   D. Clinging attachment
   E. Organized attachment

2. Complete the sentence: gender is _____ and sex is _____.

   A. biologically determined, culturally assigned
   B. customary, religious
   C. scientific, abstract
   D. socially constructed, biologically determined
   E. required, optional

3. Based on what we know about physical development in young children, which skill are children likely to develop first?

   A. Writing their name
   B. Eating with a spoon
   C. Throwing a frisbee
   D. Running
   E. Tying their shoes

4. Lydia is 14 years old, and she has just started to discover the music genres she likes best. To represent her interests, Lydia likes decorating her bedroom wall with posters of her favorite bands and artists. She has also asked her mom for permission to repaint her bedroom wall in her favorite color, purple. These behaviors are representative of Erikson's conception of the crisis of

A. trust versus mistrust
B. initiative versus guilt
C. intimacy versus isolation
D. industry versus inferiority
E. identity versus role confusion

5. What is object permanence?

A. Knowing that things can be arranged in categories
B. Developing an identity separate from one's family
C. Being aware that people and things exist, even when you can't see or hear them
D. The ability to think abstractly
E. The ability to use imagination and play pretend

Answer Key and Explanations

1. A	2. D	3. D	4. E	5. C

1. **The correct answer is A.** Ambivalent-anxious attachment is the type of insecure attachment most directly associated with an unreliable caregiver. While disorganized attachment (choice C) is also an insecure form, it usually occurs because the primary caregiver has faced a trauma or experienced a mental illness. Secure attachment (choice B) occurs when an infant trusts that a reliable caregiver will meet their needs. Choices D and E do not reference terms from attachment theory.

2. **The correct answer is D.** Gender is a social construct, meaning it is defined by a culture, while sex is biologically determined and related to the reproductive organs a person is born with.

3. **The correct answer is D.** Children develop gross motor skills before fine motor skills. Running is a gross motor skill. All the other choices are fine motor skills.

4. **The correct answer is E.** During stage 5 of psychosocial development, identity versus role confusion, Erikson asserts that adolescent individuals develop a unique identity and explore new roles to find themselves. For instance, Lydia's desire to express herself via her music interests and to paint her bedroom in her favorite color reflect her desire to express her identity through the things that she likes most.

5. **The correct answer is C.** Object permanence refers to an individual's awareness that objects and people exist even when they cannot see or hear them. Piaget asserts that individuals gain the sense of object performance during the preoperational stage of human development.

Chapter 10

Personality

OVERVIEW

- Methods of Assessment
- Personality Theories and Approaches
- Self-Concept and Self-Esteem
- Conclusion
- Readiness Check: Personality
- Test Yourself: Personality

This chapter offers a general overview of how personality develops and changes over time. It also covers theories that address the processes by which these changes can occur, the question of whether personality is immutable, and the methods researchers use to measure intangibles such as personal growth and personality traits. In the process, this chapter also addresses the concept of identity and what it means to have self-esteem. Questions regarding personality account for approximately 7%–8% of the CLEP Introductory Psychology exam.

METHODS OF ASSESSMENT

In any discussion about theories of **personality**, it is important to consider the methods used to analyze personality and why they are used. Psychologists utilize various methods to assess personality, including **self-report assessments**, **behavioral observation**, **interview methods**, and **factor analysis**. Each method offers distinct advantages and limitations, contributing to a comprehensive understanding of an individual's personality.

Self-report assessments are questionnaires or inventories that individuals complete to provide information about their own personality traits, attitudes, and behaviors. These assessments rely on individuals' self-perceptions and reflections. However, the potential biases or inaccuracies that may arise from self-reporting, such as social desirability bias, are important to consider.

Behavioral observation involves clinicians directly observing how people behave in various situations. Behavioral observation methods are often employed in controlled laboratory settings, where researchers observe the behavior of participants in different scenarios to assess personality traits. While this method is more limited in its clinical applications than self-report assessments, it is also less prone to the introduction of bias.

Interview methods include structured or semistructured interviews in which psychologists directly engage with individuals to gather information about their personalities. Interviews allow for in-depth exploration of an individual's experiences, motivations, and beliefs. The **Structured Clinical Interview for DSM Disorders (SCID)** is an interview method widely used in clinical settings to assess personality disorders. Interviews provide a more interactive and personalized approach to personality assessment, allowing psychologists to ask follow-up questions and delve deeper into specific areas of interest.

Factor analysis is a statistical technique used to identify underlying dimensions or factors that explain the pattern of correlations between different personality traits. By analyzing large sets of personality data, factor analysis helps to uncover the fundamental dimensions that contribute to an individual's personality.

PERSONALITY THEORIES AND APPROACHES

Personality is a combination of characteristics and qualities that define an individual's unique character. Personality is considered fairly stable throughout a person's lifetime, though it can adapt or evolve due to environmental factors or different types of experiences. In multiple chapters, we mention the question of "nature versus nurture" in regard to numerous facets of psychology, so it should come as no surprise that it is also pertinent to theories of personality. Early psychologists initially assumed that infants were born with certain traits that would follow them through childhood and into adulthood. Some argued that traits were inherited from the mother or developed as a result of problems during pregnancy and/or in early life (excluding congenital injury, formerly referred to as a "birth defect"). Over time, some psychologists shifted to the opinion that all traits are developed because of one's upbringing.

As with most areas in psychology, the truth lies somewhere in between the complex interplay of inheritance (nature) and a person's upbringing (nurture). Today, there are myriad theories on how to assess and evaluate personality, including methods from behaviorist, social-cognitive, psychodynamic, and humanist approaches to psychology. For many clinicians, determining personality is a matter of combining dominant methods of personality analysis with inventories and analyses that mirror their chosen approach.

Temperament

When psychologists speak of the "nature" side of personality, they are often referring to temperament. Temperament is a broad collection of biologically based and consistent individual differences in behavior that occur independent of **environmental factors** (i.e., education, values, and attitudes). The concept of temperament has a complex history that began in ancient Greece with the physician **Hippocrates** and was developed into a formal typology by the Greek physician Galen in the second century AD.

According to Galen, there were four basic temperament types dictated by the "**humors**," or bodily fluids. Each of the four temperaments was said to be governed by the dominance of a humor—when these fluids remained in balance, a person was said to be healthy, but too much of a given fluid was said to indicate the presence of illness. As the following chart lays out, these four temperaments were known as the **sanguine**, **choleric**, **melancholic**, and **phlegmatic** temperaments.

GALEN'S FOUR TEMPERAMENTS

Temperament	Governing Humor	Physical Attributes	Characteristics
Sanguine	Blood	Ruddy complexion, general healthful appearance	Balanced: sociable, hopeful, enthusiastic, talkative, extraverted, carefree Imbalanced: reckless, undedicated, overly impulsive
Choleric	"Yellow" bile	Jaundiced appearance, yellowed complexion	Balanced: ambitious, outgoing, confident, assertive Imbalanced: aggressive, domineering, perfectionistic

(continues)

GALEN'S FOUR TEMPERAMENTS (*CONTINUED*)

Temperament	Governing Humor	Physical Attributes	Characteristics
Melancholic	"Black" bile	Dark freckles or complexion, dry skin, thin hair	Balanced: introverted, conscientious, serious, reliable Imbalanced: depressive, cold, prone to illness, timid
Phlegmatic	Phlegm, clear/white bodily fluids	Light skin and hair, smooth and shiny complexion	Balanced: reserved, charitable, caring, slow to anger, tenacious Imbalanced: overly stoic, passive, sheepish, self-critical

The goal was to "balance" the bodily fluids to reach ideal physical health, contentment, and a strong moral code. This balance was known as eucrasia, and an imbalance was known as dyscrasia. Early physicians spent much of their time attempting to balance the humors, often with practices such as bloodletting and hydrating.

Infant Temperament Types

One modern theory of temperament that bears a striking resemblance to Galen's typology is the theory that there are four basic infant temperaments. Though the idea is an amalgamation of many different theories, the most prominent of which were developed by **Stella Chess** and **Alexander Thomas**, most developmental psychologists still adhere to the idea that babies are born with one of four basic and immutable infant personality types that dictates their early outlook on the world and the ease with which their caregiver(s) can bond with them. The four basic infant personality types are sociable, slow to warm, settled, and sensitive.

FOUR BASIC INFANT TEMPERAMENTS

Infant Temperament	Characteristics	Needs/Challenges
Sociable	• Interacts eagerly with both caregiver(s) and environment • Seeks stimulation	• Requires boundary setting • Prone to overstimulation and may react emotionally, requiring attentive care

FOUR BASIC INFANT TEMPERAMENTS (*CONTINUED*)

Infant Temperament	Characteristics	Needs/Challenges
Slow to warm	• Strongly prefers predictability and stability • Enjoys resting quietly in a caregiver's lap • Prefers to observe the world from a safe position	• Finds comfort in routine • Seeks stability and safety from caregiver(s)
Settled	• Sleeps and feeds well • Easily comforted by caregiver(s) • Slow to become upset • Processes stimulation very efficiently • May be referred to as "easy" by others	• Not especially challenging so long as their needs are met • Requires stimulation to avoid boredom
Sensitive	• Difficult to comfort • May struggle to adopt predictable sleep patterns • May struggle with feeding	• Struggles occur even in the absence of physical/developmental limitations • More prone to colic • Requires more time and energy from caregiver(s) to be soothed

Developmental psychologists note that an infant's temperament may affect the way a caregiver bonds with a child, which can, in turn, affect the child's temperament as they develop. For example, even the most patient and well-meaning new parents can quickly become exhausted by a sensitive baby, which can then cause a lack of sleep for both infant and parent(s) and affect the way the parents interact with their child. Most psychologists agree that defining infant temperament is not an exact science and that most infants display traits of multiple types; nonetheless, using the four infant temperaments as a guideline can be helpful to new parents looking to provide a safe and nurturing environment.

Personality Types

While science and modern research techniques have long abandoned the idea of Galen's "humors" as the underlying biological factor in shaping personality, the principles these temperaments represent remain evident in many of the evolving theories regarding personality types. Theories on personality are myriad, but this section covers a few of the most dominant in the history of the field of psychology.

Gordon Allport's Trait Theory

Gordon Allport was a 20th-century psychologist who believed that personality is fixed at the time of birth and that **personality traits** are so set in individuals that even trauma responses can be predicted by personality. Utilizing a holistic methodological approach and statistical factor analysis, Allport's research included the entirety of a person's characteristics and background, including components such as intelligence, schooling, and childhood events. In the 1930s, he studied infants and very young children, then checked in with them again a few years later. He also conducted detailed interviews with adults. Based on his research, Allport divided traits into three basic categories: **cardinal traits** (dominant traits shaping a person's entire life), **central traits** (characteristics that shaped behavior in specific situations), and **secondary traits** (inconsequential characteristics that had little to no impact on a person's specific development).

Allport suggested that while personality was set, it was also highly unique to the individual and involved internal motivations and cognitions. In his view, new traits accrue over time in a series of building blocks, with different traits informing the development of those to come. In this way, while Allport saw elements of personality as biologically determined, his theory acknowledged that environment and upbringing alike could shape the way new traits developed over time.

Hans Eysenck's Personality Theory

During the 1940s, **Hans Eysenck** developed a theory of personality while working as a psychologist debriefing soldiers being treated at a London hospital during and after World War II. Eysenck noted that many soldiers suffered from what was then called "shell shock" but has since been identified as **post-traumatic stress disorder (PTSD)**, a mental disorder that can occur in individuals who have witnessed or lived through a traumatic event. Eysenck hoped to identify which characteristics made a soldier more likely to need psychiatric treatment. He carefully interviewed soldiers to look for commonalities and found that certain traits were easily grouped together, allowing him to create a four-tiered, multidimensional metric for determining an individual's personality type.

Eysenck was one of the first personality theorists to codify personality traits across multiple dimensions rather than creating a typology wherein an individual's personality was completely dominated by one certain type. He described four basic traits that existed on two polarized continuums, allowing an individual's unique personality to be identified within a plane at the point where the two continuums intersected.

The first axis measured a person's tendencies from **introversion** to **extraversion**. **Introverts** tend to prefer quiet environments and need to "recharge" from social interaction by spending time alone. They also tend to avoid risk and become overstimulated more easily than others. **Extraverts**, on the other hand, tend to seek excitement, change, and social stimulation. They tend to prefer the company of others, recharge socially, and may deliberately take more risks to provide the stimulation they need. In the middle of this continuum are **ambiverts**, those with characteristics of both introversion and extraversion and no tendency toward either extreme.

Eysenck's second dimension of personality measured tendencies along an axis ranging from **neuroticism** to **stability**. (The term *neuroticism*, first coined by **Sigmund Freud**, is now considered an outdated way to refer to a person's tendency to experience anxiety in the face of stress.) In Eysenck's model, a neurotic person is more likely to feel anxiety in the face of stress, while a stable person is less likely to display anxiety. Eysenck posited that these traits were dictated biologically by a person's central nervous system and how reactive it was to stressors.

In the 1970s, Eysenck added another axis to his scale that measured a person's tendencies on the spectrum of **psychoticism** to **normalcy**. Psychoticism included a tendency toward self-isolation, cruelty, and a lack of empathy, while normalcy included a tendency toward compassion, sympathy, and culturally appropriate responses to events. A person with high psychoticism might react to the news of a friend's divorce with little comment or even by insulting their friend, while a person tending toward normalcy would express sympathy and condolences.

Eysenck theorized a neurological basis for each dimension; for example, he was convinced that psychoticism was linked with testosterone and that extraversion was the result of higher cortisol levels. Since the late 1990s, many psychologists have questioned the scientific basis of Eysenck's work, yet **Eysenck's Personality Inventory (EPI)** is still commonly used as a starting point for investigating personality as a combination of biological and mental components.

Raymond Cattell's 16 Personality Factor Trait Theory

In response to Eysenck's relatively simplistic approach, **Raymond Cattell** developed a theory of personality using 16 traits. At the time of Cattell's research in the 1960s, Eysenck's analysis was limited to interviews with military men and only included four dimensions. Cattell believed that researchers should assess a much larger number of traits across a much larger sample group to properly understand personality. To diversify his research, Cattell collected data in three different ways across a more extensive range of people with different ages and backgrounds. He used a combination of **L data**, **Q data**, and **T data**. L data, or "life data," is drawn from a person's background and includes their employment and academic history. Q data, drawn from **Cattell's 16 Personality Factor Questionnaire (16PFQ)**, includes self-reported information in response to questions curated by the researcher. T data includes any objective or quantitative measurements that the researcher gathered.

The 16 personality factors that Cattell identified were as follows:
- Abstractedness
- Apprehension/anxiety
- Dominance
- Emotional stability
- Liveliness
- Openness to change
- Perfectionism
- Privateness
- Reasoning
- Rule consciousness
- Self-reliance/independence
- Sensitivity
- Social assertiveness
- Tension
- Vigilance/paranoia
- Warmth

Cattell argued that these traits are present in most individuals and that determining a person's unique personality requires measuring each personality factor along a continuum. Cattell's work remains important to psychologists because he used **cross-sectional research** methods (meaning he collected from different groups and age cohorts at the same time) and differentiated between **source traits** (deeply ingrained, internal traits) and **surface traits** (the manifestation of source traits, which could be adjusted over time). Psychologists today recognize that Cattell's work provided a broader starting point for personality analysis than anyone else's before him.

The Myers-Briggs Type Indicator

Despite being one of the most popular personality type indicators in professional and personal settings (such as dating apps), the **Myers-Briggs Type Indicator (MBTI)** is largely considered **pseudoscience** by psychologists today. Developed in the mid-20th century by a mother-daughter team (**Katharine Briggs** and **Isabel Myers**) in response to personality theories initially proposed by **Carl Jung**, the MBTI is a simple self-assessment questionnaire that purportedly helps an individual understand how they perceive the world and make decisions. While the MBTI has shown little **external validity**—meaning psychologists have had difficulty meaningfully applying the assessment results to real-world situations—the military and many police departments continue to use the MBTI to help place recruits.

The MBTI uses four sets of interrelated traits measured along a continuum to develop a dimensional analysis of personality that falls into 16 basic types. The four axes of analysis in the MBTI are
1. introversion (I) and extraversion (E) (**attitudinal characteristics**);
2. sensing (S) and intuition (N) (**functional characteristics**);
3. thinking (T) and feeling (F) (functional characteristics); and
4. judgment (J) and perception (P) (**lifestyle characteristics**).

An individual's personality type is then labeled based on where they fall along these continuums. For example, an ENTP result indicates an extraverted person who relies on intuition and thinking to make decisions. This person would be more inclined to view the world based on their perceptions rather than judgments. An ISFJ person would be the inverse: introverted and inclined to rely on their sensations, feelings, and logical judgments of the world. Despite lacking scientific efficacy, the MBTI is so commonly used as a popular science metric that it is still important for psychologists to understand it and recognize how it might shape their patients' own perceptions of their personalities.

Five-Factor Model of Personality (Big Five)

Contemporary psychologists draw on any number of personality inventories that blend approaches from Allport, Cattell, Eysenck, and others in the field. Of these contemporary approaches, one of the most dominant and validated is referred to as the **five-factor model of personality**, or the **"Big Five."**

This model measures personality along the following five dimensions:
- Agreeableness
- Conscientiousness
- Extraversion
- Neuroticism
- Openness to experience

These five factors were identified as the "Big Five" because research has shown them to be highly predictive of behavior and largely cross-cultural. For example, a person who scores high in agreeableness, conscientiousness, and extraversion but low in neuroticism would predictably perform well in most customer-facing jobs. While other contemporary models may allow researchers to analyze personality across more dimensions, there is also a benefit to only focusing on five highly predictive dimensions as a starting point for more in-depth analysis.

The Minnesota Multiphasic Personality Inventory

Psychologists can use many different assessments to determine a person's personality traits. Still, psychologists consider the **Minnesota Multiphasic Personality Inventory (MMPI)** critical when making diagnostic evaluations of personality and psychological disorders. This inventory focuses on determining if a person has a "normal" or "average" personality or if their traits deviate considerably from known norms. Because of this focus, psychologists can use the MMPI to identify both psychological disorders and **personality disorders**, which are deeply ingrained behavioral patterns that deviate significantly from generally agreed-upon norms for average behavior.

Initially, the inventory required 1,000 true-or-false questions, but the current version has been reduced to 500. These questions ask about a person's attitudes toward work, friends, family, and much more. Multiple questions also simultaneously seek to determine a person's propensity for certain behaviors, such as lying or avoiding certain topics. A clinician (or even a computer) then looks for patterns that emerge across the responses.

Projective Measures

A few limitations of the MMPI, MBTI, and many other personality inventories are that they rely on self-reported responses and a person's summation of their inner world. **Projective measures** are designed to examine what occurs at the subconscious level, such as how a person might respond to unstructured stimuli. One of the most common projective tests that psychologists use is the **Rorschach inkblot test**, developed in the 1920s by **Hermann Rorschach**. In this test, a person is shown a series of 10 abstract, symmetrical inkblots, and then they are asked to explain what kinds of images or ideas they associate with each. The idea is that participants will reveal tendencies or subconscious biases toward certain topics. For instance, a person who tends to see violent images in the inkblots may have a propensity for aggression.

Other projective measures work in a similar fashion by asking participants to engage in word association, complete sentences, create art depicting social situations, or otherwise respond to stimuli open to interpretation. For example, the **thematic apperception test** (TAT) requires a person to describe what is happening in a picture that they are shown. The assumption is that themes that may be difficult for a person to discuss in recollections of their own experiences may arise when asked to tell a story about an image.

SELF-CONCEPT AND SELF-ESTEEM

In early toddlerhood, most children begin the process of **individuation**, or realizing they are separate beings from their caregiver(s). Individuation can result in boundary testing, which, while challenging, is a very normal and necessary part of development. A similar occurrence happens again during the teen years, as adolescents struggle to find their place in the world outside their family unit and family belief system. One goal of adulthood is achieving an integrated and stable sense of self, meaning that as one develops and matures, their sense of who they are will remain internally secure even if and when it changes or gets reshaped by environmental factors and external experiences.

Self-Concept

A person's **self-concept** is their idea of self, constructed from both internal beliefs and the external reactions of others to their presentation of self. A person's self-concept is significantly shaped by their belief systems, including morality and ethics, any values they've developed irrespective of outside forces, and their sense of how others perceive them. Self-concept is based on what a person finds important: Does their parenting status define them? Do they tie their career to their sense of self? Do they conceive of themselves in terms of personal traits they like or dislike? Do they view their medical diagnoses as part of their personality? Determining the questions that shape one's self-concept, as well as reshape it as one grows, matures, or heals from psychological trauma, plays a large part in determining a person's perspective on the world.

A person naturally adjusts their self-concept as they change over time. For instance, someone who defines themselves primarily as a stay-at-home parent may need to change that self-concept once their children have grown and are out of the house. However, even as they adjust their self-concept, the values that drove them to identify strongly as a parent are likely to remain intact and continue to shape how they view themselves if they have a stable self-concept. An unstable self-concept can result in interpersonal issues and mental disorders. For example, a hallmark of **borderline personality disorder** is a lack of a solid sense of self, and psychological conditions like **major depressive disorder** can erode a person's confidence in ways that make maintaining a stable self-concept difficult.

Self-Image

Self-concept is tied to **self-image**, but while self-concept is internal, self-image is external. The term *self-image* describes a person's perception of how they present themselves to the world. Since a person's self-image is based on internal assumptions about how they are perceived externally, these assumptions do not necessarily align with reality. For example, a person may think that others see them as a happy-go-lucky prankster, while others may actually see them as irresponsible, immature, or rude. Different conditions can affect a person's self-image as well. Someone with depression may falsely assume that they are perceived as a burden to those around them. **Self-efficacy**, or the confidence a person has in their abilities, is another facet of self-concept, as is **self-awareness**, which refers to the degree that a person can recognize how their actions affect others.

Self-Esteem

In the mid-20th century, humanistic psychologist **Carl Rogers** created the **self-concept theory of personality**. He felt self-image and self-awareness created a "feedback loop" that ultimately determined an individual's personality. In Rogers's view, this feedback loop helped achieve the ultimate goal of humanist theory: a state of **self-actualization** in which all of a person's needs are met and they feel they have become the best version of themselves. Rogers coined the term *self-esteem* to describe where a person falls within the feedback loop between self-image and self-awareness. He defined high self-esteem as confidence in one's worth, value, and morals. While self-esteem is vital to a person's emotional well-being, it is also a balancing act. Too little self-esteem leads to self-doubt and self-denigration and can even spawn risky behaviors as a person's self-value diminishes. At the same time, too much self-esteem can lead to narcissistic behavior patterns, lack of empathy, devaluation of others, and emotional or physical violence.

While a person's self-concept is generally stable at its core, some may have trouble finding a healthy balance of self-esteem. For those with low self-esteem, both individual actions and therapeutic interventions can help them learn to value themselves more, engage in intentional acts of self-love, and take accurate stock of how others perceive them. For example, someone with poor self-esteem who has grown accustomed to self-critical thought patterns can learn, over time, how to engage in more positive self-talk. A psychologist might encourage them to engage in activities that can help them shift their self-image, such as asking friends to give an honest account of their personality traits or writing down positive feedback they receive so they can return to it later.

CONCLUSION

The numerous psychological approaches to personality suggest that the concept is not fixed. Moreover, as society progresses, many of the ways that psychologists have evaluated personality in the past may no longer be relevant or deemed valid or useful. One need only think of the racial underpinnings of Galen's claim that temperament can partially be determined by skin color or the different inaccuracies that have emerged from widespread use of the MBTI to recognize why psychologists periodically reevaluate their assumptions about personality. As researchers continue to make headway on the concept—and particularly as concurrent advances in genetics, neurobiology, and behavioral endocrinology further elucidate the biological underpinnings of personality—personality theories are likely to change as well. However, the central philosophical question of "nature versus nurture" remains at the heart of psychological research on personality. What is certain in answering that question is that a person's core sense of self and the traits that shape them are a combination of genetics, environment, upbringing, experiences, and all the other elements of life that inform each person's worldview.

READINESS CHECK: PERSONALITY

To check how well you understand the concepts covered in this chapter, review the following questions. If you have trouble answering any of them, consider reading through this chapter again and reviewing the key terms before moving on to the next chapter.

- Can you define and differentiate between the following terms?
    - Personality
    - Temperament
    - Traits
    - Self-concept
    - Self-image
    - Self-efficacy
    - Self-awareness
    - Self-esteem
    - Self-actualization
- Can you discuss the basic ideas and history behind the following personality theories/inventories, the methods of analysis used for each, and the pros and cons of each?
    - Galen's four temperaments
    - Infant temperament types
    - Allport's trait theory
    - Eysenck's personality theory
    - Cattell's 16 personality factor trait theory
    - Myers-Briggs Type Indicator
    - Five-factor (Big Five) model of personality
    - Minnesota Multiphasic Personality Inventory
    - Rogers's self-concept theory of personality
- From a diagnostic perspective, what makes the Minnesota Multiphasic Personality Inventory different from other personality inventories?
- What are projective measures, and how are the Rorschach inkblot test and thematic apperception test examples of projective measures of personality?
- What methods have psychologists developed for measuring internal processes, like the degree to which someone exhibits certain traits? What are the pros and cons of these different methods?
- How much of personality is inherent, and how much of personality grows and adjusts as a person gains life experience?

TEST YOURSELF: PERSONALITY

Directions: Each of the questions or incomplete statements below is followed by five suggested answers or completions. Select the one best answer for each. The Answer Key and Explanations will follow.

1. Which of the following definitions best describes the concept of temperament?

   A. A social construct no longer relevant to psychologists' understanding of personality
   B. A spectrum of feelings one can have in response to stimuli
   C. The degree to which an individual is affected by negative experiences
   D. The degree to which an individual is shaped by their environment
   E. A collection of consistent biological behavioral tendencies

2. Talia is generally a happy-go-lucky infant who enjoys smiling at her caregiver(s) and others she encounters. However, Talia tends to get overstimulated in new or busy environments, resulting in emotional displays that require attentive soothing from her caregiver(s). According to theories of infant temperaments, Talia is a

   A. sociable baby
   B. slow-to-warm baby
   C. self-aware baby
   D. settled baby
   E. sensitive baby

3. Which of the following is a common criticism of the Myers-Briggs Type Indicator (MBTI)?

   A. It is not thorough enough.
   B. It is too thorough.
   C. It is considered pseudoscience by modern psychologists.
   D. Businesses that try to use the MBTI administer it incorrectly.
   E. The questions associated with the MBTI are compromised by bias.

4. Dr. Amick suspects that a patient could be dealing with a combination of depression and a cluster B personality disorder. Which of the following reasons best explains why Dr. Amick might use the Minnesota Multiphasic Personality Inventory (MMPI) to evaluate the patient?

A. It is the only personality inventory that can be used to determine if someone has a cluster B personality disorder.
B. It is the only inventory that evaluates personality in a multidimensional way.
C. It is designed for diagnostic purposes and helps evaluate traits associated with potential mental illnesses or personality disorders.
D. It is based on the Myers-Briggs Type Indicator.
E. It is one of the "Big Five."

5. Which of the following terms can best be defined as "the amount of cognizance an individual has regarding the impact of their actions on other people"?

A. Self-awareness
B. Self-efficacy
C. Self-esteem
D. Self-image
E. Self-actualization

Answer Key and Explanations

1. E	2. A	3. C	4. C	5. A

1. **The correct answer is E.** Temperament refers solely to the innate, biological nature of personality, meaning the consistent biological, behavioral tendencies an individual shows regardless of their environment or upbringing.

2. **The correct answer is A.** While an infant with a sociable temperament may be challenging to soothe at times due to overstimulation, the primary hallmark of this personality type is that they engage with their surroundings, like to explore, and tend to seem comfortable socializing with their caregiver(s) or other humans.

3. **The correct answer is C.** Modern psychologists consider the MBTI to be pseudoscience—despite its popularity for business and personal use, its application in clinical settings is quite limited.

4. **The correct answer is C.** Dr. Amick would likely want to use the MMPI in this case because research has shown it can help diagnose certain mental illnesses and/or personality disorders. The MMPI may be one of many metrics Dr. Amick uses, but she would likely choose it over the MBTI (choice D), which is not diagnostic. Choice A may seem accurate, but it is too excessive in its phrasing since clinicians may still choose to use other personality inventories in their evaluation process. Choices B and E are inaccurate statements.

5. **The correct answer is A.** Self-awareness describes the amount of awareness a person has about how their actions impact others. Self-efficacy (choice B) refers to the amount of confidence a person feels about their abilities. Self-esteem (choice C) relates to the humanistic idea that a person moves between self-awareness and self-image (choice D) on the path to self-actualization (choice E).

Chapter 11

Understanding and Treating Psychological Disorders

OVERVIEW

- Mental Disorders and the DSM-5
- Affective Disorders
- Anxiety Disorders
- Somatoform Disorders
- Disorders Related to Eating
- Personality Disorders
- Dissociative Disorders and Psychoses
- Health, Stress, and Coping
- Treatment of Psychological Disorders
- Conclusion
- Readiness Check: Understanding and Treating Psychological Disorders
- Test Yourself: Understanding and Treating Psychological Disorders

One of the most important clinical applications of psychology is in the definition, diagnosis, and treatment of psychological health concerns. While grouped together in this chapter due to thematic similarity, these topics are addressed in two different categories on the CLEP Introductory Psychology exam. The first category, "psychological disorders and health" (8%–9% of the questions), addresses various disorders recognized by the *Diagnostic and Statistical Manual of Mental Disorders*, **Fifth Edition** (**DSM-5**). The second category, "treatment of psychological disorders" (6%–7% of questions) explores interventions used to treat mental health concerns. Collectively, topics in this chapter are addressed by 14%–16% of the questions on the CLEP Introductory Psychology exam.

MENTAL DISORDERS AND THE DSM-5

Both the DSM-5 and the World Health Organization (WHO) define a **mental disorder** as "a clinically significant disturbance in an individual's cognition, emotional regulation, or behaviour" that is "usually associated with distress or impairment in important areas of functioning."[1] According to a 2019 WHO report, one in eight people globally lives with a mental disorder. The CLEP Introductory Psychology exam focuses on **psychological disorders**, including **affective disorders** (**bipolar disorders** and **depressive disorders**), **anxiety disorders**, **somatoform disorders**, eating-related disorders, **personality disorders**, and **dissociative disorders**. Notably, the DSM-5 includes additional disorder types not commonly addressed on the CLEP exam, such as neurodevelopmental disorders, schizophrenia spectrum disorders, sexual dysfunctions, and more.

Since its 1952 inception, the DSM's purpose has been to aid clinicians, students, and researchers by providing up-to-date criteria for diagnosable mental disorders. Each edition, updated by international psychology scholars and practitioners, reflects scientific advancements and new understanding in the field. The DSM-5 serves as a crucial reference for practitioners, ensuring accurate diagnoses. The DSM-5 is also a guiding resource for the CLEP test makers, so this guide makes every effort to align criteria, classifications, and terminology with the DSM-5.

Despite codification in the DSM-5 and the *International Classification of Diseases and Related Health Problems*, 11th revision (ICD-11), which is used by the WHO and to which the DSM-5 aligns, the boundaries between mental disorders remain ambiguous. The understanding of diagnostic criteria, as well as emerging mental disorders, continuously evolves. For instance, the DSM-5 does not yet recognize complex post-traumatic stress disorder (CPTSD) as a diagnosable mental disorder, though many clinicians globally now acknowledge it as a potential variation of **post-traumatic stress disorder** (**PTSD**) linked to long-term trauma. Students of psychology should be aware of the evolving nature of the understanding of mental disorders, as well as the necessity and limitations of categorizing mental health disorders in resources like the DSM-5.

The sections in this chapter that outline psychological disorders are based on information found in the DSM-5. Diagnostic criteria and other key characteristics relevant to the CLEP Introductory Psychology exam are

---

1 World Health Organization, "Mental Disorders," June 8, 2022, https://www.who.int/news-room/fact-sheets/detail/mental-disorders.

detailed in tables. For more information on prevalence, development, risk factors, diagnostic issues, and more, consult the DSM-5. For all psychological disorders, diagnosis requires the presence of symptoms severe enough to interfere with daily life, social interactions, and/or work that aren't better attributed to another mental disorder or medical condition. There are specific symptom criteria for mild, moderate, and severe forms of many disorders.

Within each disorder category in the DSM-5, there are up to four standardized subclassifications.

DSM-5 SUBCLASSIFICATIONS

Subclassification	Explanation
Substance/ medication-induced disorder	• Used when symptoms of the disorder type are present, but the root cause appears to be ingestion of a particular substance or medication that is known to produce those effects • Onset of the psychological disorder coincides with the introduction of the substance/medication and is typically alleviated by removing the substance/medication
Disorder due to another medical condition	• Used when symptoms of the disorder type are present, but the root cause appears to be the onset of a different medical condition that is known to produce those effects • In most cases, alleviating the medical condition eliminates psychological symptoms
Other disorder	• Used when symptoms of the disorder type are present but are insufficient or unclearly established enough to meet specific diagnostic criteria
Unspecified disorder	• Used when symptoms of the disorder type are present, but the clinician does not have enough time or patient history to make a clear diagnosis, such as in emergency room settings

Note: For specific variations of these subclassifications by disorder type, see their respective listings in the DSM-5.

AFFECTIVE DISORDERS

Affective disorders, also known as **mood disorders**, involve significant disruptions in emotion regulation and experience. **Mood** refers to a person's internal experience of emotion, tone, and state of mind, particularly relating to external factors. In the DSM-5, affective disorders are broadly classified as bipolar disorders and depressive disorders.

Bipolar Disorders

Bipolar disorders involve oscillation between emotional highs (**mania**), and depressive lows, leading to prolonged and persistent mood instability coupled with decreased social and occupational function. The DSM-5 notes contextual factors (e.g., adolescence and substance abuse) may cause bipolar-like phenomena and should be considered when making a bipolar diagnosis.

A **diagnostic feature** is a symptom that a person must have experienced to be diagnosed with a particular disorder, and **manic episodes** or **hypomanic episodes** that follow or precede **depressive episodes** are a major diagnostic feature of bipolar and related disorders. Manic episodes last a week or more, while hypomanic episodes last at least four consecutive days. The primary distinguishing feature between **bipolar I** and **bipolar II** is the presence of manic episodes in the former—bipolar II includes only depressive and hypomanic episodes. The table that follows briefly outlines the bipolar disorders recognized by the DSM-5 alongside their diagnostic features and other key characteristics.

BIPOLAR AND RELATED DISORDERS

Diagnostic Features	Other Key Characteristics
BIPOLAR I DISORDER	
Manic episode(s) followed or preceded by depressive episode(s): • Manic (lasting one week or more) and hypomanic (lasting four consecutive days or more) episodes are marked by at least three of the following: ○ Sleep disturbance (decreased sleep need) ○ Elevated talkativeness ○ Increased self-image ○ Racing thoughts ○ Increased distractibility ○ Increase in agitated and, often, goal-oriented activity ○ Increased risk taking • Depressive episodes are marked by depressed mood and/or loss of interest across a period of at least two weeks, plus at least five of the following: ○ Significant loss of appetite or weight ○ Insomnia ○ Decreased or agitated psychomotor activity ○ Daily fatigue or energy loss ○ Feelings of guilt or decreased self-worth ○ Diminished focus and decisiveness ○ Recurrent suicidal ideation or rumination on death	• Manic mood can appear euphoric, irritable, prone to excess • Accompanied by **lability**: the "alternation among euphoria, dysphoria, and irritability" that occurs across "rapid shifts in mood"* • Contextualization is key, as behaviors will appear inappropriate for their context • Differences may be noticeable in speech patterns, such as loud or rapid in manic episodes and slower/delayed in depressive episodes

BIPOLAR AND RELATED DISORDERS (*CONTINUED*)

Diagnostic Features	Other Key Characteristics
BIPOLAR II DISORDER	
Hypomanic and depressive episodes like bipolar I but with no history of manic episodes	Individuals may report depressive episodes to clinicians and be unaware of their hypomanic tendencies.
CYCLOTHYMIC DISORDER	
Numerous periods of both hypomanic and depressive periods that do not necessarily follow or precede one another occurring at least half the time over the course of at least two years (adults) or one year (children and adolescents)	• May apply in cases where depressive or hypomanic symptoms are present but not significant enough to constitute a bipolar I or bipolar II diagnosis • Experiencing new symptoms consistent with other disorders (such as a manic episode) will typically result in a changed diagnosis

Source: Adapted from *Diagnostic and Statistical Manual of Mental Disorders*, 5th ed. (DSM-5) (Washington, DC: American Psychiatric Association, 2013), 123–54.

Note: The DSM-5 also lists "substance/medication-induced bipolar and related disorder," "bipolar and related disorder due to another medical condition," "unspecified bipolar and related disorder," and "other bipolar and related disorder."

* DSM-5, 127–8.

Depressive Disorders

Before the DSM-5, depressive disorders were grouped with bipolar disorders due to shared characteristics like "the presence of sad, empty, or irritable mood, accompanied by somatic and cognitive changes that significantly affect the individual's capacity to function."[2] However, recognizing differences in cause, duration, and expression of depressive episodes, as well as the lack of mania in some disorders, psychologists now classify them separately. Each depressive disorder involves recurrent episodes with "clear-cut changes in affect, cognition, and neurovegetative functions"[3] as well as remissions between episodes. In depressive disorders, sadness is experienced more intensely or for longer than befits typical sadness, grief, or bereavement. The table that follows briefly outlines the depressive disorders recognized by the DSM-5 alongside their diagnostic features and

---

2 DSM-5, 155.
3 DSM-5, 155

DEPRESSIVE DISORDERS

Diagnostic Features	Other Key Characteristics
DISRUPTIVE MOOD DYSREGULATION DISORDER	
Prolonged and recurring behavioral or verbal outbursts that are disproportionate to the moment and one's current development, usually unprovoked, and: • have been occurring for at least one year without a break of more than three months and • occur in at least two of three settings (with peers, at home, in school)	• May present as persistent anger, irritability, "bad temper" • Diagnosis must be made between ages 6 and 18 • Behavior must have started before age 10
MAJOR DEPRESSIVE DISORDER	
Period(s) of more than two straight weeks that deviate from one's normal behavior and include at least five of the following: • Depressed mood for majority of every day • Loss of pleasure or interest in all/most activities • Significant weight gain or loss unrelated to diet • More intense or sedated psychomotor activity • Daily tiredness/low energy • Daily unwarranted feelings of guilt and/or worthlessness • Daily diminished focus, concentration, decisiveness • Rumination on death and/or suicidal ideations/planning, suicide attempts	• May be accompanied by sleep and appetite issues • Should not be confused with understandable grief; those who suffer from major depressive disorder may also experience loss more intensely—diagnosis requires close contextual consideration • Presence of a manic or hypomanic episode would rule out this disorder and suggest a bipolar or related disorder instead • In adolescents and children, may manifest more as irritability than sadness • Can also be exacerbated by a major medical condition (e.g., cancer does not cause depression, but it is common for cancer patients to become depressed)
PERSISTENT DEPRESSIVE (DYSTHYMIA) DISORDER	
Persistent depressed mood for most days across a minimum of two years (one year for children and adolescents), during which at least two of the following symptoms are present: • Appetite changes (under- or overeating) • Insomnia/hypersomnia • Tiredness/low energy • Loss of self-esteem • Indecision/lack of concentration • Hopeless feelings	• Two-month period without symptoms would exclude diagnosis • See other key characteristics for major depressive disorder

DEPRESSIVE DISORDERS (*CONTINUED*)

Diagnostic Features	Other Key Characteristics
PREMENSTRUAL DYSPHORIC DISORDER	
Beginning in the final week before menses starts, diminishing over the course of menses, and becoming minimal or disappearing after menses ends, the individual experiences at least one symptom of <ul><li>a feeling of losing control</li><li>anger/irritability</li><li>appetite changes</li><li>depressed or hopeless mood</li><li>insomnia/hypersomnia</li></ul> AND at least one symptom of <ul><li>loss of interest in activities</li><li>mood swings</li><li>physical symptoms (breast discomfort, joint pain, muscle pain, bloating, weight gain)</li><li>tension, anxiety, edginess</li><li>trouble concentrating</li></ul>	<ul><li>Cannot simply be a period during which symptoms of another condition become worse</li><li>Must occur in at least two menstrual cycles</li></ul>

Source: Adapted from DSM-5, 155–88.

Note: The DSM-5 also lists "substance/medication-induced depressive disorder," "depressive disorder due to another medical condition," "unspecified depressive disorder," and "other depressive disorder."

ANXIETY DISORDERS

Anxiety disorders share a key feature: the presence of excessive fear or anxiety beyond normative levels for a given situation. Diagnosing anxiety disorders requires careful consideration of context due to the subjective nature of determining "excessive" fear or worry, as well as the similarity some anxiety symptoms bear to other mental disorders. As the DSM-5 clarifies, "*fear* is the emotional response to real or perceived imminent threat, whereas *anxiety* is anticipation of future threat."[4] Those with anxiety disorders exhibit heightened arousal in the face of perceived danger, intensifying their "fight or flight" response, often leading to the avoidance of triggering situations. **Panic attacks**, most associated with anxiety disorders but present with other mental disorders, have a common diagnostic description outlined alongside anxiety disorders in the DSM-5 criteria labeled "panic attack specifier."

The table that follows briefly outlines the anxiety disorders recognized by the DSM-5 alongside their diagnostic features and other key characteristics.

---

4 DSM-5, 189.

ANXIETY DISORDERS

Diagnostic Features	Other Key Characteristics
SEPARATION ANXIETY DISORDER	

• Developmentally inappropriate and excessive fear, worry, or anxiety related to separation from an individual to whom the patient is closely attached
• Must be accompanied by at least three of the following symptoms:
  ○ Extreme and recurrent fear when separated or anticipating a separation; of losing attachment figure(s) or harm coming to them; of life events that could create separation
  ○ Refusal or reluctance to leave attachment figure(s), spend time alone, leave the home, sleep away from attachment figure(s) or outside the home
  ○ Recurring nightmares involving separation
  ○ Recurring physiological complaints when separated from attachment figure(s) (headaches, stomach trouble, etc.)
	• In children, symptoms must persist for at least four weeks, but in adults, the minimum duration is approximately six months.
	• Some symptoms are common with other disorders (such as agoraphobia and autism spectrum disorder), so practitioners should take extra care to rule out other causes before diagnosing.

SELECTIVE MUTISM DISORDER	
Consistent failure or refusal to speak in social settings where speaking is expected/required (such as at school) and where one is otherwise capable of speaking in lower-pressure settings (such as at home)	• Must last at least one month • Cannot be explained by a language barrier or communication disorder • Often accompanied by another anxiety disorder • More common in young children than adolescents or adults
PANIC DISORDER	
Pattern of unexpected, recurring panic attacks as outlined in the "panic attack specifier" description	• Some symptoms may be tied to cultural differences. • One or more panic attacks must be followed by a month that includes constant worry about having another panic attack and/or behavioral changes designed to help one avoid panic attacks.

ANXIETY DISORDERS (*CONTINUED*)

Diagnostic Features	Other Key Characteristics
PANIC ATTACK SPECIFIER	
"An abrupt surge of intense fear or intense discomfort that reaches a peak within minutes"* accompanied by at least four of the following symptoms: <ul><li>Accelerated heart rate/palpitations</li><li>Sweating</li><li>Shaking/trembling</li><li>Breathing difficulty</li><li>Choking sensation</li><li>Pain or discomfort in the chest</li><li>Nausea/stomach issues</li><li>Feeling dizzy or lightheaded</li><li>Hot/cold sensations</li><li>Tingling/numbness</li><li>Derealization (a feeling that things aren't real) or depersonalization (feeling detached from a sense of self)</li><li>Fear of losing grip on sanity or dying</li></ul>	<ul><li>Unlike other classifications in the DSM-5, this is intended to help clinicians diagnose panic attacks (which can occur due to numerous medical conditions) rather than a specific disorder.</li><li>When possible, clinicians should use panic attacks as a specifier for a known root disorder (e.g., bipolar I disorder with panic attacks).</li><li>The presence of panic attacks is implied when diagnosing panic disorder, so panic attacks do not need to be specified.</li></ul>
SOCIAL ANXIETY (SOCIAL PHOBIA) DISORDER	
<ul><li>At least six months of notable and disproportionate anxiety and fear about almost all social situations wherein the individual may be evaluated or judged by another, including the following:<ul><li>Social interactions</li><li>Observations</li><li>Public performance</li></ul></li><li>Intense fear of humiliation or embarrassment</li><li>Avoidance of social situations</li></ul>	<ul><li>In children, fears must exist with peers and not stem solely from interactions with adults.</li><li>Clinicians can specify "performance only" if the fear only arises due to public speaking or performance.</li></ul>

(continues)

ANXIETY DISORDERS (*CONTINUED*)

Diagnostic Features	Other Key Characteristics
SPECIFIC PHOBIA DISORDER	

• Notable anxiety and fear about a particular situation (such as flying, heights, public speaking, etc.) or object(s) (such as animals, blood, needles, etc.)
• Object or situation causing the phobia always elicits a fear response and is always avoided
• Amount of fear and anxiety the patient experiences
  ○ is disproportionate to situational context and
  ○ lasts at least six months
	• Common phobias are sorted into codes based on stimulus: animal, natural environment, blood-injection injury, situational, other.
	• More than one specific phobia is not uncommon—multiple diagnoses of "specific phobia" with different codes may be given.

AGORAPHOBIA	

• At least six months of notable anxiety or fear in response to at least two of the following situations:
  ○ Taking public transportation
  ○ Visiting open spaces
  ○ Visiting enclosed spaces
  ○ Being in crowds/standing in line
  ○ Leaving the house alone
• Fear or avoidance of anxiety-causing situations, particularly around the inability to "escape" or retreat to privacy
	• Individuals commonly require a companion to complete activities.
	• A diagnosis does not preclude the diagnosis of other mental disorders, including panic disorder.
	• Reactions must seem disproportionate to context.

GENERALIZED ANXIETY	

• At least six months in which a majority of days the individual experiences excessive and difficult-to-control worry and anxiety
• Anxiety is related to at least three of the following symptoms:
  ○ Feeling restless or edgy
  ○ Tiring easily
  ○ Concentration difficulties
  ○ Irritability
  ○ Tense muscles
  ○ Sleep difficulties/changes
	Multiple medical and mental disorders can cause anxiety symptoms; practitioners should take extra care to rule out other causes before diagnosing.

Source: Adapted from DSM-5, 189–233.

Note: The DSM-5 also lists "substance/medication-induced anxiety disorder," "anxiety disorder due to another medical condition," "unspecified anxiety disorder," and "other anxiety disorder."

* DSM-5, 214.

SOMATOFORM DISORDERS

CLEP identifies somatoform disorders as those related to **somatic** symptoms, meaning physiological reactions to intense stress. The DSM-5 notes that patients with these disorders are more likely to be encountered in medical settings than in mental health settings, emphasizing the category's creation for the DSM-5 to aid nonpsychiatric clinicians in recognizing the psychological origins of physiological symptoms. The manual notes the commonality of physical symptoms with other psychological disorders and the potential coexistence or exacerbation of somatic disorders with other mental disorders. The classification as somatoform arises from the general misconception of these symptoms as physical rather than mental health concerns.

The table that follows briefly outlines the disorders listed in the section "Somatic Symptom and Related Disorders" in the DSM-5 alongside their diagnostic features and other key characteristics.

SOMATIC SYMPTOM AND RELATED DISORDERS

Diagnostic Features	Other Key Characteristics
SOMATIC SYMPTOM DISORDER	

• Intense recurring thoughts related to somatic symptoms, causing distress and complications in daily functioning
• Associated with one or more of the following:
  ○ Inordinate, persistent thoughts about symptom severity
  ○ High anxiety about health and symptoms
  ○ Exorbitant energy devoted toward symptoms and health
	• Symptoms of discomfort may be specific (pain) or nonspecific (fatigue)
	• Persistence of symptoms that typically exceed six months

ILLNESS ANXIETY DISORDER	

• Captivation and anxiety stemming from having or developing a serious health condition
• Concern about personal health status
• Excessive health-related behaviors or problematic avoidance of medical care
	• Symptoms present for six months or more
	• Two symptom presentation types:
	  ○ Care seeking (frequently pursuing medical care)
	  ○ Care avoidant (medical care rarely utilized)

(continues)

SOMATIC SYMPTOM AND RELATED DISORDERS (*CONTINUED*)

Diagnostic Features	Other Key Characteristics
CONVERSION (FUNCTIONAL NEUROLOGICAL SYMPTOM) DISORDER	

• At least one symptom related to atypical sensation or movement
• Substantial anxiety and distress in performing daily functions
• Presentation of symptoms inconsistent with a known medical condition
• Onset may follow a psychological stressor
	• Symptom presentation may be acute (less than six months) or persistent (greater than six months)
	• Symptom types include the following:
	  ○ Anesthesia
	  ○ Attacks
	  ○ Atypical movement
	  ○ Atypical sensation
	  ○ Atypical speech
	  ○ Atypical swallowing
	  ○ Mixed symptoms
	  ○ Paralysis
	  ○ Seizures
	  ○ Sensory loss
	  ○ Weakness

PSYCHOLOGICAL FACTORS AFFECTING OTHER MEDICAL CONDITIONS	

• Physical medical condition or symptom present
• Physical medical condition adversely affected by psychological or behavioral factors
	• Medical condition impacted in one of the following ways:
	  ○ Influences the course of the medical condition (e.g., delayed recovery)
	  ○ Interferes with treatment
	  ○ Creates additional health risks
	  ○ Negatively influences physiological processes related to medical condition

FACTITIOUS DISORDER	

• Involves making false claims of pathological or injurious symptoms about oneself or another
• Comes in two varieties:
  ○ Factitious disorder imposed on oneself
  ○ Factitious disorder imposed on another
• Presentation of oneself (or another) as disabled, injured, sick
	• Formerly called Munchausen syndrome
	• Deception used to maintain the false narrative supporting an individual's pathological or injurious claims, which may relate to their own health or the health of another individual

Source: Adapted from DSM-5, 309–27.

Note: The DSM-5 also lists "other specific somatic symptom and related disorder" and "unspecific somatic symptom and related disorder."

DISORDERS RELATED TO EATING

In the DSM-5, **eating disorders** and **feeding disorders** are grouped together due to their impact on a person's relationship with eating-related behavior. Often mutually exclusive, diagnosing one type excludes others in isolated episodes, except for pica, which can coexist with other disorders.

The table that follows briefly outlines eating-related disorders in the DSM-5 alongside their diagnostic features and other key characteristics.

EATING-RELATED DISORDERS

Diagnostic Features	Other Key Characteristics
PICA	
• Continuous consumption of nonfood substances for longer than one month • Nonfood consumption practices that are not developmentally appropriate or related to established social or cultural practices	Consumption of nonfood substances occurring in the context of another mental disorder (e.g., autism, schizophrenia) necessitates additional clinical attention
RUMINATION DISORDER	
• Habitual regurgitation of food that is held in the mouth and rechewed before swallowing or spitting out the partially digested food • Not attributable to a medical condition (e.g., gastroesophageal reflux)	• Does not occur exclusively in association with anorexia nervosa, bulimia nervosa, binge-eating disorder, avoidant/restrictive food intake disorder • Symptoms occurring in the context of another mental disorder (e.g., autism, schizophrenia) necessitate additional clinical attention
AVOIDANT/RESTRICTIVE FOOD INTAKE DISORDER	

• Prohibitive food consumption behavior that leads to an inability to meet one's nutritional needs
• Lack of interest in eating, preoccupation with perceived negative consequences of eating, aversion to sensory characteristics of food
• Associated with at least one of the following:
  ○ Substantial weight loss
  ○ Substantial nutritional deficiency
  ○ Negative impact on one's social life
  ○ Dependence on nutritional supplements or feeding tubes
	• In severe cases, especially in cases involving infants or children with developmental disorders, avoidant/restrictive food intake disorder can lead to life-threatening malnutrition
	• Atypical food consumption patterns not attributable to a co-occurring medical condition
	• Likely unrelated to one's experience of their body weight or physical condition
	• Does not occur exclusively in association with anorexia nervosa or bulimia nervosa

(continues)

EATING-RELATED DISORDERS (*CONTINUED*)

Diagnostic Features	Other Key Characteristics
BINGE-EATING DISORDER	

• Repeated binge-eating episodes defined as
   ○ consumption of food greatly exceeding the amount most individuals would consume in a similar time frame and
   ○ feeling that one cannot control their excessive consumption behaviors
 • Binge-eating episodes associated with at least three of the following:
   ○ Rapid eating
   ○ Eating to the point of physical discomfort
   ○ Eating when not hungry
   ○ Eating alone due to embarrassment associated with the amount consumed
   ○ Feeling shame, guilt, disgust with overeating
 • Eating habits cause feelings of distress
	• Overeating typically occurs at least weekly over a period of three or more months
	 • Binge-eating periods are not associated with compensatory behaviors seen in bulimia nervosa
	 • Partial remission involves a reduction in the frequency of binge-eating episodes
	 • Full remission involves the extinction of all binge-eating episodes
	 • Severity based on the number of binge-eating episodes per week

BULIMIA NERVOSA	

• Recurring periods of binge-eating behavior; includes
   ○ consumption of food greatly exceeding the amount most individuals would consume in a similar time frame and
   ○ a feeling that one cannot control their excessive consumption behaviors
 • Unhealthy compensatory behaviors to minimize weight gain (e.g., excessive exercise or fasting, self-induced vomiting, or the abuse of medications, diuretics, laxatives)
 • Weekly periods of binge eating and compensatory behaviors for a period of three months or longer
	• Bulimic episodes must not occur only during periods with anorexic behaviors
	 • Partial remission involves the sustained reduction of symptom presentation
	 • Full remission involves the extinction of all bulimia-related behaviors
	 • Severity based on the frequency of unhealthy compensatory behaviors

EATING-RELATED DISORDERS (*CONTINUED*)

Diagnostic Features	Other Key Characteristics
ANOREXIA NERVOSA	

• Substantially reduced food consumption that leads to nutritional deficits and health issues
 	
• Preoccupation with the idea of gaining weight
 	
• Psychological distress associated with one or more of the following:
  ○ Experience of body weight or shape
  ○ Self-evaluation of one's body weight or shape
  ○ Failure to recognize the health issues associated with one's critically low body weight
	• Two subtypes:
	  ○ Restricting type involves excessive dieting, fasting, or exercise; binge-eating behaviors, self-induced vomiting, or misuse of laxatives, enemas, and diuretics have not occurred in three or more months
	  ○ Binge-eating/purging type involves cycling with episodes of binge eating, self-induced vomiting, or misuse of laxatives, enemas, and diuretics for three or more months
	• Categorization of severity relates to body mass index (BMI) percentile

Source: Adapted from DSM-5, 329–54.

Note: The DSM-5 also lists "other specified feeding or eating disorder" and "unspecific feeding or eating disorder."

PERSONALITY DISORDERS

The DSM-5 defines a personality disorder as "an enduring pattern of inner experience and behavior that deviates markedly from the expectations of the individual's culture, is pervasive and inflexible, and has onset in early adolescence or adulthood."[5] While this definition is relatively broad, it helps clinicians understand that personality disorders include a stable set of behaviors that define a person's personality (in contrast to traditional psychological disorders, which affect but do not define personality). Diagnostic criteria for personality disorders are thus less focused on specific symptoms so much as pervasive personality traits. Note that many of these personality disorders are comorbid with other mental disorders. For example, studies have shown that diagnoses of bipolar and related disorders correlate strongly with a diagnosis of **borderline personality disorder**, meaning that a clinician who suspects borderline personality disorder may want to investigate bipolar-related disorders as a potential **comorbidity**.

While the traditional definitions of 10 specific personality disorders in the following table match those outlined in the DSM-5, the manual also points

---

5 DSM-5, 645.

to evolving views on how personality disorders are diagnosed, suggesting that definitions are likely to be updated in the next edition of the manual.

PERSONALITY DISORDERS BY CLUSTER

CLUSTER A: PERSONALITY DISORDERS DEFINED BY ECCENTRIC BEHAVIORS OR THOUGHTS	
Paranoid	• Distrusts other people • Tends to suspect others have sinister motives • Prone to outbursts of anger, violence, aggression • May appear emotionally cold, stoic, guarded, intensely serious, jealous • May "challenge" others to make them demonstrate their devotion
Schizoid	• Is extremely withdrawn and may seem unwilling or too introverted to form close relationships • Stays in their own head and prefers their own company • May be described as a "loner" or "daydreamer" • Has underdeveloped social skills
Schizotypal	• Can be described as extremely eccentric, peculiar, atypical in their manner of fashion, speech, other outward presentations • Struggles to form relationships • May have "magical" beliefs, such as claiming to be telepathic • May engage in odd behaviors like talking to themselves or refusing to respond when spoken to • May have associated mental illnesses on the schizophrenia spectrum

CLUSTER B: PERSONALITY DISORDERS DEFINED BY EXCEPTIONALLY EMOTIONAL, DRAMATIC, UNPREDICTABLE THOUGHTS OR BEHAVIORS	
Antisocial	• May have a history of crime or legal trouble particularly related to violent or aggressive impulses • Lacks a "conscience;" others may describe them as manipulative, cruel, calculating • Does not tend to ascribe to the typical moral values of their society • Is at high risk for alcoholism and substance abuse
Borderline	• Has wide variations in moods; often swings sharply between anger and joy • Struggles with an unstable self-image • Tends to see people and situations as either all positive or all negative; is inclined toward polarized thinking • May act impulsively or take risks to manipulate others or get attention • Tends to have tumultuous relationships • May struggle with different forms of depression • Tends to be at high risk of suicidal ideation and self-mutilation

(continues)

CLUSTER B: PERSONALITY DISORDERS DEFINED BY EXCEPTIONALLY EMOTIONAL, DRAMATIC, UNPREDICTABLE THOUGHTS OR BEHAVIORS (*CONTINUED*)	
	• Believes that everyone loves them • Engages in provocative, over-the-top, melodramatic behaviors for attention • Comes across as overly enthusiastic, flirtatious, emotional • Lies or exaggerates situations for attention
Narcissistic	• Has an excessive ego and sense of self-importance • Exaggerates or lies about their achievements, abilities, prestige • Assumes they are superior to others and that other people should recognize them as such; may also present as a victim, believing their suffering matters more than that of others • Makes good first impressions or has a positive public image but struggles to maintain long-term relationships or form close emotional bonds • Exploits and manipulates others for their own gain

CLUSTER C: PERSONALITY DISORDERS DEFINED BY FEARFUL OR ANXIOUS BEHAVIORS OR THOUGHTS	
Avoidant	• Has high social anxiety • Behaves similarly to those with schizoid personality disorder but differs by intensely desiring social contact • Feels extremely sensitive to and fearful of criticism, rejection, and embarrassment • Avoids social situations in which they are not sure they will be liked and accepted
Dependent	• Lacks independence because of their constant need for approval, direction, reassurance • Acts clingy and submissive • Has extremely low self-confidence • Does not enjoy time spent alone • Feels particularly sensitive when close relationships end and is at increased risk of suicide after a breakup
Obsessive-compulsive	• Comes across as perfectionistic, overly orderly, strict, controlling • Worries about the "right" way to do things and is inflexible about routines • Has exceptionally high standards that can interfere with their life and productivity • Fears making errors and is excessively cautious • Has difficulty expressing emotions • Has characteristics similar to those seen in obsessive-compulsive disorder

Source: Adapted from DSM-5, 645–85.

Note: The DSM-5 also lists "other general personality disorder," "personality change due to another medical condition," "other specified personality disorder," and "unspecified personality disorder."

DISSOCIATIVE DISORDERS AND PSYCHOSES

Dissociative disorders are particularly intense because they have a lasting impact on multiple dimensions of psychological health. Those who suffer from dissociative disorders experience disconnection or disruption in certain cognitive functions, including conscious thought, emotion, memory, perception, motor control, behavior, sense of identity, and more.

While the DSM-5 does not devote much space to **psychoses**, mentioning them primarily in terms of substance use or alcoholism, the CLEP Introductory Psychology exam groups psychoses with dissociative disorders because they represent episodes in which individuals lose contact with reality.

Dissociative Disorders

Dissociative disorders are commonly marked by a sense of **depersonalization** and/or **derealization** and are often the result of traumatic experiences. The DSM-5 notes that "many of the symptoms, including embarrassment or confusion about the symptoms or a desire to hide them, are influenced by [one's] proximity to trauma."[6]

The table that follows briefly outlines dissociative disorders in the DSM-5 alongside their diagnostic features and other key characteristics.

DISSOCIATIVE DISORDERS

Diagnostic Features	Other Key Characteristics
DISSOCIATIVE IDENTITY DISORDER	

• Identity disturbances involving at least two distinct personality traits
• Disturbances related to a discontinuous sense of self or autonomy, accompanied by alterations in one's behavior, cognition, sensorimotor functions
• Atypical recollection of events that involves gaps in memory
• Personally and/or socially distressing symptoms
	• Identity disturbances may be culturally described as an individual experiencing possession
	• Sustained for long periods when psychosocial stressors are severe or maintained across time
	• Identity disturbances must not be related to the following:
	  ○ Broadly accepted sociocultural behaviors
	  ○ Imaginary play in children
	  ○ Physiological effects of substance use or a medical condition

---

6 DSM-5, 291.

DISSOCIATIVE DISORDERS (*CONTINUED*)

Diagnostic Features	Other Key Characteristics
DISSOCIATIVE AMNESIA DISORDER	

• Unable to recall important details in one's life; often associated with stressful or traumatic events but inconsistent with ordinary lapses of memory
• Personally and/or socially distressing symptoms
• Possibility of experiencing dissociative fugue or periods defined by loss of awareness of one's identity
	• Amnesic experiences must not be related to the following:
	  ○ Physiological effects of substance use
	  ○ Neurological condition or brain injury
	• Multiple categories of amnesia:
	  ○ Localized—most common form; amnesia typically occurs over a broad period
	  ○ Selective—individuals can recall some details of an event but not others
	  ○ Generalized—complete loss of one's autobiographical and historical memory
	  ○ Systematized—amnesia involves a certain category of information across contexts
	  ○ Continuous—forgetting events as they occur

DEPERSONALIZATION/DEREALIZATION DISORDER	

• Continuous or repeated experiences of one, or both, of the following:
  ○ Depersonalization—feeling detached from one's own body, senses, thoughts, behaviors, sense of time
  ○ Derealization—feeling detached from one's surroundings and perceiving environment in a visually distorted, dreamlike manner
• Personally and/or socially distressing symptoms
	• Depersonalization or derealization experience must not be related to the following:
	  ○ Physiological effects of substance use
	  ○ Medical condition (e.g., seizures)
	• One's ability to test reality maintains intact during the episode

Source: Adapted from DSM-5, 291–307.

Note: The DSM-5 also lists "other specified dissociative disorder" and "unspecific dissociative disorder."

Psychoses

Psychoses can manifest as hallucinations, delusions, magical thinking, speech disruptions (such as rapid or slowed speech), or as intense manifestations of other psychological symptoms like depression or mania. There are also numerous psychological disorders associated with psychosis, most notably **schizotypal personality disorder**, but also **delusional disorder, schizophreniform disorder, schizophrenia**, and **schizoaffective disorder**.

Trauma and Stressor-Related Disorders

While the CLEP exam guide does not explicitly mention trauma and stressor-related disorders, their close relationship with dissociative disorders means that it is a good idea to recognize the names of common trauma and stress-related disorders such as PTSD and **reactive attachment disorder**. Like dissociative disorders, these onset because of a traumatic or highly stressful event.

HEALTH, STRESS, AND COPING

Psychological disorders often have a significant impact on an individual's overall health, especially when untreated. Challenges associated with these disorders can lead to physical health problems, such as sleep disturbances, appetite changes, and weakened immune system functioning. **Stress** is common for those with mental disorders due to the energy required to manage symptoms while navigating daily life as well as the stigma and **social isolation** often associated with these conditions.

Chronic stress can negatively impact mental health and exacerbate the symptoms of the disorders; therefore, it is crucial for mental health professionals to provide effective coping strategies to help individuals manage stress, regulate emotions, and address the challenges they face. Common coping strategies include cognitive strategies, behavioral strategies, and social support.

Cognitive coping strategies involve changing negative thought patterns and beliefs. Examples of cognitive coping strategies include **cognitive restructuring**, through which individuals challenge and reframe negative thoughts, and **mindfulness techniques**, which promote present-moment awareness and acceptance.

Behavioral coping strategies involve behaviors that promote well-being and reduce stress. These strategies can include exercise, relaxation techniques, and enjoyable activities.

Social coping strategies rely on having a strong social support system in place. Social support can come from family, friends, support groups, or mental health professionals. Social coping strategies provide individuals with emotional support, practical assistance, and a sense of belonging.

TREATMENT OF PSYCHOLOGICAL DISORDERS

There are various types of **therapy** available to treat psychological disorders, and each involves unique techniques and strategies. Their diversity makes some more suitable for certain types of disorders or patients than others; for example, pediatric therapy options are tailored to meet the unique needs of children. Most treatment approaches can be divided into two categories: therapeutic interventions, which rely on different forms of talk therapy, and **psychotropic drugs**.

Therapeutic Interventions

Play therapy recognizes that the natural language of children is play. Play therapists create a safe and supportive environment where children can freely explore, process, and communicate their emotions through play activities. Play therapy can be used to treat a variety of mental and behavioral disorders in children, including trauma, anxiety, depression, and behavioral issues. For example, a child who has experienced a traumatic event may use play therapy to process and express their emotions about the trauma through symbolic play even if they are not equipped to talk about it directly.

Cognitive-behavioral therapy (CBT) is commonly used for both pediatric and adult patients. It is a goal-oriented and evidence-based therapy that aims to identify and modify **negative thought patterns** and behaviors. CBT focuses on the connection between thoughts, emotions, and behaviors and how they influence one another. CBT is particularly effective in treating anxiety disorders, depression, **attention deficit hyperactivity disorder (ADHD)**, and **obsessive-compulsive disorder (OCD)**. By challenging irrational beliefs and teaching individuals healthier coping strategies, CBT helps people manage their symptoms, develop more positive thought patterns, and improve their overall functioning.

Dialectical behavior therapy (DBT) is a specialized form of CBT that was initially developed to treat individuals with borderline personality disorder (BPD). It combines elements of CBT with **mindfulness techniques**, acceptance, and validation. DBT is highly effective in treating BPD, as well as other disorders characterized by emotional dysregulation, such as self-harm behaviors, suicidal ideation, and chronic suicidal tendencies. It focuses on teaching individuals the skills to regulate their emotions, improve **interpersonal relationships**, and develop a sense of **self-worth**.

Psychodynamic therapy is an insight-oriented therapy that explores the **unconscious processes**, early experiences, and **unresolved conflicts** that contribute to psychological distress. It emphasizes the therapeutic relationship and the exploration of the client's thoughts, feelings, and memories. Psychodynamic therapy is most effective in treating personality disorders. By gaining insight into unconscious patterns and resolving underlying conflicts, individuals can develop healthier ways of relating to themselves and others.

Humanistic therapy, also known as person-centered therapy, places a strong emphasis on the individual's capacity for self-awareness, personal growth, and **self-determination**. This approach views mental health problems as the incongruence between one's self-concept and actual experiences. The goal of humanistic therapy is to provide a supportive, empathetic, and nonjudgmental environment for clients to explore their feelings, thoughts, and experiences. Techniques used in humanistic therapy include active listening, reflection, and unconditional positive regard. This form of therapy is often used to treat issues related to self-esteem, identity, and personal growth.

Group therapy is a form of therapy where individuals with similar challenges or experiences come together in a supportive and structured environment facilitated by a therapist. It provides a space for clients to share their thoughts, feelings, and experiences, while also offering support and **feedback** to one another. Group therapy is effective in treating a range of psychological disorders, such as substance abuse, eating disorders, and social anxiety disorders. By participating in a group setting, individuals can gain a sense of belonging, learn from others' experiences, and develop interpersonal skills.

Eye movement desensitization and reprocessing (EMDR) is a therapy primarily used to treat PTSD and other trauma-related disorders. EMDR involves the use of **bilateral stimulation**, such as eye movements or tapping, to help individuals process and reframe traumatic memories. It aims to reduce the distress associated with traumatic experiences and promote adaptive coping mechanisms. EMDR has also been found to be effective in treating other psychological disorders, including anxiety disorders, phobias, and depression.

Interpersonal therapy (IPT) is a time-limited therapy that focuses on improving interpersonal relationships and resolving **interpersonal problems**. It is particularly effective in treating mood disorders like major depressive disorder and dysthymia. IPT targets specific areas of interpersonal functioning, such as grief, role disputes, role transitions, and interpersonal deficits. By addressing these interpersonal challenges, IPT helps individuals improve their social support, communication skills, and overall well-being.

Family-based therapy (FBT)—also known as family-based treatment, family therapy, or family systems therapy—is an approach that recognizes the **interconnectedness** of family members and how their interactions influence individual behavior and mental health. FBT aims to improve family communication, resolve conflicts, and promote healthy relationships. It has been found to be particularly effective in treating eating disorders. By involving the entire family in the therapy process, FBT helps address the underlying family dynamics that contribute to the development and maintenance of eating disorders.

Internal family systems (IFS) therapy is a therapeutic approach that focuses on the **internal system** of an individual's mind. According to IFS, individuals have different parts within them, each with their own thoughts, emotions, and beliefs. These parts can sometimes be in conflict, leading to psychological distress. IFS aims to help individuals understand and reconcile these internal conflicts by fostering self-compassion, self-awareness, and self-leadership. IFS has shown effectiveness in treating a range of psychological disorders, including trauma-related disorders, anxiety disorders, and mood disorders.

While there are many different approaches to therapy, all aim to provide individuals with tools and strategies to alleviate symptoms, improve functioning, and enhance overall well-being. Therapists often integrate techniques from different approaches to tailor treatment to the individual.

Psychotropic Drugs

Psychotropic drugs, also known as psychiatric medications, are designed to target specific symptoms and imbalances in the nervous system, helping individuals manage their conditions and improve their overall well-being. When used appropriately, psychotropic medications can significantly improve the quality of life for individuals with psychological disorders. Psychotropic medications should be prescribed and monitored by health care professionals, as they can have various side effects and interactions with other drugs.

Individual responses to psychotropic drugs may vary, and finding the right medication and dosage often requires ongoing evaluation. Many drugs have multiple effects on an individual's physiology and behavior. For example, benzodiazepines are known to have effects consistent with tranquilizers (sedatives), hypnotics (sleep-inducing drugs), mood-stabilizers, anxiolytics (antianxiety drugs), and muscle relaxants—paying attention to how drugs interact is especially important for this reason.

The major psychotropic drugs used in the treatment of psychological disorders are outlined in the table that follows.

MAJOR PSYCHOTROPIC DRUGS BY CLASS

Examples	Effects	Application
ANTIPSYCHOTICS (NEUROLEPTICS)		
• First generation: Haldol, Thorazine, Prolixin • Second generation: Risperdal, Zyprexa, Seroquel	• Physiological: block dopamine receptors, reducing the overactivity of dopaminergic circuits that often contribute to states of psychosis • Behavioral: help restore a sense of reality and reduce the severity of the hallucinations, delusions, and disorganized thinking that often accompany manic or psychotic episodes	Psychotic disorders (e.g., schizophrenia), mood disorders (e.g., bipolar I and bipolar II)
ANTIDEPRESSANTS		
• Selective serotonin reuptake inhibitors (SSRIs) • Serotonin-norepinephrine reuptake inhibitors (SNRIs) • Monoamine oxidase inhibitors (MAOIs)	• Physiological: generally inhibit activity of the enzymes that break down serotonin (SSRIs), serotonin and norepinephrine (SNRIs), or all monoamine neurotransmitters (serotonin, dopamine, epinephrine, norepinephrine). • Behavioral: alleviate symptoms of depression, feelings of hopelessness, and loss of interest in activities; can also help reduce anxiety, improve sleep patterns, and stabilize mood	Mood disorders (e.g., major depressive disorder, generalized anxiety disorder, OCD)
MOOD STABILIZERS (PHASE PROPHYLACTICS)		
• Lamotrigine (Lamictal) • Lithium • Valproat	• Physiological: restore balance of excitatory and inhibitory neurotransmitter levels; lithium influences neurotransmitter balance and neuronal excitability, Valproate increases gamma-aminobutyric acid (GABA) levels; lamotrigine reduces glutamate levels • Behavioral: help stabilize mood by reducing the frequency and severity of manic and depressive symptoms	Mood disorders (e.g., bipolar I and bipolar II)

MAJOR PSYCHOTROPIC DRUGS BY CLASS (*CONTINUED*)

Examples	Effects	Application
HYPNOTICS		
• Zolpidem (Ambien) • Eszopiclone (Lunesta)	• Physiological: bind to a select few receptors in the brain that increase the inhibitory effects of GABA • Behavioral: promote sleep onset, enhance overall sleep quality, reduce insomnia, improve sleep maintenance and daytime functioning	Sleep disorders (e.g., insomnia, restless leg syndrome, sleep apnea) and sleep symptoms related to psychological disorders
SEDATIVES (MINOR TRANQUILIZERS, ANXIOLYTICS)		
• Benzodiazepines (e.g., Valium, Xanax, Ativan) • Muscle relaxants, cyclobenzaprine (Flexeril)	• Physiological: benzodiazepines bind to several receptors in the brain that enhance the inhibitory effects of GABA; cyclobenzaprine binds to norepinephrine and serotonin receptors and acts on the brainstem • Behavioral: benzodiazepines reduce anxiety, improve sleep, promote relaxation; muscle relaxants reduce muscle spasms, help relieve pain, improve range of motion, promote relaxation	Anxiety disorders, musculoskeletal conditions, muscle spasms
PSYCHOSTIMULANTS		
• Methylphenidate (Ritalin, Concerta) • Amphetamines (Adderall, Vyvanse) • Eugeroics (modafinil, armodafinil)	• Physiological: increase dopamine and norepinephrine levels, usually by blocking their reuptake; some also influence serotonin and histamine levels • Behavioral: improve attention, concentration, impulse control, motivation, productivity; decrease hyperactivity in individuals with ADHD and episodes of sudden sleep attacks in individuals with narcolepsy	ADHD and sleep disorders (e.g., narcolepsy)

CONCLUSION

While the topics covered in this chapter are extensive, it's important to recognize that the DSM-5 groups particular disorders together for a reason. Developing a basic understanding of how these groups are characterized will help any test taker better address questions that are likely to come up about the identification and treatment of psychological disorders. The collective understanding of psychological disorders continues to advance, preparing the way for future psychological interventions for mental health concerns.

READINESS CHECK: UNDERSTANDING AND TREATING PSYCHOLOGICAL DISORDERS

To check how well you understand the concepts covered in this chapter, review the following questions. If you have trouble answering any of them, consider reading through this chapter again and reviewing the key terms before moving on to the next chapter.

- What is a mental disorder?
- What are the four standardized subclassifications for each disorder category?
- What are panic attacks? Which psychological disorders are they associated with?
- How do factors like age, duration of symptoms, and severity of symptoms influence the diagnostic process?
- What does it mean for psychological disorder diagnoses to be mutually exclusive?
- Can you summarize the diagnostic characteristics associated with the following psychological disorder categories and provide three examples of disorders in each category?
  - Affective disorders
  - Depressive disorders
  - Anxiety disorders
  - Somatoform disorders
  - Eating-related disorders
  - Personality disorders
  - Dissociative disorders
  - Personality disorders
- What are the differences between hypomanic episodes, manic episodes, and depressive episodes, and with which disorders are each of these associated?
- What are the three clusters of personality disorders, and how do they differ from each other?

- What are psychoses and how do they relate to psychological disorders?
- What are comorbidities?
- What is chronic stress, and how can it influence an individual's overall health?
- Can you provide three examples of coping strategies?
- Can you outline each of the following types of therapy and provide a justification for their application in the treatment of at least two psychological disorders?
  - Play therapy
  - Cognitive-behavioral therapy (CBT)
  - Dialectical behavior therapy (DBT)
  - Psychodynamic therapy
  - Humanistic therapy
  - Group therapy
  - Eye movement desensitization and reprocessing (EMDR)
  - Interpersonal therapy (IPT)
  - Family-based therapy (FBT)
  - Internal family systems (IFS) therapy
- Can you summarize the effects of the following psychotropic drug classes and provide examples of the conditions they're commonly prescribed for?
  - Antipsychotics (neuroleptics)
  - Antidepressants
  - Mood stabilizers
  - Hypnotics
  - Sedatives (minor tranquilizers, anxiolytics)
  - Psychostimulants

TEST YOURSELF: UNDERSTANDING AND TREATING PSYCHOLOGICAL DISORDERS

Directions: Each of the questions or incomplete statements below is followed by five suggested answers or completions. Select the one best answer for each. The Answer Key and Explanations will follow.

1. Prohibitive eating behavior, significant weight loss, dependence on nutritional supplements, lack of interest in food, and aversion to certain food-based sensory experiences (such as smells or textures) are all symptomatic of

   A. pica
   B. avoidant/restrictive food intake disorder
   C. anorexia nervosa
   D. selective mutism
   E. panic disorder

2. Which of the following categories could be defined as disorders related to significant disruption of cognitive functions like memory, conscious thought, identity, and perception?

   A. Bipolar disorders
   B. Depressive disorders
   C. Somatoform disorders
   D. Anxiety disorders
   E. Dissociative disorders

3. Vincent has extreme social anxiety when meeting new people or going out in public. He wants to find a romantic partner but has an intense fear of rejection that prevents him from trying to meet anyone. Sometimes, Vincent is afraid to leave his apartment because he worries that he'll embarrass himself in public. For which of the following personality disorders might Vincent most need to be evaluated?

   A. Paranoid
   B. Schizoid
   C. Antisocial
   D. Avoidant
   E. Dependent

4. Myles is experiencing sadness, regret, and hopelessness after an unexpected and intense falling out with his best friend. To address his rumination, Myles's therapist, Dr. Wong, challenges him to reframe the negative thoughts by considering the valuable lessons that he's learned through this difficult process. Which of the following methods best describes Dr. Wong's suggestion?

   A. Social coping strategy
   B. Behavioral coping strategy
   C. Cognitive restructuring
   D. Mindfulness techniques
   E. Relaxation techniques

5. Rachel began therapy to work through some difficult experiences in her past. Rachel's therapist has her identify different parts within herself and consider each of their thoughts, motivations, and beliefs, as well as any conflicts there may be between Rachel's distinct parts. The approach that Rachel's therapist is using is most consistent with

   A. cognitive behavioral therapy (CBT)
   B. internal family systems (IFS) therapy
   C. dialectical behavior therapy (DBT)
   D. psychodynamic therapy
   E. humanistic therapy

Answer Key and Explanations

1. B	2. E	3. D	4. C	5. B

1. **The correct answer is B.** All these symptoms are indicative of avoidant/restrictive food intake disorder. While pica (choice A) and anorexia nervosa (choice C) are also eating disorders, they do not have the same symptoms. Selective mutism (choice D) and panic disorder (choice E) are both anxiety disorders that do not relate to eating.

2. **The correct answer is E.** Dissociative disorders are marked by a disruption in the way one executes cognitive functions, including memory, conscious thought, identity, and perception as well as behavior, emotion, motor function, and more. Bipolar disorders (choice A) and depressive disorders (choice B) are both affective disorders, meaning they affect mood. Somatoform disorders (choice C) relate to physiological symptoms with psychological components and anxiety disorders (choice D) are characterized by excessive fear or worry.

3. **The correct answer is D.** The description of Vincent's personality and his desire for social contact that he can't seem to get are consistent with avoidant personality disorder. While it may seem quite like schizoid personality disorder (choice B), Vincent's desire for close relationships (such as a romantic partner) differentiates his behavior from schizoid types, who generally prefer to be alone. The other choices are not consistent with Vincent's behavior.

4. **The correct answer is C.** Cognitive restructuring, a type of cognitive coping strategy, involves challenging and reframing one's negative thoughts. Choices A and B are incorrect, as these methods involve actively seeking social connection or engaging in activities. Choice D is incorrect, as mindfulness techniques promote present-moment awareness rather than reflection on an event in the past. Processing intense and difficult emotions is not a relaxing undertaking, so choice E is also incorrect.

5. **The correct answer is B.** According to the internal family systems (IFS) therapy framework, individuals have different parts within them, each with their own thoughts, emotions, and beliefs that may conflict with one another. All other choices can be ruled out, as the unique emphasis on the distinct parts of a single individual is a characteristic of IFS therapy alone.

Chapter 12

Social Psychology and Statistical Methods

OVERVIEW
- Group Dynamics
- Attribution Processes
- Discrimination and Antisocial Behavior
- Attitudes and Attitude Change
- Prosocial Behavior and Attraction
- Statistical Methods
- Conclusion
- Readiness Check: Social Psychology and Statistical Methods
- Test Yourself: Social Psychology and Statistical Methods

Social psychology examines how individuals' thoughts, feelings, and behaviors are shaped by social environments, merging psychological principles with the study of social interactions and group dynamics. Approximately 9%–10% of the questions on the CLEP Introductory Psychology exam address this topic.

Closely intertwined with social psychology and its general integration with the social sciences are statistical methods, which are addressed by approximately 3%–4% of the questions on the CLEP Introductory Psychology exam. Statistical methods offer the analytical tools necessary for interpreting data across various scientific disciplines, as reflected in the interdisciplinary aims of social psychology. Together, these disciplines advance our collective scientific understanding of how individuals are influenced by their social environments.

GROUP DYNAMICS

Groups are an inherent part of human life, ranging from small social circles to large organizations and societies. **Group dynamics** is a branch of psychology that explores how individuals interact and behave within groups and the processes that emerge when people come together in a social setting, including roles and norms.

Roles are the expected behaviors, rights, and obligations associated with a particular position or status within a group. Roles can be formal, such as that of a leader or facilitator, or informal, emerging from interactions and dynamics within a group. **Norms**, on the other hand, are the unwritten rules or expectations that guide behavior within a group. Norms vary across different groups and cultures, influencing individuals' behavior, decision making, and social interactions.

Group dynamics involve the concept of **social influence**, through which individuals' thoughts, feelings, and behaviors are shaped by the presence and actions of others. Social influence takes numerous forms, including conformity, compliance, obedience, and group polarization. Larger, unanimous groups often increase an individual's conformity, compliance, and obedience, while dissenting voices or alternative opinions tend to decrease them. Individual differences, such as personality traits, cultural background, and social identity, can also affect the likelihood of conformity, compliance, and obedience.

Conformity

Conformity refers to the tendency to adjust one's thoughts, beliefs, and behaviors to match those of a larger group. Motivated by the desire to fit in, gain social acceptance, and avoid social rejection, individuals may feel pressured to conform, leading them to behave in ways that contradict their own beliefs or judgments. Conformity can result from **informational influence**, where individuals conform based on the belief that others possess accurate information, and/or **normative influence**, where individuals are driven by the desire to be liked and accepted or to avoid social disapproval. Factors affecting conformity include group size and unanimity, the perceived expertise or status of members, and the level of public observability.

Compliance

Compliance involves changing one's behavior in response to a direct request or suggestion from another person. Unlike conformity, compliance is often a result of explicit social pressure rather than the desire to fit in. Compliance techniques, such as the **foot-in-the-door technique**, **door-in-the-face technique**, and **low-ball technique**, are commonly used to increase the likelihood of compliance. These techniques exploit psychological principles, such as the desire for consistency, reciprocity, and commitment, to increase the chances of compliance. Understanding compliance strategies is crucial in various domains, including sales, marketing, and persuasion.

COMMON COMPLIANCE TECHNIQUES

Technique	Strategy	Example
Foot-in-the-door	Make a small initial request and then follow it up with a larger request.	A charity organization asks someone to sign a petition for a cause and later asks for a donation. After signing the petition, the individual feels more inclined to donate, having already shown support for the cause.
Door-in-the-face	Make an initial request that is unreasonable and likely to be rejected, then make a smaller, more reasonable request.	A salesperson offers a customer an expensive product, knowing they will reject it, and follows up with a reasonable option, which the customer may be more open to after declining the first offer.
Low-ball	Make an initial attractive offer or agreement, then change the terms or conditions to be less favorable after the person has committed to it.	A car salesperson initially offers a customer a great deal on a car. Once the customer agrees to buy it, the salesperson informs them that the price does not include additional features or accessories.

Obedience

Obedience—compliance with the demands or commands of an authority figure—is another important aspect of group dynamics. Yale social psychologist **Stanley Milgram** conducted influential experiments on obedience in the 1960s that shed light on the extent to which individuals are willing to obey authority, even when doing so conflicts with the individual's own moral judgment. Milgram's experiments revealed the potential for individuals to engage in destructive behaviors under the influence of **authority** and the **power dynamics** within a group.

Group Polarization

Group polarization occurs when like-minded individuals reinforce each other's views through group discussions and interactions, making their initial attitudes or beliefs more extreme or **polarized**. This phenomenon is driven by the desire for social approval and the diffusion of responsibility within the group. The consequences of group polarization can be both positive, fostering innovative ideas, and negative, reinforcing harmful ideologies.

ATTRIBUTION PROCESSES

Attribution processes involve interpreting and explaining behavior. **Attribution** refers to the process of assigning causes to behavior, whether it be one's own or someone else's. Attributions help individuals make sense of their social environment and guide their interactions with others.

Attribution theory makes a key distinction between **internal attributions,** which explain behavior based on abilities, traits, or motives, and **external attributions**, which connect behavior to external or situational factors. For example, if someone performs well on a test, internal attribution ascribes their success to their intelligence or hard work. If someone fails a test, external attribution chalks up their failure to a difficult exam or distractions in the testing environment.

Attribution processes are often influenced by cultural factors. **Individualist cultures**, such as those found in Western societies, tend to emphasize personal attributes and individual achievements. In these cultures, internal attributions are more common. In contrast, **collectivist cultures**, prevalent in many Eastern societies, prioritize group harmony and social norms. In these cultures, external attributions may be more prevalent, as individuals are more likely to consider the impact of the situation and the expectations of the group.

Attribution Biases

Attribution biases have significant implications in social psychology. They influence how individuals perceive and judge others, which in turn affects interactions and relationships. Challenging the biases that can result from attribution processes helps promote more empathetic, accurate, and fair judgments of others.

The **fundamental attribution error** is a common bias involving the tendency to overemphasize internal attributions and underestimate external factors when explaining the behavior of others. This error occurs because individuals often focus on others' personal characteristics and disregard the possible influence of situational influences. For instance, if someone is late to a meeting, one might assume the person is irresponsible without considering external factors like unexpected traffic or a family emergency. This error can result in unfair judgments and stereotypes, driving one to attribute undesirable behavior to personal flaws rather than considering external circumstances.

The **actor-observer bias** refers to the tendency to attribute one's own behavior to external factors while attributing others' behavior to internal factors. When individuals engage in inappropriate behavior, they tend to attribute it to the situation or external circumstances. However, when they observe inappropriate behavior in others, they may be more inclined to attribute it to those individuals' personal characteristics. This bias can lead to misunderstandings and conflicts in interpersonal relationships, as individuals may fail to consider the situational factors that contribute to the behavior of others.

DISCRIMINATION AND ANTISOCIAL BEHAVIOR

Antisocial behavior involves actions that violate social norms, disregard the rights of others, and often lack empathy and remorse. Similarly, **stereotypes** can lead individuals to form beliefs and attitudes about **social outgroups**, which can lead to biased judgments and **discrimination**. Studying the psychological processes behind antisocial, aggressive, and discriminatory behavior aids in developing strategies to prevent and address harmful actions stemming from stereotypes and prejudicial beliefs.

Theories of Antisocial Behavior

Social learning theory, proposed by social psychologist **Albert Bandura** in 1977, is a prominent theory on antisocial behavior and **aggression**. According to this theory, individuals learn aggression, or behaviors that intend to cause harm to others, through observation and imitation. Learning can occur through direct modeling of aggressive or antisocial acts or through exposure to aggressive media content. **Observational learning**, covered in Chapter 8, also plays a significant role in the acquisition of aggressive behavior, as individuals learn from observing consequences and rewards associated with aggression. For example, if a person observes that aggressive behavior is rewarded or leads to desired outcomes, they may be more likely to engage in aggressive acts themselves. Additionally, social learning theory suggests that individuals are more likely to engage in aggression if they perceive it as socially acceptable or normative within their social environment.

According to the **frustration-aggression-displacement theory** (also called the frustration-aggression hypothesis), aggression is a response to frustration or the blocking of **goal-directed behavior**. Frustration can arise from various sources such as interpersonal conflicts, unmet needs, or perceived injustices. When individuals experience frustration, they may be more prone to engage in aggressive behavior to relieve their frustration and regain a sense of control. Frustration can amplify aggressive tendencies, especially when coupled with other factors such as emotional arousal or the presence of aggressive cues in the environment.

Socialization and situational factors greatly influence aggressive and antisocial behaviors. Social norms can either promote or discourage aggression, depending on the prevailing beliefs and values of a particular social group or culture. Socialization processes, including those occurring in an individual's family and peer groups as well as in media, shape attitudes and beliefs about aggression. Studies have shown that frequent exposure to violence and aggression in media may increase aggressive tendencies, especially in children and adolescents, who are more susceptible to observational learning.

Situational factors can also influence antisocial behavior and aggression. Environments or situations, such as crowded or frustrating conditions, may heighten the probability of aggression. The presence of weapons or aggressive cues can trigger aggressive behavior by activating corresponding thoughts and emotions. Furthermore, situations that offer a perception of **anonymity** or reduced accountability, such as online interactions or large crowds, can lower inhibitions and elevate the likelihood of antisocial and/or aggressive conduct.

Stereotypes and Prejudice

Stereotypes are simplified beliefs and generalizations about specific groups that serve as mental shortcuts for categorizing the social environment. Despite being based on limited information, stereotypes frequently result in biased judgments and expectations regarding members of social outgroups. While stereotypes can be either positive or negative, **negative stereotypes** tend to be more widespread and influential than **positive stereotypes**. These beliefs stem from various sources, including direct experiences, media portrayals, and cultural norms. Stereotypes are often perpetuated through **confirmation bias**, where individuals selectively focus on information confirming their existing beliefs, and the **outgroup homogeneity effect** leads to perceiving members of other groups as more alike than they truly are.

Prejudice refers to negative attitudes, emotions, and beliefs held toward individuals based on their group membership. Prejudice can take the form of either overt expressions of hostility or subtler biases, encompassing both explicit and implicit components. **Explicit prejudice** is conscious and deliberate, whereas **implicit prejudice** is unconscious and automatic, often shaped by societal norms and cultural stereotypes. Prejudice can also be influenced by factors such as socialization, social identity, and **intergroup contact**. Socialization processes, such as upbringing and media exposure, can shape individuals' beliefs and attitudes toward different social groups. Developed by social psychologists **Henri Tajfel** and **John Turner** in the 1970s, **social identity theory** suggests that individuals derive their self-esteem from their group memberships, leading to in-group favoritism and outgroup diminishment.

In 1954, Harvard psychology professor **Gordon Allport** proposed **intergroup contact theory**. Allport's theory suggests that positive interactions between members of different groups can reduce prejudice and promote positive attitudes. To discourage prejudicial behavior, it is essential to encourage prosocial attitudes, create environments that foster empathy, and promote cooperation between individuals of varied socioeconomic and ethnic backgrounds.

Discrimination

Discrimination involves treating individuals unfairly or differently based on their group membership. Discrimination can be overt; **explicit discrimination** can include acts of exclusion, harassment, or violence. However, discrimination can also be subtle—**implicit discrimination** can involve differential treatment or biased decision making. Discrimination can occur at various levels, including interpersonal, institutional, and structural contexts.

Interpersonal discrimination refers to discriminatory acts or behaviors between individuals, while **institutional discrimination** refers to discriminatory practices and policies within organizations and institutions. **Structural discrimination** refers to societal disparities and inequalities that systematically disadvantage certain groups. Discrimination can be influenced by factors such as social norms, power dynamics, and institutional practices. Social norms may support or challenge discriminatory behavior depending on the prevailing beliefs and values of a society. Power dynamics and **unequal resource distribution** can create conditions that perpetuate discrimination and maintain social hierarchies.

ATTITUDES AND ATTITUDE CHANGE

The study of **attitudes** and attitude change delves into collective and individual influences on opinions, beliefs, and evaluations of people, objects, and ideas, along with the processes that can alter these attitudes. Because of the significant impact of attitudes on perceptions and behaviors, it is crucial to actively challenge attitudes that contribute to prejudice, discrimination, and inequality.

Encompassing one's evaluations and feelings toward different aspects of society, attitudes are shaped by diverse factors like **socialization**, **personal experiences**, and **cultural influences**. Socialization is the acquisition of attitudes and beliefs from the social environment, including family, peers, and media, and it imparts societal norms, values, and ideologies that influence attitudes toward various social issues. Personal experiences, whether positive or negative, significantly contribute to attitude formation. Positive encounters may lead to favorable attitudes, while negative experiences can result in unfavorable ones. Cultural influences, such as norms and values, further mold attitudes by providing a framework for evaluating different aspects of the social world.

Various processes can lead to attitude change, and a significant theory in comprehending this phenomenon is the **elaboration likelihood model (ELM)**, formulated in 1980 by psychology professors **Richard E. Petty** and **John T. Cacioppo**. According to this model, there are two routes to attitude change: the central route and the peripheral route. The **central route to attitude change** involves a careful and thoughtful evaluation of the arguments and information presented, while the **peripheral route to attitude change** relies on superficial cues and **heuristics**. The central route is more likely to lead to lasting attitude change, as it involves a thorough consideration of information coupled with cognitive processing. Meanwhile, the peripheral route is more susceptible to temporary attitude change, as it relies on superficial factors such as the attractiveness or credibility of the source.

An additional factor contributing to attitude change is **cognitive dissonance**. Cognitive dissonance refers to the discomfort or dissonance an individual feels when their attitudes and behaviors are in conflict. This discomfort serves as motivation for individuals to adjust their attitudes to match their behaviors, thereby alleviating the dissonance. For instance, if someone who considers themselves environmentally conscious becomes aware that they engaged in environmentally harmful behaviors, they may experience cognitive dissonance and feel compelled to modify their attitudes and behaviors to reduce the inconsistency.

Social influences, such as conformity, compliance, and obedience, play a crucial role in shaping attitude change. Persuasion, another social influence, entails intentional attempts to modify attitudes through convincing or influential messages. These messages may incorporate logical arguments with credible sources or illogical arguments that rely on emotional appeals or deceptive evidence without a solid foundation. The effectiveness of persuasive tactics is influenced by factors such as the credibility of the source, the quality of the argument, and the characteristics of the audience.

PROSOCIAL BEHAVIOR AND ATTRACTION

Prosocial behavior refers to acts that benefit others or society, often driven by **empathy**, **altruism**, or a sense of moral responsibility. Empathy is the ability to understand and share the feelings of others, and altruism refers to selfless concern and actions to benefit others, even at a personal cost. Both play a key role in driving prosocial behavior. **Interpersonal attraction**, on the other hand, refers to feelings of attraction and connection between individuals. Understanding the social psychological processes inherent to prosocial behavior and interpersonal attraction can help foster positive relationships and promote a more compassionate, supportive society.

Theories of Prosocial Behavior

A notable theory explaining prosocial behavior is the **social exchange theory**, formulated by French anthropologist **Claude Lévi-Strauss**. According to this theory, individuals participate in prosocial behavior when they perceive that the benefits of helping others outweigh the costs. People conduct a **rational assessment** of potential rewards and costs associated with helping, and they are more inclined to assist when the benefits surpass personal costs. For instance, individuals may help others gain social approval, maintain positive relationships, or enhance their self-esteem. Social exchange theory also proposes that individuals may practice **reciprocal altruism**, helping others with the expectation of receiving assistance in return later.

Another influential view of prosocial behavior is the **empathy-altruism** hypothesis promoted by American social psychologist **C. Daniel Batson**. Empathy-altruism theory suggests that individuals may engage in prosocial behavior out of genuine concern for the well-being of others and that they are driven by empathy and altruism to do so. Empathy-altruism theory suggests that when individuals experience empathy toward someone in need, they are more likely to engage in prosocial behavior, regardless of the potential rewards or costs involved. This theory highlights the importance of fostering empathy and promoting a sense of interconnectedness and compassion toward others.

Interpersonal Attraction

Interpersonal attraction relates to the factors that influence the formation and development of relationships between individuals. The **similarity-attraction effect** describes the tendency of individuals to be more attracted to others who are like them in their attitudes, beliefs, values, and interests. **Similarity** provides a sense of familiarity, validation, and shared experiences, which enhances likability and connection between individuals. Additionally, the **mere exposure effect**, sometimes called the familiarity principle, suggests that repeated exposure to someone or something increases another person's affinity and attraction to that person or thing. The more familiar individuals become with each other, the more they tend to develop positive feelings and preferences toward one another.

Another important factor in interpersonal attraction is **physical attractiveness**. Physical appearance plays a significant role in initial attraction, as individuals tend to be attracted to others who are perceived as physically attractive, even outside romantic contexts. This preference for physical attractiveness is influenced by **societal beauty standards** and cultural norms. However, it is important to note that attraction is not solely based on physical appearance. Personal qualities such as kindness, intelligence, and a good sense of humor also contribute to interpersonal attraction and the development of meaningful relationships.

STATISTICAL METHODS

Much of social psychology relies on **statistical analysis**, which provides a framework for drawing meaningful conclusions from data. It involves the application of statistical methods to analyze and interpret data, allowing researchers to make inferences about populations based on samples. Understanding the key concepts related to statistical analysis allows the selection of appropriate experimental design and the subsequent interpretation of the myriad and complex phenomena investigated in psychological research.

Statistics Overview

Central tendency is a statistical measure that helps psychologists understand the most representative value in a dataset. The three commonly used measures of central tendency are the **mean**, **median**, and **mode**. The mean, or arithmetic average of a set of numbers, provides an overall representation of the data, but it can be influenced by extreme values. The median is the middle value in a dataset when the values are arranged in ascending or descending order. It is not affected by extreme values and provides a more reliable measure of central tendency. The mode represents the most common value in the data and can be useful when dealing with **categorical data** (qualitative) or **discrete data** (numbered values).

MEASURES OF CENTRAL TENDENCY

Measure	Definition	Characteristics
Mean	The arithmetic average of a set of numbers; provides an overall representation of the data	Can be influenced by extreme values
Median	The middle value in a dataset when the values are arranged in ascending or descending order	Not affected by extreme values; provides a more reliable measure of central tendency
Mode	The most common value in the data	Useful when dealing with categorical data (qualitative) or discrete data (numbered values)

Variability refers to the spread or dispersion of data points in a dataset. It helps researchers understand how much the values in a dataset deviate from the central tendency. **Range** and **standard deviation** are commonly used measures of variability. Range is the difference between the highest and lowest values in a dataset. It provides a simple measure of variability but is sensitive to extreme values. Standard deviation measures the average amount by which the values in a dataset deviate from the mean. It provides a more robust measure of variability and is commonly used in psychology research to assess the spread of data.

In psychological research, a **sample** refers to a subset of individuals or cases selected from a larger group known as the **population**. The population represents the entire group of interest to the researcher, while the sample is a smaller representation used to make inferences about the population. The selection of a **representative sample** is important to accurately reflect the characteristics of the entire population and ensure the **generalizability** of findings.

In statistics, **norms** refer to reference points against which individuals or groups are measured and provide a basis for evaluating and interpreting psychological phenomena. For example, in **intelligence testing**, an individual's score may be compared with a **normative sample** to determine their relative performance. Norms can be derived from large-scale studies or established through consensus within a specific field.

In an experimental or research study, the **independent variable** is a factor or condition that the researcher manipulates or controls to observe its effect on the **dependent variable**. The independent variable is the presumed cause or predictor variable, while the dependent variable is the outcome or response variable that is measured or observed. For example, in a study examining the effects of exercise on mood, exercise would be the independent variable and mood would be the dependent variable. The researcher would manipulate the level or amount of exercise and measure its impact on mood.

In statistical **hypothesis testing**, researchers typically formulate two competing hypotheses: the **null hypothesis (H_0)** and the **alternative hypothesis (H_1 or H_a)**. The H_0 states that there is *no* significant difference, relationship, or effect between variables in the population. The H_1 or H_a suggests that there *is* a significant difference, relationship, or effect. Researchers collect data and use statistical tests to determine whether the evidence supports rejecting the null hypothesis in favor of the alternative hypothesis. The level of statistical significance, often set at $p < 0.05$, determines the threshold for rejecting the null hypothesis.

Type I and **type II errors** are associated with hypothesis testing. A type I error occurs when a researcher rejects a true null hypothesis, mistakenly concluding that there is a significant effect or relationship when there isn't one. A type II error occurs when a researcher fails to reject a false null hypothesis, mistakenly concluding that there is no significant effect or relationship when there is one. Both errors can have significant implications for research findings and subsequent interpretations.

In recent years, psychology and other scientific fields have faced a **reproducibility crisis**, raising concerns about the **reliability** and **validity** of research findings. Reliability refers to the consistency and stability of measurements or results. Research is reliable when its findings can be reproduced by a follow-up experiment conducted under similar conditions. Validity, on the other hand, refers to the accuracy and meaningfulness of measurements or results. Effective studies measure what they claim to measure and have results that are truly representative of the construct being investigated. By selecting an appropriate experimental design and implementing sufficient experimental controls, researchers can limit potential biases and increase the internal validity of their studies.

Experimental design involves carefully planning and conducting studies so that valid and reliable conclusions can be drawn regarding causal relationships between variables. One common experimental design is the **randomized controlled trial (RCT)**, where participants are randomly assigned to different conditions or treatments. This design helps minimize the influence of confounding variables and allows researchers to infer causality. Another design is the **factorial design**, wherein researchers manipulate multiple independent variables to investigate both their individual and interactive effects.

Experimental controls are necessary to minimize the influence of extraneous variables that could confound the relationship between the independent and dependent variables. Control over experimental conditions can be achieved through various means, such as the **randomized assignment** of participants to different conditions, the use of **control groups**, and the implementation of **standardized procedures**. By controlling extraneous variables, researchers can attribute any observed effects to the independent variable with greater **statistical confidence**.

Descriptive and Inferential Statistics

Two commonly used methods in psychological research include **descriptive statistics** and **inferential statistics**. While both methods aim to summarize and draw conclusions from data, they have distinct purposes, strengths, weaknesses, and appropriate contexts, as outlined in the table that follows.

PSYCHOLOGICAL RESEARCH APPROACHES

Method	Purposes	Strengths	Weaknesses
Descriptive	• Presents data in a meaningful, concise manner • Focuses on describing the main characteristics of a dataset, such as mean, median, mode, variability (range, standard deviation)	• Is simple to calculate and interpret • Presents summarization of data patterns, trends, outliers • Provides clear, straightforward communication of findings to a wide audience	• Is not generalizable to a larger population • Has less inferential power; does not test hypotheses or make predictions about relationships between variables
Inferential	• Makes inferences or generalizations about a population based on a data sample • Involves statistical tests and experimental techniques to make probabilistic predictions about relationships between variables	• Generalizes to a wider population, increasing external validity • Involves hypothesis testing and determining the likelihood that observed relationships are not due to chance • Can establish causal claims regarding the relationships between variables	• Is highly complex; challenging to implement correctly • Relies on assumptions such as random sampling, which may not be met • Risks an increased possibility for errors from hypothesis testing

CONCLUSION

The intersection of social psychology research and statistical methods offers valuable insights into human behavior and the complexities of the social world. Social psychology delves into phenomena like group dynamics, attribution, discrimination, antisocial behavior, and prosocial behavior. Experimental design and statistical methods serve as crucial tools in social psychology research and in the field of psychology in general, enabling psychologists to test hypotheses, control variables, and draw valid conclusions. Through the application and scrutiny of established social psychology theories, coupled with statistical analysis for interpreting research results, psychologists not only gain an understanding of human behavior but also contribute to social well-being. This process informs interventions aimed at improving individuals' lives and society as a whole.

READINESS CHECK: SOCIAL PSYCHOLOGY AND STATISTICAL METHODS

To check how well you understand the concepts covered in this chapter, review the following questions. If you have trouble answering any of them, consider reading through this chapter again and reviewing the key terms before moving on to the next chapter.

- Can you define the following terms?
  - Roles
  - Norms
  - Group polarization
  - Persuasion
  - Independent and dependent variables
  - Experimental control
- Can you discuss the following concepts?
  - Group dynamics
  - Social influence
  - Attribution processes, biases, and errors
  - Discrimination
  - Prosocial behavior
  - Interpersonal attraction
  - Samples, norms, and variability
  - Experimental design
- Can you explain each of these theories?
  - Attribution theory
  - Social learning theory
  - Frustration-aggression-displacement theory
  - Social identity theory
  - Intergroup contact theory
  - Social exchange theory
  - Empathy-altruism theory
- What are attribution processes, including internal and external attributions, and how are their manifestations influenced by cultural variables?

- What is the role of social learning in the development of antisocial and aggressive behaviors?
- How can stereotypes lead to prejudicial and discriminatory views?
- What are the processes that can lead to attitude changes, such as the elaboration likelihood model?
- What are the differences between descriptive and inferential statistical methods, and when is each method appropriate?
- What are some examples of the research methods researchers can use to increase experimental validity and reproducibility?

TEST YOURSELF: SOCIAL PSYCHOLOGY AND STATISTICAL METHODS

Directions: Each of the questions or incomplete statements below is followed by five suggested answers or completions. Select the one best answer for each. The Answer Key and Explanations will follow.

1. Susan is a psychology researcher whose work explores the ways individuals behave in groups and the processes that emerge in social situations. Which of the following subfields offers the most accurate categorization of Susan's research?

   A. Cognitive psychology
   B. Evolutionary psychology
   C. Group dynamics
   D. Attribution processes
   E. Clinical psychology

2. When Andre's boss did not contact him after requesting to meet later in the afternoon, Andre felt anxious and assumed his boss must be upset with his performance. Andre's assumption is an example of which of the following?

   A. Internal attribution
   B. External attribution
   C. Cognitive dissonance
   D. Confirmation bias
   E. Normative influence

3. Which of the following describes the process through which individuals acquire their beliefs and feelings toward the world via the influence of their peers, family, and media?

   A. Group dynamics
   B. Normative influence
   C. Informational influence
   D. Socialization
   E. Attribution

4. A psychologist studying the ways individuals interpret and explain the behavior of others wants to create a chart to summarize the data patterns, trends, and outliers he observed in his cross-cultural research. Which of the following options indicates the researcher's area of study and the appropriate statistical methods to utilize in this scenario?

A. Attribution processes, inferential statistics
B. Attribution processes, descriptive statistics
C. Group dynamics, inferential statistics
D. Group dynamics, descriptive statistics
E. Social exchange theory, inferential statistics

5. Which strategy would be the least effective method to ensure the generalizability of experimental findings?

A. Ensuring the sample size is representative of the wider population
B. Using a randomized, controlled trial experimental design
C. Ensuring the validity of all measurements
D. Carefully considering the independent variable's influence on the dependent variable
E. Analyzing data using descriptive statistical methods to present a clear summary of data trends

Answer Key and Explanations

1. C	2. A	3. D	4. B	5. E

1. The correct answer is C. Group dynamics are an important component in the study of how individuals behave in group settings. Choices A, B, and E do not relate specifically to social phenomena, and choice D focuses only on the ways individuals interpret and explain the behavior of others.

2. **The correct answer is A.** Attribution processes describe the ways individuals interpret and explain the behavior of others. Andre's assumption that his boss didn't contact him because of being disappointed in Andre's performance at work is an assumption about his boss's motives, an internal attribution. External attributions (choice B) relate to external, situational factors, such as an unexpected event occurring. Choices C, D, and E are not specifically related to attribution.

3. **The correct answer is D.** Socialization describes the process through which individuals acquire attitudes and beliefs from their social environment, such as family, peers, and media. Group dynamics (choice A) relate to how individuals behave and interact within groups, rather than to the formation of one's beliefs and attitudes toward the world. Normative and informational influences (choices B and C) relate to the concept of conformity, while attribution (choice E) describes how individuals explain the behavior of others.

4. **The correct answer is B.** Attribution processes refer to ways people interpret and explain the behavior of others, so choices C, D, and E can be eliminated. Descriptive statistics are used when summarizing data patterns, trends, and outliers, so choice A is incorrect.

5. **The correct answer is E.** Descriptive statistical methods are not appropriate for generalization to a wider population. Choices A through D are appropriate suggestions to increase the generalizability of an experiment.

Chapter 13

Practice Test

OVERVIEW

- Practice Test
- Answer Key and Explanations

An answer sheet for this test can be found on page 259.

PRACTICE TEST

This practice test and the time allotted are approximately half the length of a full CLEP Introductory Psychology exam.

48 Questions—45 Minutes

Directions: Each of the questions or incomplete statements below is followed by five suggested answers or completions. Select the one best answer for each. The Answer Key and Explanations will follow.

---

1. The discredited belief that one's skull shape and facial features define their personality and intelligence is called

   A. trepanning
   B. phrenology
   C. pseudoscience
   D. Adlerian theory
   E. biological theory

2. "Unobservable mental processes like language, memory, and attention are important for psychologists to study in order to understand how the human mind works."

   This statement is most closely associated with which of the following approaches?

   A. Behavioral
   B. Biological
   C. Humanistic
   D. Cognitive
   E. Biopsychosocial

3. Which of the following genetics concepts explains why traits affecting the X chromosome disproportionately appear in males?

   A. Protein synthesis
   B. Autosomal inheritance
   C. Sex-linked inheritance
   D. Gene-environment interplay
   E. Recessive allele inheritance

4. The depolarization that accompanies an action potential causes the

    A. electrical charge inside of a neuron to become less negative

    B. electrical charge inside of a neuron to become less positive

    C. influx of negatively charged sodium ions

    D. influx of negatively charged calcium ions

    E. release of neurotransmitters into the synaptic gap

5. The feature of human vision that is responsible for the ability to perceive the world as three dimensional is

    A. trichromatic vision

    B. binocular vision

    C. protanopia

    D. tritanopia

    E. monocular depth cues

6. Which class of drugs includes substances that slow down the activity of the central nervous system, leading to relaxation, sedation, and reduced inhibition?

    A. Stimulants

    B. Psychedelics

    C. Cannabinoids

    D. Hallucinogens

    E. Depressants

7. The four key processes involved in observational learning are

    A. shaping, retention, reproduction, and motivation

    B. attention, retention, reproduction, and motivation

    C. shaping, attention, retention, and reproduction

    D. attention, retention, observation, and reproduction

    E. cognition, attention, retention, and observation

8. In operant conditioning, the concept of positive punishment consists of

   A. adding an aversive stimulus in response to an undesired behavior to discourage its continuation

   B. adding a desirable stimulus in response to the discontinuation of an undesired behavior

   C. removing a desired stimulus in response to an undesired behavior to discourage its continuation

   D. removing an aversive stimulus to increase the frequency of desired behaviors

   E. adding a desired stimulus in response to an undesired behavior to encourage its continuation

9. On her way to work one morning, Asha briefly noticed a new billboard on the highway. She didn't see it long enough to retain all of the information, but she remembers that it involved a person eating a hamburger. Asha's memory of what she saw on the billboard is an example of which of the following?

   A. Procedural memory
   B. Emotional memory
   C. Iconic memory
   D. Echoic memory
   E. Semantic memory

10. After a long morning hiking, Paul turns around when he begins to feel hungry. Despite his exhaustion, Paul is motivated to get lunch as soon as he gets back to his car. Which of the following theories best describes Paul's behavior?

   A. Three needs theory
   B. Two-factor theory
   C. Drive-reduction theory
   D. Social exchange theory
   E. Self-determination theory

11. Which of the following represents a challenge associated with the use of cross-sectional study design in developmental research?

    A. Obtaining data from different participants reduces reliability.
    B. Participants frequently drop off before the completion of the study.
    C. Studies require a large amount of time to complete.
    D. Varied age groups cannot be included.
    E. Statistical analysis of the data obtained is not possible.

12. According to Piaget's stages of childhood development, the stage during which children develop object permanence is the

    A. sensorimotor stage
    B. preoperational stage
    C. concrete operational stage
    D. formal operational stage
    E. postoperational stage

13. The theory that attributes personality to repeated patterns of behavior, thought, and emotion that are generally stable over time is

    A. Gordon Allport's trait theory
    B. Hans Eysenck's theory of personality
    C. Raymond Cattell's 16 personality factor trait theory
    D. The Myers-Briggs Type Indicator
    E. Five-factor model of personality

14. Everett is 28 years old and is prone to unprovoked verbal outbursts and violent bouts of aggression; he has also suffered severe depressive episodes. Everett's symptoms are consistent with all of the following disorders EXCEPT:

    A. Bipolar I disorder
    B. Bipolar II disorder
    C. Medication-induced bipolar disorder
    D. Major depressive disorder
    E. Disruptive mood dysregulation disorder

15. Meryl tends to make good first impressions, but she generally cannot form lasting friendships. She also tends to lie about and exaggerate her accomplishments and experiences to improve how others perceive her. Meryl's symptoms are consistent with

   A. avoidant personality disorder
   B. narcissistic personality disorder
   C. histrionic personality disorder
   D. borderline personality disorder
   E. paranoid personality disorder

16. Which of the following statements is true about play therapy?

   A. It is not as effective for patients with personality disorders.
   B. It involves pure observation and no direct interaction between clinician and patient.
   C. It is not recommended for pediatric patients.
   D. It is one of the best ways to conduct therapy for pediatric patients.
   E. It cannot be used in a diagnostic setting.

17. Paula is unsure about which mayoral candidate best reflects her values. After seeking guidance from trusted community leaders, she feels confident that her knowledge of the candidates is sufficient to cast her vote for the best candidate. Paula's approach to this situation is consistent with

   A. informational influence
   B. normative influence
   C. external attribution
   D. generational influence
   E. deindividuation

18. Requesting an unreasonably high price for a service before making a more reasonable second offer is consistent with which of the following compliance techniques?

   A. Low-ball
   B. Foot-in-the-door
   C. Door-in-the-face
   D. High-ball
   E. Door-open-at-rejection

19. Which of the following study features is manipulated by a researcher to assess its influence on the experimental subjects?

A. Normative sample
B. Dependent variable
C. Independent variable
D. Central tendency
E. Categorical data

20. The choice to withhold information from both the researchers and the participants about each participant's placement in the placebo group or the treatment group indicates the use of a

A. correlational method
B. experimental method
C. clinical study
D. blind experiment
E. double-blind experiment

21. The school of individual psychology, which focuses on the integration of all aspects of an individual's personality and environment, was founded by

A. Alfred Adler
B. Carl Jung
C. Sigmund Freud
D. James B. Watson
E. B. F. Skinner

22. Which of the following neurotransmitters functions by inhibiting neuron impulses to regulate excitability in the nervous system?

A. Acetylcholine
B. Glutamate
C. Dopamine
D. GABA
E. Vasopressin

23. Which of the following is responsible for one's perception of fine details, textures, and spatial location when feeling an object?

A. Discriminative touch
B. Crude touch
C. Somatosensation
D. Mechanoreception
E. Proprioception

24. Which of the following is known for its role in the amplification of nociceptive signals?

A. Acetylcholine
B. GABA
C. Substance P
D. Substance N
E. Vasopressin

25. Which of the following drugs would be most likely to cause strong feelings of relaxation and euphoria?

A. Antidepressant
B. Stimulant
C. Opioid
D. Hallucinogen
E. Neuroleptic

26. Mr. Vyas rings a bell when it is time for his third graders to be excused for lunch. One day, Mr. Vyas accidentally drops a notebook on the bell 20 minutes before lunchtime, and his students begin packing up before he can inform them of his mistake. In this case, packing up early is a(n)

A. unconditioned stimulus
B. unconditioned response
C. conditioned stimulus
D. conditioned response
E. neutral stimulus

27. Anchoring bias describes a tendency for people to

A. search for information that confirms their existing beliefs
B. cling to the first piece of information they receive about a topic
C. make decisions based on personal experience rather than data
D. adopt beliefs based on social pressure
E. modify behavior in response to the requests of authority figures

28. Paige is a graphic designer being considered for a promotion. Her boss commends her for coming up with novel ideas and approaches to completing her projects, which indicates that Paige excels at

A. divergent thinking
B. convergent thinking
C. functional fixedness
D. metacognitive knowledge
E. iconic memory

29. As a young adult, Kesha struggles with feelings of self-doubt and shame. Her lack of motivational drive makes it difficult for her to begin to pursue her goals. These difficulties may be related to maldevelopment during which stage in Erikson's theory of psychosocial development?

A. Trust versus mistrust
B. Identity versus role confusion
C. Intimacy versus isolation
D. Initiative versus guilt
E. Generativity versus stagnation

30. A 5-year-old child named Sasha visits a psychologist who observes that Sasha shows little interest in interacting with her mother, including when her mother leaves or reenters the room. Sasha's behavior aligns most closely with

A. secure attachment
B. anxious-ambivalent attachment
C. anxious-avoidant attachment
D. ambivalent-avoidant attachment
E. disorganized attachment

31. The Rorschach ink blot test is categorized as which of the following?

A. Thematic apperception test
B. Self-esteem test
C. Self-concept test
D. Self-image test
E. Projective test

32. A patient is diagnosed with a personality disorder by a psychologist who conducts an in-depth exploration of their unique experiences, motivations, and beliefs in a clinical setting. Which of the following methods is consistent with this style of assessment?

A. Self-report assessments
B. Structured clinical interviews
C. Projective tests
D. Behavioral observations
E. Factor analyses

33. Which of the following is categorized as an anxiety disorder?

A. Anorexia nervosa
B. Selective mutism
C. Persistent depressive disorder
D. Depersonalization disorder
E. Premenstrual dysphoric disorder

34. If a patient is prescribed a medication classified as a phase prophylactic (mood stabilizer), such as valproate or carbamazepine, they have most likely been diagnosed with

A. bipolar I disorder
B. major depressive disorder
C. dissociative amnesia
D. reactive attachment disorder
E. bulimia nervosa

35. Ren is often late to work and tends to blame his lateness on factors beyond his control. However, when one of Ren's coworkers arrives late for a meeting one day, Ren is upset that his coworker is not being respectful of their colleagues' time. Ren's behavior is consistent with

A. confirmation bias
B. negative stereotypes
C. outgroup homogeneity effect
D. normative influence
E. actor-observer bias

36. A situation in which interactions between members of a group lead to the strengthening of their initial beliefs and attitudes is described as

A. internal attributions
B. external attributions
C. compliance
D. obedience
E. group polarization

37. Dr. Logan examines his patients' physiological markers, such as their hormonal levels, to gain insight into the factors that may be influencing their behavior. This is consistent with which of the following approaches?

A. Behavioral
B. Biological
C. Humanistic
D. Cognitive
E. Psychodynamic

38. When a researcher has made a type II error, which of the following has occurred?

A. Failure to incorporate a control group during the experimental design phase
B. Identification of a relationship between variables, when there is none
C. Failure to identify a relationship between related variables
D. Attributing features of the control group to the experimental group
E. Invalid application of inferential statistical methods

39. Damage to which of the following structures would be most likely to cause issues processing sensory information, including one's sense of touch and proprioception?

A. Gustatory cortex
B. Frontal lobe
C. Occipital lobe
D. Temporal lobe
E. Parietal lobe

40. Damage to the inner ear would be most likely to cause issues with which of the following senses?

A. Audition and proprioception
B. Audition and nociception
C. Thermoception and balance
D. Audition and balance
E. Balance and nociception

41. Which of the following processes involves the generation of new neuronal cells in the nervous system?

A. Neuroplasticity
B. Long-term depression
C. Long-term potentiation
D. Consolidation
E. Neurogenesis

42. An individual's ability to plan, monitor, and evaluate their own cognitive activities is called

A. attentional spotlight
B. divergent thinking
C. convergent thinking
D. metacognitive regulation
E. metacognitive knowledge

43. Stacy experiences a strong sense of calmness and peace while engaging in a meditation exercise, and she decides to incorporate meditation into her daily morning routine. Stacy's decision to persist in this behavior is associated with which of the following?

    A. High social motivation
    B. Low extrinsic motivation
    C. High extrinsic motivation
    D. Low intrinsic motivation
    E. High intrinsic motivation

44. Dr. Lee's research focuses on the cultural influences of personality and involves the collection and analysis of data from individuals representing all age classes and multiple cultures. Which of the following terms best describes Dr. Lee's research method?

    A. Factor analysis
    B. Self-report assessment
    C. Observational research
    D. Cross-sectional research
    E. Structured clinical interviews

45. Lacey experiences hypomanic and depressive episodes but has also been diagnosed with Cushing syndrome, a hormonal condition that can cause bipolar-like symptoms. Which of the following is most likely to be the appropriate diagnosis?

    A. Bipolar I disorder
    B. Bipolar II disorder
    C. Other bipolar or related disorder
    D. Cyclothymic disorder
    E. Bipolar or related disorder due to another medical condition

46. Liza cares deeply about the environment and is troubled by the fact that the company she works for does not recycle. Her discomfort at the inconsistency between her values and her job is an example of

    A. observational learning
    B. personal history
    C. cultural influences
    D. cognitive dissonance
    E. intergroup contact

47. Corryn notices that Jordan shares many of her interests, including staying active and volunteering at an animal shelter. As a result, she finds herself attracted to Jordan. Which of the following explains Corryn's attraction to Jordan?

    A. Similarity-attraction effect
    B. Mere exposure effect
    C. Cultural influences
    D. Personal experiences
    E. Altruism

48. All of the following are effective strategies to increase an experiment's validity EXCEPT:

    A. Establishing the accuracy of measurements
    B. Using a design that includes an experimental control group
    C. Selecting a representative sample of participants
    D. Ensuring that data collection methods are appropriate for statistical analysis
    E. Establishing the dependent variable's correlative effect on the independent variable

ANSWER KEY AND EXPLANATIONS

1. B	11. A	21. A	31. E	41. E
2. D	12. B	22. D	32. B	42. D
3. C	13. A	23. A	33. B	43. E
4. A	14. E	24. C	34. A	44. D
5. B	15. B	25. C	35. E	45. E
6. E	16. D	26. D	36. E	46. D
7. B	17. A	27. B	37. B	47. A
8. A	18. C	28. A	38. C	48. E
9. C	19. C	29. D	39. E	
10. C	20. E	30. C	40. D	

1. **The correct answer is B.** Phrenology is a pseudoscientific theory developed by Franz Joseph Gall in the late 18th century that posited that an individual's cranial and facial features were related to their personality and intelligence. While phrenology is indeed a pseudoscience (choice C), this is a broad term that applies to all nonscientific ideas inappropriately represented as having an evidentiary basis. Choice A is incorrect, as trepanning is a distinct, ancient pseudoscientific idea involving the opening of human skulls. Choices D and E are modern approaches in psychology.

2. **The correct answer is D.** The cognitive approach focuses on unobservable mental and cognitive processes like language, memory, and attention. This approach is a break from the behavioral approach (choice A), which was rooted in the belief that unobservable processes should be considered separate from empirical science. Choices B and E focus on physiological insights in their therapeutic approach, so they are incorrect. Choice C is also incorrect as the humanistic approach views people as individuals, rather than looking for patterns to study.

3. **The correct answer is C.** Sex-linked inheritance refers to certain traits that are inherited based on one's sex. Since males have only one X chromosome, traits affecting the X chromosome (such as color deficiency) disproportionately affect males, making them sex-linked traits. Only choice C describes the inheritance of traits located on the sex-determining chromosomes.

4. **The correct answer is A.** Depolarization involves the influx of positively charged ions, which results in the interior of the neuron becoming less negatively charged. Choices C and D are incorrect as the sodium and calcium ions involved in the propagation of action potentials have a positive charge. Choice E is also incorrect since the release of neurotransmitters happens after the wave of depolarization has traveled down the length of the presynaptic neuron.

5. **The correct answer is B.** The brain's processing of the overlap between the visual fields of the forward-facing right and left eyes, described as binocular vision, underlies human perception of the world as three dimensional. Choices A, C and D relate to the properties of color perception; choice E relates to a single eye's perception of depth.

6. **The correct answer is E.** Depressants include drugs such as alcohol, barbiturates, and benzodiazepines, and they slow down the central nervous system, leading to relaxation, sedation, and reduced inhibitions. Hallucinogens, psychedelics, and stimulants (choices D, B, and A) often increase alertness and energy, and cannabinoids (choice C) may have stimulant or hallucinogenic effects, so these answers are incorrect.

7. **The correct answer is B.** The four processes involved in observational learning, outlined by Albert Bandura, include attention (focusing on a model's behavior), retention (encoding the memory of observed behavior), reproduction (physically imitating observed behavior), and motivation (drive to imitate the model's behavior). Cognition (choice E) is a broad concept that relates to all forms of learning, and shaping (choices A and C) is a concept that relates to forms of learning that involve conditioning.

8. **The correct answer is A.** Punishment aims to reduce the frequency of undesired behaviors, and reinforcement aims to increase the frequency of desired behaviors. The use of the terms *positive* and *negative* refers to whether a stimulus is being added or removed during the processes of punishment and reinforcement. Choice C represents negative punishment, and choice E is illogical as this approach would reinforce undesired behaviors. Choices B and D are also incorrect as they represent positive and negative reinforcement, respectively.

9. **The correct answer is C.** Iconic memory is a type of sensory memory related to a visual stimulus. Sensory memories are a brief, transient form of memory that allow individuals to retain sensory information from their environment for a short period of time. Echoic memories (choice D) are sensory memories involving sounds. All other choices relate to forms of long-term memory.

10. **The correct answer is C.** Drive-reduction theory posits that hunger is triggered when the body's energy reserves are depleted, which, in turn, motivates individuals to partake in behaviors that restore their energy equilibrium and homeostasis. Choice B is incorrect because it relates to emotions, rather than motivation. All other choices involve achievement-based or social theories of motivation, so they are also incorrect.

11. **The correct answer is A.** Cross-sectional research methods in developmental research can be challenging because obtaining data from different samples of participants tends to be less reliable, and it is also harder to identify confounding variables. Choices B and C are incorrect; they represent drawbacks of conducting longitudinal studies. Choices D and E are also incorrect as they don't represent challenges associated with either longitudinal or cross-sectional studies.

12. **The correct answer is B.** Object permanence, or one's comprehension of the continued existence of out-of-sight objects, develops early in the preoperational stage, which lasts from age 2 to age 7. Choice A occurs before the preoperational stage, and choices C and D occur after the preoperational stage. Choice E is not one of Piaget's stages of childhood development.

13. **The correct answer is A.** Allport's theory posits that personality is generally fixed at the time of birth and that personality traits are so ingrained that even trauma responses can be predicted by personality type. While personality is widely considered to be relatively stable throughout one's life, Gordon Allport's trait theory is the least flexible in its view of the fixedness of personality.

14. **The correct answer is E.** All the choices mentioned include depressive episodes and potential temper issues. However, while Everett's doctor would need more information before making any kind of diagnosis, they could safely rule out disruptive mood dysregulation disorder because the DSM-5 stipulates that this diagnosis can only be given to patients between the ages of 6 and 18. Since Everett is 28, his doctor can safely assume that Everett's behavior stems from a different mental disorder.

15. **The correct answer is B.** Meryl's behaviors are most consistent with descriptions of narcissistic personality disorder, which is characterized by an inflated ego; a tendency toward manipulation, exaggeration, and self-aggrandizement; and an ability to make good first impressions without developing longer-term social connections.

16. **The correct answer is D.** Because play is such a dynamic part of a child's growth and development, play therapy is especially well-suited for pediatric patients who may not be able to speak as freely or with as much nuance as an adult patient would in a traditional therapeutic setting. It is especially well-suited to preschool and school-age children, as well as children with developmental disorders. None of the other statements are true.

17. **The correct answer is A.** Paula sought the guidance of others she trusted to have more accurate information and adjusted her beliefs and behaviors to match those of the larger group (informational influence). Paula's behavior was not influenced by a desire to be liked or avoid social disapproval (normative influences—choice B). Attribution processes (choice C) are not related to social influence, and there is no indication that generational influence (choice D) impacted her decision. Choice E is too general to be unique to this scenario.

18. **The correct answer is C.** The door-in-the-face technique involves making an initial request that is unreasonable and likely to be rejected, followed by a smaller, more reasonable request. Foot-in-the-door techniques (choice B) involve making a small initial request and then following it up with a larger request. Low-ball techniques (choice A) involve changing the terms or conditions to be less favorable after the person has committed to more favorable terms. Choices D and E are not compliance techniques.

19. **The correct answer is C.** During an experiment, the independent variable, sometime called the presumed cause or the predictor variable, is manipulated by a researcher. The dependent variable, sometimes called the outcome or response variable, is measured to assess the influence of the independent variable. The question does not indicate the type of data, samples, or statistical measures used in the experiment, so all other choices are incorrect.

20. **The correct answer is E.** A double-blind experiment refers to a clinical trial where neither the researchers nor the participants are aware of which participants receive the experimental treatment or the control (placebo). Correlational studies (choice A) do not attempt to draw conclusions regarding causal associations, such as the efficacy of a drug. Only participants (not researchers) are unaware which drug is being administered in blind experiments (choice D). Choices B and C are too broad to be the most appropriate choice for this scenario.

21. **The correct answer is A.** Alfred Adler adopted a holistic view of personality, which stood in contrast to the psychodynamic framework used by Sigmund Freud (choice C) and Carl Jung (choice B), which focused on the unconscious mind. James B. Watson (choice D) and B. F. Skinner (choice E) worked within the behaviorist framework, focusing on observable behaviors and the stimuli that trigger them.

22. **The correct answer is D.** GABA is the major inhibitory neurotransmitter in the CNS of mammals. Acetylcholine (choice A) is primarily involved in the transmission of signals between motor neurons and muscle fibers, glutamate (choice B) is the major excitatory neurotransmitter, and dopamine (choice C) is a neuromodulator involved in motivation and reward-seeking behaviors. Vasopressin (choice E) is a hormone.

23. **The correct answer is A.** Discriminative touch, or fine touch, is associated with the perception of fine details, textures, and spatial localization. Crude touch (choice B) involves the perception of nonlocalized touch and mechanical pressure changes on the skin's surface. Choices C and D are too general, and choice E involves the sensation of one's body position and movement rather than touch.

24. **The correct answer is C.** Substance P is the neurotransmitter whose release amplifies nociceptive signals. Acetylcholine (choice A) is primarily active in neuromuscular junctions, and GABA (choice B) is the major inhibitory neurotransmitter in the CNS of mammals. Vasopressin (choice E) is a hormone associated with the regulation of water content in the blood. Substance N (choice D) is not a neurotransmitter.

25. **The correct answer is C.** Opioids such as heroin, morphine, and prescription pain killers are known to induce strong feelings of relaxation and euphoria. The intense psychoactive effects of opioids contribute to their extremely addictive nature. Antidepressants and neuroleptics (choices A and E) are psychotropic drugs prescribed for the treatment of psychological disorders and don't typically cause individuals to experience intense relaxation or euphoria. Hallucinogenic and stimulant drugs tend to increase alertness rather than inducing relaxation, so choices B and D are also incorrect.

26. **The correct answer is D.** In this scenario, the students' anticipatory packing behavior because of Mr. Vyas's accidental bell ringing represents a conditioned response (choice D). Before the students understood the association between the sound of the bell and being released for lunch, the bell would be considered a neutral stimulus (choice E). After forming an association between the sound of the bell and being released for lunch, the bell sound would be a conditioned stimulus (choice C). The students' apparent understanding of the meaning of the bell indicates that successful conditioning has already occurred, so choices A and B can be ruled out.

27. **The correct answer is B.** Anchoring bias refers to the tendency of individuals to favor information they've already been exposed to over modification of their current beliefs. Choice A describes confirmation bias, and choice C describes the availability heuristic. Choices D and E are both examples of social influence.

28. **The correct answer is A.** Divergent thinking refers to the creative ability to generate multiple novel ideas. Convergent thinking (choice B), on the other hand, relates to the ability to refine existing ideas. Functional fixedness (choice C) limits creative potential. Choices D and E are not specifically related to creativity.

29. **The correct answer is D.** The signs associated with maldevelopment differ for each of the 8 stages outlined in Erik Erikson's model of psychosocial development, and maldevelopment occurring during the initiative versus guilt stage of Erikson's psychosocial development (age 3-6) can be associated with self-doubt, guilt, and a lack of initiative in adulthood.

30. **The correct answer is C.** Children with anxious-avoidant attachment styles show little interest if their caregivers depart or return, perhaps showing hesitant interest before turning away. These children also show minimal interest in exploring or engaging with individuals they don't know. Choices A and E involve behaviors that are distinct from the anxious varieties of insecure attachment, and choice D is not a form of attachment. Children with anxious-ambivalent attachment (choice B) also show little interest in their caregiver; however, these children become very distressed when their caregiver leaves.

31. **The correct answer is E.** Projective tests are designed to examine what occurs at the subconscious level, such as how a person might respond to unstructured stimuli. Choice A is a distinct type of projective test that requires a person to describe what is happening in a picture, which sets it apart from a Rorschach test. Choices B, C, and D are associated with the process of individuation; while these concepts have relevance in personality research, they are not associated with tests.

32. **The correct answer is B.** The Structured Clinical Interview for DSM Disorders (SCID) is widely used to assess personality disorders and allows psychologists to ask follow-up questions and delve deeper into specific areas of interest. Choices A, D, and E provide valuable insight into an individual's personality, but these methods of assessment do not support in-depth, highly personalized exploration of an individual's unique experiences. Choice C is also incorrect as projective tests are specifically designed to examine what occurs at the subconscious level.

33. **The correct answer is B.** Selective mutism, characterized by a persistent inability or unwillingness to speak in certain social settings, is a type of anxiety disorder. Anorexia nervosa (choice A) is classified as an eating disorder, depersonalization disorder (choice D) is classified as a dissociative disorder, and both persistent depressive disorder (choice B) and premenstrual dysphoric disorder (choice E) are classified as depressive disorders.

34. **The correct answer is A.** Phase prophylactics, more commonly referred to as mood stabilizers, are intended to help regulate mood and address the complications of manic episodes, which are associated with bipolar I disorder. It is possible that in some cases, these drugs might be used to treat other mental disorders, but they are most likely to be prescribed for the treatment of bipolar or related disorders. Outside of psychological settings, it is also common for these drugs to be used to treat neurological issues such as epilepsy and neuralgia.

35. **The correct answer is E.** Ren exhibits actor-observer bias as he attributes the lateness of his coworker to internal factors while attributing his own lateness to external factors. The question does not describe confirmation bias (choice A), the tendency of individuals to favor information that confirms their preexisting beliefs. The situation is not consistent with stereotypes since no details are shared about the coworker (choice B), nor does it suggest that Ren's bias was due to a perception of his coworker as belonging to an outgroup (choice C). Normative influence (choice D) relates to conformity; it is not an accurate descriptor here as Ren's behavior was not influenced by pressure to conform to the view of a larger social group.

36. **The correct answer is E.** Group polarization is a phenomenon in which group discussions and interactions lead to the strengthening of initial attitudes or beliefs. Choices A and B are incorrect as attribution processes relate to the ways individuals interpret and explain the behavior of others. The question does not involve direct suggestions or the demands of an authority figure, so choices C and D are also incorrect.

37. **The correct answer is B.** Of these approaches, the only choice that prioritizes the relationship between one's physiology and psychology is the biological approach.

38. **The correct answer is C.** Type II errors occur when a researcher mistakenly concludes that there is no significant effect or relationship between variables when there is one. Choice B represents a type I error, which is mistakenly concluding that variables are related when they are not. Choices A, D, and E are not directly related to type II (or type I) errors.

39. **The correct answer is E.** The parietal lobe contains the primary somatosensory cortex, which is responsible for the processing of sensory information such as temperature, touch, and proprioception.

40. **The correct answer is D.** Audition (hearing) and balance (vestibular sense) both involve structures embedded within the inner ear. Proprioception, nociception, and thermoception do not involve inner-ear structures, so you can eliminate all other answer choices.

41. **The correct answer is E.** Neurogenesis refers to the generation of new neurons while neuroplasticity (choice A) refers to the formation of new neural connections between existing neurons. Long-term potentiation (choice C) and long-term depression (choice B) are processes associated with neuroplasticity, representing the strengthening and weakening of neural connections, respectively. Consolidation (choice D) refers to the stabilization and strengthening of information during memory formation.

42. **The correct answer is D.** Metacognitive regulation refers to an individual's ability to plan, monitor, and evaluate their own cognitive activities; metacognitive knowledge (choice E) refers to an individual's understanding of the strategies most compatible with their ability to learn. Choice A broadly relates to the concept of attention while choices B and C are aspects of creativity.

43. **The correct answer is E.** Being motivated to perform well because of one's inner sense of pride, happiness, and satisfaction is consistent with having high intrinsic motivation. Extrinsic and social motivation involve obtaining external rewards or avoiding external punishment, so all other choices are incorrect.

44. **The correct answer is D.** Cross-sectional research methods involve obtaining and analyzing data from different groups and age cohorts at the same time. Since the question does not specify Dr. Lee's means of data collection (for example, whether Dr. Lee conducts interviews or has individuals complete a self-report assessment), only choice D is supported by the question.

45. **The correct answer is E.** When bipolar-like symptoms stem from a clear, separate medical issue, the best practice is to diagnose a patient with bipolar under the "Bipolar and Related Disorder due to Another Medical Condition" heading as outlined by the DSM-5. The one exception would be if bipolar-like symptoms existed before the onset of the medical condition, but the question does not offer enough information, so the most likely diagnosis should be attributed to the medical condition.

46. **The correct answer is D.** Cognitive dissonance refers to the discomfort people feel when dealing with contradictory aspects of their beliefs, values, environment, and identity. While all other choices can also influence one's attitude, only cognitive dissonance relates to the contradiction described in the question.

47. **The correct answer is A.** The similarity-attraction effect describes an individual's tendency to be more attracted to others who are like them in their attitudes, beliefs, values, and interests. Mere exposure effect (choice B) describes the tendency to become more attracted to others because of spending more time with them. While the other choices can influence who an individual finds attractive, they do not account for Corryn's preference of pursuing a partner with similar characteristics.

48. The correct answer is E. Experiments seek to establish whether there is a correlation between the independent variable and the dependent variable. A valid experiment would develop a hypothesis regarding how the dependent variable may respond to the independent variable, not the other way around. Choices A through D are all sound strategies to increase experimental validity.

MY PRACTICE TEST SCORES BY CATEGORY		
Category	**Question Numbers**	**Raw Score**
History, approaches, and methods	1, 2, 20, 21, 37, 38	_____ /6
Biological bases of behavior	3, 4, 22, 39	_____ /4
Sensation and perception	5, 23, 24, 40	_____ /4
States of consciousness	6, 25	_____ /2
Motivation and emotion	10, 43	_____ /2
Learning	7, 8, 26, 41	_____ /4
Cognition	9, 27, 28, 42	_____ /4
Developmental psychology across the lifespan	11, 12, 29, 30	_____ /4
Personality	13, 31, 32, 44	_____ /4
Psychological disorders and health	14, 15, 33, 45	_____ /4
Treatment of psychological disorders	16, 34	_____ /2
Social psychology	17, 18, 35, 36, 46, 47	_____ /6
Statistics, tests, and measurement	19, 48	_____ /2
Total Raw Score		_____ /48
Full Test Raw Score Projection*		_____ /96**

* Multiply total raw score by 2

** CLEP's full length exam is approximately 95 questions; this practice test will provide a rough estimate.

Chapter 3

Diagnostic Test Answer Sheet

1. Ⓐ Ⓑ Ⓒ Ⓓ Ⓔ   9. Ⓐ Ⓑ Ⓒ Ⓓ Ⓔ   17. Ⓐ Ⓑ Ⓒ Ⓓ Ⓔ

2. Ⓐ Ⓑ Ⓒ Ⓓ Ⓔ   10. Ⓐ Ⓑ Ⓒ Ⓓ Ⓔ   18. Ⓐ Ⓑ Ⓒ Ⓓ Ⓔ

3. Ⓐ Ⓑ Ⓒ Ⓓ Ⓔ   11. Ⓐ Ⓑ Ⓒ Ⓓ Ⓔ   19. Ⓐ Ⓑ Ⓒ Ⓓ Ⓔ

4. Ⓐ Ⓑ Ⓒ Ⓓ Ⓔ   12. Ⓐ Ⓑ Ⓒ Ⓓ Ⓔ   20. Ⓐ Ⓑ Ⓒ Ⓓ Ⓔ

5. Ⓐ Ⓑ Ⓒ Ⓓ Ⓔ   13. Ⓐ Ⓑ Ⓒ Ⓓ Ⓔ   21. Ⓐ Ⓑ Ⓒ Ⓓ Ⓔ

6. Ⓐ Ⓑ Ⓒ Ⓓ Ⓔ   14. Ⓐ Ⓑ Ⓒ Ⓓ Ⓔ   22. Ⓐ Ⓑ Ⓒ Ⓓ Ⓔ

7. Ⓐ Ⓑ Ⓒ Ⓓ Ⓔ   15. Ⓐ Ⓑ Ⓒ Ⓓ Ⓔ   23. Ⓐ Ⓑ Ⓒ Ⓓ Ⓔ

8. Ⓐ Ⓑ Ⓒ Ⓓ Ⓔ   16. Ⓐ Ⓑ Ⓒ Ⓓ Ⓔ   24. Ⓐ Ⓑ Ⓒ Ⓓ Ⓔ

Practice Test Answer Sheet

1. Ⓐ Ⓑ Ⓒ Ⓓ Ⓔ
2. Ⓐ Ⓑ Ⓒ Ⓓ Ⓔ
3. Ⓐ Ⓑ Ⓒ Ⓓ Ⓔ
4. Ⓐ Ⓑ Ⓒ Ⓓ Ⓔ
5. Ⓐ Ⓑ Ⓒ Ⓓ Ⓔ
6. Ⓐ Ⓑ Ⓒ Ⓓ Ⓔ
7. Ⓐ Ⓑ Ⓒ Ⓓ Ⓔ
8. Ⓐ Ⓑ Ⓒ Ⓓ Ⓔ
9. Ⓐ Ⓑ Ⓒ Ⓓ Ⓔ
10. Ⓐ Ⓑ Ⓒ Ⓓ Ⓔ
11. Ⓐ Ⓑ Ⓒ Ⓓ Ⓔ
12. Ⓐ Ⓑ Ⓒ Ⓓ Ⓔ
13. Ⓐ Ⓑ Ⓒ Ⓓ Ⓔ
14. Ⓐ Ⓑ Ⓒ Ⓓ Ⓔ
15. Ⓐ Ⓑ Ⓒ Ⓓ Ⓔ
16. Ⓐ Ⓑ Ⓒ Ⓓ Ⓔ

17. Ⓐ Ⓑ Ⓒ Ⓓ Ⓔ
18. Ⓐ Ⓑ Ⓒ Ⓓ Ⓔ
19. Ⓐ Ⓑ Ⓒ Ⓓ Ⓔ
20. Ⓐ Ⓑ Ⓒ Ⓓ Ⓔ
21. Ⓐ Ⓑ Ⓒ Ⓓ Ⓔ
22. Ⓐ Ⓑ Ⓒ Ⓓ Ⓔ
23. Ⓐ Ⓑ Ⓒ Ⓓ Ⓔ
24. Ⓐ Ⓑ Ⓒ Ⓓ Ⓔ
25. Ⓐ Ⓑ Ⓒ Ⓓ Ⓔ
26. Ⓐ Ⓑ Ⓒ Ⓓ Ⓔ
27. Ⓐ Ⓑ Ⓒ Ⓓ Ⓔ
28. Ⓐ Ⓑ Ⓒ Ⓓ Ⓔ
29. Ⓐ Ⓑ Ⓒ Ⓓ Ⓔ
30. Ⓐ Ⓑ Ⓒ Ⓓ Ⓔ
31. Ⓐ Ⓑ Ⓒ Ⓓ Ⓔ
32. Ⓐ Ⓑ Ⓒ Ⓓ Ⓔ

33. Ⓐ Ⓑ Ⓒ Ⓓ Ⓔ
34. Ⓐ Ⓑ Ⓒ Ⓓ Ⓔ
35. Ⓐ Ⓑ Ⓒ Ⓓ Ⓔ
36. Ⓐ Ⓑ Ⓒ Ⓓ Ⓔ
37. Ⓐ Ⓑ Ⓒ Ⓓ Ⓔ
38. Ⓐ Ⓑ Ⓒ Ⓓ Ⓔ
39. Ⓐ Ⓑ Ⓒ Ⓓ Ⓔ
40. Ⓐ Ⓑ Ⓒ Ⓓ Ⓔ
41. Ⓐ Ⓑ Ⓒ Ⓓ Ⓔ
42. Ⓐ Ⓑ Ⓒ Ⓓ Ⓔ
43. Ⓐ Ⓑ Ⓒ Ⓓ Ⓔ
44. Ⓐ Ⓑ Ⓒ Ⓓ Ⓔ
45. Ⓐ Ⓑ Ⓒ Ⓓ Ⓔ
46. Ⓐ Ⓑ Ⓒ Ⓓ Ⓔ
47. Ⓐ Ⓑ Ⓒ Ⓓ Ⓔ
48. Ⓐ Ⓑ Ⓒ Ⓓ Ⓔ